Auld Acquaintance

AULD ACQUAINTANCE

by Guy Lombardo

with Jack Altshul

Introduction by Jules Stein

DOUBLEDAY & COMPANY, INC.   GARDEN CITY, N.Y.
1975

Grateful acknowledgment is made by the authors to the following:

Dell Publishing Company, for permission to reprint excerpts from "Radio Royalty Steps Out," by Jerry Wald, from *Radio Stars*, October 1933. Copyright © 1933 by Dell Publishing Company, Inc., reprinted by arrangement with Dell Publishing Company, Inc.;

The Los Angeles *Times*, for permisson to reprint "Lombardo: Past and Present," from the Los Angeles *Mirror-News*, copyright © 1959. Reprinted by permission of the Los Angeles *Times*;

Motor Boating, for permission to reprint selections from "New World's Records in Gold Cup Race," by H. Clay Cotter, from *Motor Boating* magazine, October 1946, copyright © 1946 by The Hearst Corporation, all rights reserved;

Random House, for permission to reprint material from A *History of Popular Music in America*, by Sigmund Spaeth, copyright © 1948 by Random House, Inc., reprinted by permission of the publisher;

And to *Variety*, for permission to reprint sections from articles by Louis Armstrong, Abel Green, and Ben Gross.

Library of Congress Cataloging in Publication Data

Lombardo, Guy, 1902–
Auld acquaintance.

1. Lombardo, Guy, 1902– 2. Musicians—
Correspondence, reminiscences, etc. I. Altshul,
Jack, joint author. II. Title.
ML422.L76A3   785'.092'4 [B]

TO CARM

Contents

Contents

Introduction

The year was 1927. The city, Chicago. The scene, an obscure, dimly lit night club on the South Side. It was blocks away from the busy corners of Cottage Grove and Sixty-third Street, where all the action was, and there seemed to be no more life in the neighborhood than in the cemetery across the street. Inside the cafe most of the tables were empty and the dance floor almost deserted. This was the first engagement of Guy Lombardo and His Royal Canadians in the Windy City, and it was booked by the Music Corporation of America.

Our road scout, my brother Bill, was on the road looking for new attractions, and was taken to a roadhouse on the outskirts of Cleveland. He came back raving about the Lombardo band, a name none of us had ever heard. His enthusiasm and our company's need for new names in the orchestral field led us to Al Quodbach, the owner of a little cafe at Sixty-eighth Street and Cottage Grove. He was induced to take a trip to Cleveland and on his return signed a contract for the Royal Canadians to open the Granada Cafe in September.

Very few customers turned up for the opening; mostly song pluggers, our agency employees, and food purveyors to the cafe. There were no newspaper ads or radio announcements. The people who somehow strayed in seemed to enjoy the dancing, but there were not enough to support the orchestra cost.

After a week or so of desultory business, a group of us met at the cafe to try and figure out what to do. It was surprising it took that long. The answer, of course, was radio. All the hotel dance rooms and prominent amusement places had nightly radio broadcasts which reached the budding audience on their new contrivances, or even on the old crystal sets. Finally, WBBM agreed to carry a fifteen-minute nightly spot if they were reimbursed for the line costs. This tab was split among Lombardo, MCA, and the Granada. Imagine today an orchestra like Lombardo paying a station to carry his program!

Before the first broadcast was finished, the phones started ringing, and by one o'clock the first night there were more customers than had attended the entire previous week. The next night the place was jammed, and from then on it was New Year's Eve every night.

Never in our entire booking experience had an orchestra attained such overwhelming success in such short time. Besides capacity business at the Granada, the Royal Canadians received a Decca record contract, and Carmen Lombardo composed several smash song hits. From then on everything was up—a summer tour of theaters and single dates which brought the band as much in one night as it had earned in a month.

New York came next, where the orchestra was as big a success at the Roosevelt Hotel as they had been in Chicago. As time went on, there came commercial radio programs—first, the Robert Burns Cigar Show with Burns and Allen, and later the prestigious Standard Oil of Jersey account, which combined a dance tour with the radio broadcasts from various cities.

Starting in 1929, there was no question that the Guy Lombardo Orchestra was the biggest dance band attraction in the entire country, and it held this rank for many years. Thirty years later, Lombardo had become THE symbol of the American dance orchestra; the greatest popularity, highest grosser, and most probably the most beloved, as attested by the following article quoted from the amusement pages of the Los Angeles *Mirror-News*, October 31, 1959:

LOMBARDO: PAST AND PRESENT

What can one say about the music of Guy Lombardo who curtsied this week in the Cocoanut Grove, particularly if he can recall the days when the Lombardo strains were on hand in Chicago's old Granada Cafe? They ain't changed much.

It is still the same sugary serving. And if any transplanted mid-westerners have forgotten this era, maybe such items as crystal sets and Capone's cement shoes will help their recollections.

Meanwhile back in this world . . . you'd never know it by listening to current disc jockey offerings, but the Guy ranks as the world's No. 1 recording artist! Really!

Lombardo recently set an all-time high in records sold by any entertainer and will receive an award in honor of Record No. 100,-000,000 in a special presentation by the Record Industry of America next month in New York.

Guy's perennial "sweetest music this side of heaven" is presently packing in the dinner and dance crowd at the Cocoanut Grove. While rock'n'roll or jazz fans are conspicuous by their absence, the cheek-to-cheek set, old and young, still glide over the waxed floor with closed eyes, God bless 'em.

Many times I have been asked to explain this sudden and phenomenal success. In early days, some of the other orchestras tried to simulate Lombardo and were quite adept at it, but not for long. When one leader complained to me that Lombardo played out of tune, I adapted Lincoln's answer about General Grant's whiskey, and told him I wished we had a dozen orchestras that played out of tune the same way.

Was it style alone that has kept this orchestra on top for such a long time? Surely the Lombardo style, slow beat and clean melody, all had a lot to do with the initial success, but this alone wouldn't have kept the band up there so long. If we can use a little psychology in analyzing the Lombardo longevity, there are two intangibles which may be part of the explanation, but these are philosophical, rather than statistical, and may be only the personal opinion of this particular Lombardo fan.

If we psychoanalyze ourselves in a modest way as to why certain things or events are retained as happy memories, we often find that wonderful feeling called nostalgia linked with melodies. Some melodies remain with us forever, which is why people still can remember the words and music of "Moonlight Bay," "Harvest Moon," and many more, while other songs of the same era and equal popularity are long forgotten. Somehow these songs have become associated in our minds with pleasureful and youthful events. I believe this same formula can be applied to the Lombardo music. The young people who danced to Lombardo in the early days received a mood, a pleasure, and, used in its best sense, even a thrill from the pleasant, relaxing music of this then different orchestra. The Lombardo music made a "gentle" impression, and as we advance in years our gentle memories become the fondest. To those who enjoyed dancing to Lombardo in those early days, it has remained a pleasurable experience in memory which may be renewed by listening to the band again and again through the years. If you don't believe this, notice the crowd in the room the next time you go to a Lombardo dance. Sure, there are the young people as always, where there is music and gaiety, but notice the preponderance of those couples who look now to be just about the age of someone who might have first enjoyed dancing twenty-five or thirty years ago. Not only do they come back to hear some of the same old Lombardo tunes, "Sweethearts on Parade," "Little Coquette," and many others, but they even induce their now grown-up children to go and see Lombardo. Sometimes the kids laugh and call us old-fashioned, but sometimes they go and enjoy the evening as their parents did so long ago. This must be the case, or Lombardo would not have survived all the changes in the band and dance world and kept his position through swing, boogie-woogie, and even now during our present rock 'n' roll. If the band keeps going much longer, there may even be a third generation of Lombardo fans, the grandchildren of the original pioneers.

There may be one other reason for the orchestra's long career, and one entirely separate from its music. Back in the thirties, the Blackhawk Restaurant had introduced more name bands to Chicago dancers than any other night club. Here is an exact quote made forty years ago by Otto Roth, owner of the Blackhawk: "If the Lombardo band ever starts edging off the top, everyone in the business would hold out his hand to keep them up."

So maybe it was the helping hands, as well as the dancing feet, that have kept Guy Lombardo and His Royal Canadians on top for nearly half a century.

                                                                        Jules Stein

Auld Acquaintance

1. *London, Ontario, Was the Genesis*

There are only Lebe and I, now, to come back to London. Mama and Papa and Carm aren't with us any longer and the rest of the Lombardo clan hardly has the time or occasion to visit the bustling little city in Ontario, where all of us were born and grew up. My brother and I return to our beginnings at least once a year, not so much to indulge our memories as to keep the faith with three generations of Londoners who consider the Royal Canadians their own and keep asking us back for annual concerts.

We have been making music in and around London for almost sixty years, since the formation of an adolescent quartet that consisted of brothers Carmen and Lebert on the flute and drums, Freddie Kreitzer on the piano, and me on the fiddle with a bow that doubled as a baton. From that beginning grew Guy Lombardo and His Royal Canadians. Now Lebe and I are the sole survivors of the original band.

We have played continuously through two world wars and Korea and Vietnam. We started when ragtime was evolving into jazz; developed our style by listening to Paul Whiteman on records in the early twenties, when he introduced a symphonic sound into dance bands; and later in that delirious decade, matriculated into professionals.

The band has appeared in virtually every one of the United States and all the provinces of Canada, in every major city and in hamlets you won't find on the map without microscopic help.

We have played in dance halls and hotel dining rooms, cafes and night clubs, country clubs and country fairs, indoor and outdoor theaters. We have participated in every aspect of the American entertainment medium, from vaudeville to television, and helped pioneer the introduction of dance music into the living room when radio was in its infancy.

Through it all we have never deviated from the Lombardo sound and style that saw us through all the musical trends of the last half century—the Charleston and Black Bottom, swing and be-bop, Dixieland and progressive jazz, the rhumba and cha-cha, country and western, and the electronic cacophony of today's rock.

We were the best known of all the wondrous combinations that made up the Big Band era between 1930 and 1950, and no musical aggregation has approximated our sale of 300,000,000 records. We may be the longest running act in show business that still goes out on the road ten out of every twelve months a year.

We have played every Inaugural Ball (except President Kennedy's) since Franklin Roosevelt took office in 1933. And as I travel around the country and people come up to the bandstand, it seems sometimes that we haven't missed playing an engagement, wedding, and anniversary party for anybody who ever celebrated a milestone by dancing.

Still, we are best known as a synonym for New Year's Eve. We ushered out 1929 over the radio from the Roosevelt Grill and not a year has gone by since that countless listeners have failed to tune into the airwaves to hear the Royal Canadians play "Auld Lang Syne." There have been years when we were booked on NBC to play until a minute to midnight and on CBS on the stroke of the new year.

Longevity does create certain problems. There are people, for instance, who come up to me to reminisce about the time they first heard the band—when my father was leading it! They are wrong, but it was Papa who was entirely responsible for the genesis of that little band in London and it was he who laid down all the precepts we followed to whatever we achieved.

Papa was Gaetano Lombardo, a boy of fourteen when he arrived in London in 1887 from the tiny island of Lipari, which lies off the northern coast of Sicily. His route to the New World had deviated from the one normally taken by Italian immigrants whose ultimate destination was New York City. Papa would stop in the metropolis only long enough to clear Ellis Island and take a train to London, where there was a trade to be learned and family waiting for him.

His own father was a thriving dyemaker on the volcanic island best known for producing pumice. The three oldest sons—Vincent, Fred, and Frank—had been sent off to America as soon as they were old enough to become eligible for arduous military service. A distant cousin named Paladino was in London and he needed apprentices for his tailoring shop.

Carmelo Paladino had founded his own minute Italian colony in the small city in southwest Ontario some years before. London had been settled in 1790 by English colonists and named for the capital of their homeland. Everything about the city that was razed by fire in 1845 and rebuilt soon after had an adoptive ring to it. The principal waterway, for instance, ran through the heart of London and was known as the Thames River. When Carmelo Paladino arrived, London was an expanding industrial town inhabited by English, Scottish, French, and Indians. There were no Italian families.

Paladino had never heard of Canada, much less London, when he left Lipari with his bride. A young tailor, he was headed for Buenos Aires, but his ship was turned off its course by a storm and limped, instead, into New York. There he read an advertisement in an Italian newspaper paid for by a Count Rhubigino, an Italian engineer. The count was searching for petroleum deposits in Ontario and had established his base of operations in London. Everything suited the nobleman about the frontier city except the absence of a custom tailor to provide him with his accustomed finery. So the count placed his ad in the New York paper, hoping to find an Italian tailor willing to migrate.

The Paladinos and a baby daughter, Mary, came to London to set up shop and home. A few years later Carmelo had become so busy, he wrote back to Lipari that he could use apprentice helpers. My father's brothers answered the call. Each was to learn the tailoring trade and set up his own shop as London continued expanding. As for Gaetano, his father was saving his youngest son to take over his own business. The boy seemed content with the future laid out for him and might even have risked the military draft but for an adolescent disappointment.

He had been born with an ear and a love for music. As he grew older, he expressed a desire to train the voice that had changed from boy soprano to rich baritone, or perhaps to learn to play an instrument. On Lipari there was one place to learn music, the small public school he attended. The trouble was that music lessons were given almost as an afterthought. The music class started at 4:30 in the afternoon after regular school was over and most of the pupils had gone home to help with family chores. Gaetano was needed in the dyemaking shop and his one aspiration seemed hopeless.

He could not, apparently, hide his disappointment from Grandfather Lombardo, who perceived that something was bothering his youngest son, the one with the bright and sunny disposition who rarely complained. Papa would remember the day he was asked what was bothering him. He said it was music and added that he would like to go to America to learn it.

"If I could join my brothers," he told his father, "I would work hard to become a tailor and then when I could afford it, I would like to take music lessons. Perhaps I will be disappointed, but when I have my own family, I will see that my children learn music, even if I have to sell every brick in the house to pay for it."

Grandfather did not wish to lose his last son, but neither did he want to quench what he considered an admirable ambition. He came up with the passage money and a few months later Gaetano Lombardo arrived in London, speaking not a word of English and wearing a name sign on his chest.

Uncle Vincent was at the railroad station to meet him, wondering if he would recognize the brother he had last seen as a small boy. He is the uncle my father would refer to in laters years as Adolphe Menjou, because he resembled the actor and always dressed in the height of fashion. The first words my father was to hear from his brother were: "*Madonna, mia,* we are going to have to teach you to dress like an American."

That my father would learn in time, as he quickly learned every

aspect of the tailoring trade from Carmelo Paladino. In a few
years, it developed, he learned even more than his brothers, each
of whom had acquired a specialty. One could make patterns, the
other pants, the other jackets. Papa became proficient in every
aspect of the trade and by the time he was twenty-eight he had set
up his own shop on Dundas Street in the heart of London's main
shopping district and not far from City Hall.

He had also found time to go to school, had taken voice lessons,
and sang a resounding baritone in the YMCA choir. And he had
fallen in love with the Paladinos' second daughter, Angelina, the
first child of Italian parentage born in London. But Angelina's
mother did not look with favor on the courtship. There would be
a breaking of tradition in that the oldest daughter, Mary, would
not be the first to marry. Angelina had already broken another
tradition by choosing a career in business rather than learning to
become a housewife.

She had insisted on going to and graduating from high school
and had surprised her family by taking a postgraduate course in
the new techniques of typewriting and shorthand. Unlike Italian
girls of her day, she had not been content after high school to help
around the house or in her father's tailor shop. Instead she
became London's first woman secretary and took a position with
Hume Cronyn, an attorney and banker whose grandson was to
become a celebrated actor.

"Marry Mary," Mrs. Paladino told Gaetano. "Angelina is not
yet ready to be a good wife. She can hardly cook or sew."

"But I do not love Mary. I love Angelina and I will never stop
asking for her hand."

Carmelo Paladino, mentor to four tailors named Lombardo,
was more willing to defy tradition, especially for the one he considered most promising. He told his wife that, if Angelina was
willing to marry Gaetano, he would not oppose it.

Angelina said yes, Gaetano went out and purchased a small
white cottage on Oxford Street, and by the time of the nuptials
had filled it piece by piece with new furnishings. The wedding
took place in the first year of a new century and the honeymoon
in what my mother was later to refer to as her "bridal cottage."

The family began arriving in 1902. I was the first-born, named

Gaetano for my father, who had no objection when my earliest schoolmates shortened it to Guy. A year later Carmen arrived, named for his maternal grandfather. Two years after that, it was Lebert. Elaine, Victor, Joseph, and Rose Marie followed in that order.

Papa was prospering as his family grew. He had a steady source of income from the students, interns, and doctors at the University of Western Ontario's Medical School in London. He made their white jackets. By the time I was nine, he had eleven tailors working for him and had purchased a much larger house on Simcoe Street in a fine residential district. I remember that it had two large outdoor verandas, one of them jutting from the second-story bedrooms, and that Carm, Lebe, and I would sleep there on cots during the summer.

Mama, meanwhile, had long ago dispelled her own mother's fears about her qualifications as a housewife. She became a remarkable cook, and until the day she passed away half a century later it was at her table that all my brothers and sisters best enjoyed eating. It is fair to say that on our future travels we would all dine at one time or another in the world's best restaurants, but the real treat in eating was to sample Mama's pasta and indelibly remembered sauces.

The earliest memory of Mama was in her role as diction teacher. My parents spoke no Italian around the house because Papa was so anxious to speak good, unaccented English. I often regret this policy as I travel around and meet so many people with the same ethnic background who will greet me with an Italian phrase or expression and find to their dismay that I don't understand what they're talking about.

It was Mama's belief that diction and pronunciation would be important for her children in whatever career they chose. Look at how it had helped her get a position with the prestigious Mr. Cronyn. And so as the places at the dinner table grew, I can remember her pulling us up short if we mispronounced a word, slurred a consonant or were less than precise in completing words with a hard g sound.

It was training that would serve the band handsomely in later years when Carmen became our vocalist, almost against his will.

Carm sang as he played the flute and sax—with a tremolo that underscored his feeling about a song. His lyrics were precise and he made each syllable count the way Mama had taught us all. He was one of the first singers of popular music to discard the flowing tones associated with opera and musical comedy, so when the words came out "I love you," instead of "I loh-ve you," women listeners believed and felt he was delivering a personal message. Carmen never had a rich or a trained voice, but he became one of the best-known and imitated vocalists of the Big Band era, and his vocals were as much of an identifying part of our band's style as the vibrato that came out of his instrumentals.

Papa was shaping his children's lives on another front. He could hardly wait for us to grow old enough to begin our musical education. I was about nine and Carmen eight, when we got our first instruments, a three-quarter-size violin for me and a flute for Carmen. At the time, we were going to St. Peter's Parochial School after transferring from the public school near our home on Simcoe Street. The parish priest had been putting pressure on Mama to enroll us at St. Peter's as soon as we were old enough for kindergarten. But St. Peter's was two miles away and Mama was too busy having children to walk us to school.

But now that his oldest sons could venture a distance without maternal protection, Papa set out to fulfill the promise he had made on Lipari. He would not have to sell a single brick of his house to pay for instruments and instruction as each of us became old enough to learn music. Papa Precept No. 1 was something we would all hear repeated time and again.

"Music is a light load to carry," he would say.

I don't believe Papa meant that he expected us to make a career out of music, much less be part of what would become the best-known dance band in the world. He meant that no matter what we decided to be we would always have music to fall back on as a source of enjoyment. I have a sneaking suspicion that Papa had in back of his mind, too, the thought that, while his children were absorbing their musical education, some of it would rub off on him.

Now he set up a routine and discipline that would be part of our lives for the next five years. It went like this: Carm and I would be expected to be in the tailor shop at eight o'clock every morning of a school day. There we practiced the scales for an hour, before walking to school. At four o'clock we returned to the store, halfway between school and home, and practiced under the tutelage of music teachers until six o'clock, when it was time for dinner. Then we would ride home in Papa's horse and buggy.

Naturally, neither Carmen nor I was enamored of the routine. Both of us were sturdy, active, and nonstudious types. If there was any fun to going to school, it was walking home with schoolmates, playing kids' games, skating on the Thames in the winter, and fishing and swimming in it during the warmer months. Education is enough of a chore for a youngster and when you put another layer on top if it, as Papa did with our music lessons, it takes a strong hand to make pedagogy successful.

Papa had a strong hand. He was an old-fashioned disciplinarian, not averse to reaching for a switch or slapping at an errant backside. When neighbors complained one day that Carmen had climbed their plum tree and helped himself to most of the fruit, he gave him such a whipping that Carmen never ate another plum for the rest of his life.

I remember another time when he was helping me tune my little fiddle. I had it under my chin and was scraping away on the strings while Papa was adjusting the pegs. We got into an argument when it came to the A-string, which Papa deemed flat. I contended it was sharp and Papa yanked away the fiddle, hit me over the head with it, and caused it to splinter into tiny pieces.

It really didn't hurt but I was so startled I must have presented a comic spectacle, mouth open, splinters and strings decorating my face.

Papa wasn't incensed any longer. He started laughing and I began laughing with him. Moments later, he took me by the hand, walked me to the music store and bought another violin. "It was worth it," he said as he handed the proprietor the money.

Lebert had an engaging way of escaping paternal clout. He was a shy little boy with an aversion to girls his own age. Whenever one came around, he would choke up and begin giggling. It was annoying to Papa and one day after such an incident he tried to slap some sense into him. In a trice, Lebe went to the floor on his back, curled himself into a ball, and kicked his feet, a self-protected porcupine without quills. Papa took a few swipes but missed by a mile. It was such a ludicrous sight, Papa's ire disappeared and he broke into laughter. Lebe hardly ever took any lickings after that because he always knew he could turn away Papa's wrath by going into his porcupine act.

If spare the rod was the accepted method of bringing up children of my day, at least Papa interspersed the discipline with visible evidence of high, good humor and frequent displays of affection. Although we sometimes chafed at the regimen, Carm and I both sensed that our father had our best interests at heart. As the music lessons continued, we noticed that Papa would more often exhibit a velvet glove than an iron fist.

He instituted a system of rewards. A word of praise from either Carm's teacher or mine brought an immediate bonus. Papa had made two purchases to go along with his new-found prosperity. One was the finest trotting horse in London; the other was one of the city's first motorboats. A ride on one or the other would be the payoff for a good lesson.

Carmen was much more precocious at his flute than I was on my violin. In a year or two, Papa was being told his second son was displaying prodigy-like talents and that if he continued studying he could become one of the youngest concert flutists in Canada. This made it rather tough for me to earn the quarter a day Papa also awarded to the one who best performed his lesson. But Papa managed to distribute the quarters evenly, and kept me from getting discouraged.

Lebe was another matter. Papa decided his third son ought to learn the harp. But during one of his first lessons, Lebe ran afoul of his professor, a notoriously ill-tempered man, who slapped him before Lebe could bring up his porcupine defense. From that day on, he refused to take lessons. Instead he began playing around with an old Canadian Army bugle. When he got tired of that, he traded for a much-used trumpet with valves sticking out. When he knocked out a front tooth playing hockey, he relegated the trumpet to the branch of a tree where he would use it as a target for his BB gun.

Papa then turned his attention on Elaine, for whom he purchased a piano. Since she couldn't transport the piano to the tailor shop, Elaine had her music lessons at home, but not under Papa's watchful eyes. My sister remembers that Mama was not as rigid as Papa in supervising practice. As a matter of fact, when six o'clock approached, Mama would stand by the window and as Papa brought his sons home from the store she would tell Elaine, "Sit down at the piano. Papa's coming."

But Mama did not deprecate the musical proceedings. She had become somewhat of a social butterfly around London, was president of the Mothers' Club of the Simcoe Street School and immersed in war-relief, fund-raising events when Canada began organizing its expeditionary force at the beginning of World War I.

Carm and I were unaware that Mama had us on her society calendar until the day she accompanied us to the tailor shop, where Papa took our measurements. A few nights later he brought home two outfits that Mama proudly announced we would be wearing for our musical debut at a lawn party. Carm and I looked at each other, pointing derisive fingers at Mama's version of what well-dressed young musicians ought to be wearing. They were not exactly the kind of outfit you would want to wear in the company of your peers without being prepared to fight.

The jackets and knee breeches were of black velvet. Buster Brown collars covered our necks. Large black, scarf-like bow ties flowed over the collars. Knee-length black stockings completed the Little Lord Fauntleroy look. Thus attired, the Lombardo duet made its debut in 1914 on a lawn in back of a church.

Carm played the flute and I played the fiddle, which snapped a string. The duet was intended to be harmonious, but Carm kept finishing first. The guests applauded mildly but nobody asked for autographs. Strangely, Papa did not seem displeased.

"It was not too bad," he ventured. "At least you tried to follow the melody and that is what is important. Music is easy to play and easy to listen to if you don't forget the melody and choose songs people can sing, hum, or whistle."

That was Papa Precept No. 2, the one that became the formula for the Royal Canadians and remains unchanged today. Call it simplicity, but remember that by the time we became nationally known the band was composed of sophisticated musicians with fifteen years of hard work and training behind them.

The lawn party debut brought demands for repeat perform-ances at garden parties, teas, strawberry festivals, and war-relief benefits. Mama was our first booking agent, but had she been ten-per-centing us, her commissions would have amounted to exactly zero.

Mama had become friendly with another Mothers' Club pres-ident, Mrs. Agnes Kreitzer of the London South School. Her son Freddie played the piano, and both mothers thought it would be nice if he helped the Lombardo brothers dispense free music at the socials. A little while later we grew into a quartet when Lebert joined us. Lebe hadn't taken lessons, but somehow, on his own, he had learned to become a fairly proficient drummer. He would take the spindles out of the backs of chairs, use them as drumsticks, and bang away at assorted furniture. Papa finally bought him a big bass drum to pound on and later a complete drummer's outfit. Lebe was eleven when he rounded out the quartet.

The Lombardo name, once exclusively identified with tailoring around London, began to be associated with music. We were always on hand for those everlasting functions of Mama's. Before long, they were asking us to play in nearby towns and we even began getting paid for our efforts. I think the going rate was six-teen dollars a performance, four dollars for each of us.

Square dancing was one of the few forms of entertainment around a countryside that had yet to hear of radio. On weekends, the quartet would play engagements, Papa driving us proudly in the buggy. Since most of the engagements were at night, we would have a little trouble keeping our eleven-year-old drummer awake. After an hour or so, he would generally nod off and Papa would take over at the snares and cymbals. This would change the character of the square dance, because Papa could keep up with only one type of beat—the waltz. So we played waltzes, and Papa would happily beat the drums, content that the dancers were en-gaging in what he considered a much more civilized rhythm. After the dance, he'd bundle us all into the back of the buggy under a buffalo robe and take us home.

A year or so later he purchased a 1915 Studebaker with a hand brake on the side. This was so we could travel greater distances. One night, the car broke down and we had to sleep in a farmhouse. Freddie Kreitzer considered it a happy circumstance since it meant missing school the next morning, and on future trips he kept wishing the car would break down.

Whenever we were about to start on the return trip, Papa would always point a finger at Freddie and say, "I don't want to hear a word out of you. We want to get home tonight."

We enjoyed the excursions and the pocket money it earned us, but I don't believe any of us, with the possible exception of Carm, envisioned a lifetime career in music. As a matter of fact, the summer I was sixteen, I took a job in a bank as a messenger for four dollars a week. I think the job really gave me a perspective about my future. By the time it was over, I learned that I was not cut out to be a banker, that I was much handier at earning money as a musician. One experience, especially, convinced me.

John S. Moore was president of the Western Trust Company, and one day he called me in, apparently pleased that I had handled my routine chores satisfactorily. I would deliver messages and pick up the mail in the post office in the morning and carry the bank's mail back in the afternoon.

He said, "Guy, I've noticed you do everything that is asked of you, that you're never late, and that you have a nice smile, which I consider a walking advertisement for the bank. I would like you to try an assignment, which if successful could guarantee your future with the bank."

He explained that the bank owned a mansion that had been occupied by a wealthy widow. She had died and the bank was the trustee of her estate. The house would have to be sold to pay off taxes. There was one hitch. It was occupied by the widow's housekeeper, an elderly Irish lady who refused to leave the premises. My job, Mr. Moore explained, was to convince her to move. I could promise her, he said, that the bank would give her enough money to return to Ireland, and to purchase a smaller house.

I took a trolley to the mansion and its lone occupant came out to greet me, asking if I would like a cup of "tay." She proceeded to put on a kettle and listen to my proposition. After I stammered through it, she laughed. "Imagine the bank sending a little boy way out here to take an old lady's home away from her. You go back and tell the bank I don't want to go to Ireland. This is my home."

And, noticing the stricken look on my face that must have mirrored the demise of my banking aspirations, she said gently, "Don't worry, my boy, everything turns out for the best."

I told my father the story that night and learned a third precept. "The lady is right," he said. "Maybe you're too soft-hearted to be a banker. Remember what she said: 'Everything turns out for the best.'"

It was a line that would stay with me for the rest of my life. Through all the frustrations and disappointments that would accompany our ladder-scaling, events would occur to balance them out. Sometimes it would be sheer luck; other times we would be in the right place at the right time; and oftentimes we would be in a position to scale another rung by simple perseverance. I would always console myself during a dark period with the Irish housekeeper's axiom to which Papa subscribed.

We went back to playing music, sharpening our skills, beginning to sound more like a foursome in harmony than a battle of instruments. By the time I was seventeen, I was a bandleader, not so much because I was the most talented musician in the quartet, but because I was the oldest. The talent, of course, was chiefly embodied in Carmen, a bundle of energy, quick and intense about everything musical and constantly seeking more knowledge. I had come to the conclusion I would never be a great violinist. My fingers were too stiff and inflexible.

If I had inherited anything from Papa, it was his ear for music. I knew what sounded right for us, and Carmen and the others leaned on me for final decisions. Not that they wouldn't argue during rehearsals (the arguments would continue during the lifetime of the band). But when I would finally say, "This is it," the word would be accepted without rancor.

Papa was having as much fun as we were with our road engagements, which were increasing in frequency as we branched out into what had become known as "The Lombardo Brothers Concert Company." Most of the outlying towns had a large Scottish population, so we added a Scottish comedian and Scottish dancer to our entourage. We could even offer our audiences a troupe of singers. We began bringing little Elaine with us and she and Carm would sing duets. For solos we had Papa's baritone.

The Studebaker wasn't equipped as a bus but it served the same function, and when an engagement called for the entire company, eight of us would squeeze into it with all our instruments and props. When we arrived at the date, I'm sure we looked like that circus act that disgorges passengers ad infinitum out of a tiny car.

We performed only on weekends because Papa refused to permit the concert company from interfering with our schoolwork. To digress, he had also managed to schedule our time so that we could engage in other activities not connected with school or music lessons. Lebert, for instance, had found a home away from home in the local movie house, where he helped the projectionist and the pianist in the pit. Later on, he would build his own crystal set and that first radio in our house would heighten our interest in the dance music of the outside world.

Carmen was trendy. He would become interested in all the sports the kids were playing around town and attack them until he figured he had mastered their intricacies. Then he would move on to the next one. I think the one that took up most of his time was swimming, and he developed a powerful stroke that was to last through his lifetime. But more than the rest of us, he continually pursued his musical education.

I had developed my own interests as we were progressing through the music lessons. First, there was physical culture study. I was always sending away for Bernarr MacFadden books after reading those ads about the puny weakling who builds himself into a Samson by pursuing the prescribed course of exercise.

Then Papa bought me an English bike, lighter and faster than the ones manufactured in Canada. I think it was as a reward for a particularly good music lesson. With my new-found MacFadden muscles, I soon became the fastest kid cyclist in London. I even replaced the handle bars with a steering wheel from a junked auto, and at every chance I was showing off my skill to the boys who congregated around the Thames for impromptu races. Leading down to the river was a hill so steep it had been converted into a public stairway with about a hundred concrete steps. One summer

night after supper, I was challenged to ride down those steps on
the bike. I only made it halfway and the next thing I knew I was
flying over the steering wheel.

Ten hours later I awakened, and my mother, father, and assorted aunts and uncles were praying over me. I'd been unconscious all that time. They didn't have X-ray in those days and the
doctor's prognosis was that I had a sumptuous bump on my head.
His prescription was to avoid concrete steps on a bicycle. I walked
around with a headache for a month.

After that I got into boxing through the good offices of an
older boy who was about to make a professional career out of
pugilism. He used to spar with me, all the time teaching me the
jabs and crosses and how to protect myself. I learned enough to
later become champ of my weight division at St. Peter's. The title
hardly impressed an Indian boy I would meet one afternoon when
I was pressed into service to umpire a baseball game.

I really wasn't dressed for the occasion. The folks always
insisted that their children be immaculately attired. Maybe it was
an outcropping of Papa's early lessons in learning how to dress like
an American. Besides he was a custom tailor whose business it was
to outfit his customers fashionably. This day I was wearing a blue
felt hat, flat on the top, the latest style of the day. It was called a
porkpie.

I carefully removed the hat, put it on a bench under a tree, and
proceeded to call balls and strikes. At the end of the first inning, I
looked at the bench and saw the hat squashed. It was obviously
the result of good footwork. I straightened it out and, confident in
my newly acquired pugilistic skill, announced, "Whoever did that,
I want to hear from you."

From the tree dropped a very large boy, a resident of the Indian
reservation on the outskirts of London. He wasn't at all hesitant
about announcing he was the culprit. I said, "Do it again." He did
it.

For the next forty-five minutes, we rough-and-tumbled around
that baseball field, kicking, scratching and jumping on each other
like a scene out of a cowboy and Indian picture. I never did get a
chance to jab and parry like I had been taught. We finally both
lay on the ground, too exhausted to do further damage, and I

walked the five blocks to my house, carrying that porkpie, before collapsing on the front stoop.

Papa arrived a few minutes later, taking in a very dirty, bruised and unfashionable son. The only excuse he would tolerate for fighting was if somebody provoked us with an ethnic slur. "The guy called me a wop," I said.

The next day was May 24, the Queen's birthday, Canada's version of July 4 in the States. The family was on the porch watching fireworks exploding over the Thames, when my father noticed a young man walking on the other side of the street. He was as bruised and patched up as me. I nodded at Papa's silent question. "That's the guy."

Papa put it all in perspective as he poured water on my pugilistic aspirations. "Fighting is like war," he said. "Nobody wins. I would say you both lost this fight."

The Lombardo Brothers Concert Company was slowly replacing all my earlier ambitions of becoming the strongest man in the world, a champion cyclist, a banker, and a John L. Sullivan. As more and more requests came pouring in for dates, I was unconsciously succumbing to the bite of the show business bug.

It is a bite that must be felt to be appreciated. For a boy standing in front of an audience, dancing and listening to your music, the reaction is the reward, far beyond the compensation that will come in an envelope at the end of the night. The couples dance by the little bandstand, smiling and euphoric. Their eyes carry the message that you are making them happy. You end a number with a flourish of the violin bow and the applause cascades through the room. You begin to see a life in which you are paid to be applauded.

In 1919, the summer after I tried banking, we got our first steady job. It almost ended our career before it was started. Our reputation had reached the ears of the owner of an outdoor dance pavilion in Grand Bend on Lake Huron, forty-five miles from London. Outdoor pavilions were popular in Canada at the time; they were usually at the end of a trolley line, making them accessible to people living within a radius of ten miles or so.

The job would pay the band forty dollars a week, but, more important, we got to sleep in a tent, and all of us liked that idea.

We played from one to five in the afternoon, took a short break for dinner, and resumed at six, playing another four-hour stint. The setting was romantic and we were thoroughly enjoying the job until one Sunday afternoon when Papa came to visit, carrying supper in a picnic basket.

He had watched our four-man band through the afternoon session, and as he spread Mama's goodies on a blanket in the tent, he was positively bubbling with enthusiasm and advice. I remember his saying, "Always give the people a little more than they pay for. That way, you'll always be invited back again."

It was another Papa precept that would remain with us. But on this fine summer day, Papa himself didn't buy it. As we were digging into the spread, the owner of the pavilion came into the tent. "You'll have to go out there right now," he said. "We got a lot of people standing out there, wanting to dance."

Papa looked at his watch. Hardly twenty minutes had gone by since we broke for our dinner hour. "My boys have to have time enough to eat," he said. "They told me they had an hour off for dinner." The proprietor said huffily, "I decide how much time they have and I've decided that the people paid to dance, not to stand around while the band is eating."

We went out and played and Papa waited until we finished. Then he announced he was taking us home. He would not permit us to work for a man who didn't live up to his word. As a matter of fact, he delivered a pronunciamento. We were finished with the band business. "If that's the way they treat you in this business," he said, "I don't want you to have any part of it."

He was unrelenting for several months. I was in my final year at St. Peter's and I wasn't studying. I kept thinking of all the time we'd put into learning how to play together, of the satisfaction we got out of entertaining people. Carm, Lebe, and Freddie felt the same way. We decided to quit school and make our way as professional musicians.

Papa was horrified, but he could hardly stand in our way. He had after all set us on our path. Reluctantly he gave us back our instruments with a final Papa precept. "I don't like the idea that you do not wish to finish school. But if you want to make music your career, be the best. Be the best."

We tried. We went back to that concert company routine and we were supporting ourselves as teen-agers. I was old enough to drive Papa's Studebaker and we always managed to get two or three nights' work a week. Perhaps the sharpest memory of that period is one that had nothing to do with the little orchestra.

Uncle Vincent had a customer who was a newspaper reporter. The reporter told him that the word had just come into his office that World War I was over, that an armistice had been signed. At ten o'clock on the evening of November 11, 1918, Uncle Vincent called our house and said the London *Free Press* would have its armistice edition on the streets at two o'clock in the morning.

I took Papa's Studebaker and Carm and Lebe piled in. We went to the newspaper office and waited around for two hours before the papers were finally put on sale on the first floor of the building. They cost a penny each and we bought three hundred. Lebe had brought along his beat-up trumpet and we drove through the pitch-black streets of London with Lebe's trumpet notes backgrounding Carm and me as we bellowed, "The war's over. The war's over."

House lights began turning on and people came running out to get the news. Radio was still a few years away and historic events could be learned only from the newspapers. So the householders came running and paid as much as a quarter apiece for the papers. They didn't ask for change. We sold out in an hour, went back for more, and by dawn's early light we had sold a thousand papers and had made about fifty dollars each. With the papers that were left over, we built a victory bonfire on Dundas Street.

As momentous as the Armistice was, an event occurred sometime later that was to prove even more historic in the career of the Lombardo brothers. Carmen got interested in the saxophone, an instrument that had never before played an important role in dance music. But around 1920, a saxophone player named Benny Krueger had come into prominence and was being featured on phonograph records. A year later, Paul Whiteman became the big name on records when he introduced "The Song of India."

The number added a new dimension to popular songs. Saxophones were featured in the arrangement and helped bring for the first time a symphonic sound to dance music. No longer would such music be denigrated by the critics. Paul Whiteman had made it respectable.

We all decided that Carmen ought to buy a saxophone. Of course, we knew we would have to contend with Papa, a traditionalist who would not look with favor at the idea of his second son converting from a flutist who could play with a symphony into a saxophonist who would fritter away his time on this newfangled music some people called jazz. If the Whiteman style was achieving respectability, it had not yet won Papa's acceptance.

We sent away for the sax without informing Papa. Not knowing any better, we requested the C-melody type, probably the one least used in orchestras. It arrived with a book of instructions one day, shortly after lunch when Papa left for the store.

Carmen took to it like a duck to water. The fingering on the flute and the sax are very much alike, and through that entire afternoon he kept playing it. Lebert and I listened and marveled at the rich sounds. There was only one problem. When you play a sax, you bring the lower lip back over the teeth to form a cushion for the reed. Carmen didn't realize that his lip wasn't used to that kind of treatment, and by dinnertime it was raw and swollen. He picked up the flute, because we had an engagement that night in St. Thomas, a town not far from London. And he found the swollen lip wouldn't permit him to play a note. So he took the sax along to the engagement and played it for the first time professionally on the same day he had taught himself the new instrument.

Papa learned about the sax a few days later and naturally delivered an opinion. We were all crazy. He had noticed that I had been fooling around with new sounds on the violin and it had made him mad, but this new development he considered even more serious. He just couldn't imagine why we would want to tamper with a flutist who had a future as a concert artist.

What he didn't realize is that his sons were expanding their horizons. We were beginning to dream of a big band like that of Paul Whiteman, who had taken the new sounds in music and arranged and orchestrated them into melodic and controlled harmony. We were dying to imitate that symphonic sound.

Whiteman made it easy for us. He kept putting out records,

and whenever the music store had a new one, we bought it and played it over and over again on the hand-wound phonograph. Even Papa began enjoying the records. They had a beauty he could understand.

Besides the records, Whiteman orchestrations were also on sale at the music store for small bands trying to achieve his sound. Carm, Lebe, Freddie, and I would rush to the store the day they came out, put the sheets on stands, and begin playing them right there.

Carmen, meanwhile, was enjoying meteoric success on the saxophone. He still listened to Benny Krueger records and was frank to admit that he tried to copy his style. The empathy with Krueger was that the famous musician's sound was more like a voice than an instrument. That's the way Carmen played his flute. Carm would later become as imitated a saxophonist as he was a vocalist, but he would always give credit to Benny Krueger as the master.

So by the time Carmen was seventeen, he was an accomplished saxophonist, and I guess as good as he would ever become. The trouble was he was the only kid in town who knew how to play it, and we needed two more saxes to back him up if we were to enlarge the band. We also needed recruits on the trumpet, trombone, string bass, and guitar. These we found but Carm had to start giving saxophone lessons before we were able to add them to the crew. Finally, he had two young men ready and we began organizing.

We hired a room above a music studio and started rehearsing. Now we could accept dates calling for combinations ranging from four to nine. There was plenty of work around. Everybody was dancing to that new music coming out of the States and every little town had a dance hall. The war was over and more and more cars were traveling Canada's dusty roads, many to the dance pavilions that flourished in the summer resort areas of the numerous lakes around London. I directed the rehearsals, handled the bookings, and made the travel arrangements.

In the fall of 1922, we got our first big job, right in our home town, in the London dance hall known as the Winter Garden. We were the first Canadian band ever hired for this job and played weekends, Friday to Sunday. We didn't think we sounded like Paul Whiteman, yet, but we were on our way.

Another event occurred that would finally lay the foundation for the future Lombardo band and its sound and its style. Just as some months before Carmen had fallen in love with the sax, Lebe, the drummer, became enamored of the trumpet. He had fooled around with it through childhood, but his musical dedication had been reserved for the drums.

Carm's saxophonic interest had been generated by the records of Benny Krueger and Paul Whiteman. Lebe's discovery of the trumpet was also phonographic. Next to Whiteman, perhaps the best-known band in America was that of Isham Jones of Chicago. He made almost as many records as Whiteman and featured the same symphonic quality that was generating the new interest in dancing throughout the States and Canada.

From the Isham Jones records, Lebe picked out the haunting trumpet tones of the band's featured attraction, Louis Panico. He'd play the record, rummage around for his old trumpet, and then try to imitate the Panico solos and choruses. After a while he'd begin bringing the trumpet to the Winter Garden and occasionally he'd put his drumsticks aside at a point when a trumpet chorus seemed a good idea. He had just enough breath, enough lip to play one chorus of the Panico-like obbligato. On engagements, when we couldn't find a trumpet player, Lebe would take his horn along and double as drummer and trumpeter.

If Carm and I had learned our music the traditional way, through long hours of instruction and practice, our younger brother was self-made. He had learned the drums with no instruction, but had spent endless hours in the Loew's Theater as a boy, not only helping the projectionist but accompanying the pit pianist, who provided background music for the silent pictures.

Lebe approached the trumpet the same way. On his own. He would play the Isham Jones records over and over, and when Louis Panico took a chorus or played an obbligato to the melody, Lebe would repeat it. He never bothered with notes or scales. He simply copied Panico's playing until he could do it by himself.

We had a trumpet player who hadn't pleased us, either with his skill or deportment. We were putting all those Papa precepts into that first big engagement at the Winter Garden: "Give a little more than you're paid for," "Be the best," etc. And we were happy with our personnel. Carm, of course, was unbeatable on the sax, and you'd have had to travel a long way around Canada to find a better pianist than Freddie Kreitzer, who everybody called "Enemy" because of his German ancestry. Lebe was an accomplished drummer, but he had had his front tooth fixed so he could concentrate on his extracurricular study of the trumpet. Frances "Muff" Henry was a great guitarist, and our left-handed trombone player, Jeff Dillon, was coming along.

As I say, the only man in the band who bothered me was the trumpet player. He had a habit of looking at his watch and yawning. One night, he yawned so loud that he almost drowned out a rather flamboyant trumpet solo Lebe was finishing, holding the trumpet in the air with one hand and beating on the drums with the other. The yawn did it. I pointed to the young man and said, "You're fired."

It was a big decision but I had my next step planned before I made it. I was convinced Lebe was now good enough to be our trumpet player. And I had a replacement for him at the drums in the person of George Gowans, a London kid who had been hanging around the band for the last few years. He'd come up to the bandstand and play Lebe's drums whenever Lebe would decide it was time to get out on the dance floor and cut in on a pretty girl. I beckoned to George and said, "Lebe's our new trumpet player. You're our new drummer." He sat down to the drums and didn't leave them until he retired from our band almost fifty years later.

So by the time we began playing our first big engagement at the Winter Garden, the nucleus of the band had been set.

We didn't exactly regard that engagement as bush league, but we knew it wasn't the majors. The major leagues consisted of Whiteman and Jones and Ted Fiorito and those bands that were playing the big Midwestern cities of Chicago, Detroit, Cleveland, and Kansas City. Detroit, burgeoning with Henry Ford, had dozens of bands, and since it was only a hundred miles from London, Carm, Lebe, and I would often visit on a day off to hear the new trends in dance music.

Two Detroit bands especially intrigued us. One was the Jean

Goldkette aggregation, which would later graduate such future bandleaders as Tommy and Jimmy Dorsey, Glenn Miller, and Benny Goodman. Carm would bring along his sax and the great Goldkette would let him sit in with his musicians. At those sessions Carm would learn to practice long notes to develop his tone.

The Wolverine Hotel had another band that attracted novice musicians who came to hear and learn from the masters. The co-leaders were Steve Pasternak, a piano virtuoso, and Irving Rubinstein, an equally talented violinist. Carmen asked to sit in with Pasternak-Rubinstein, too, and was told the band might hire him if he got rid of his C-melody sax and obtained an E-flat alto. Carmen immediately purchased one in Detroit and the next thing he knew he had been hired to play for the band at $125 a week. He was only nineteen years old.

He stayed with Pasternak-Rubinstein for nine months, and what he learned about tempo he brought back to our band in London to give us the beat that would get us ready for the big leagues. Almost every band played the same beat. Fast. We used to call it "the businessman's bounce." Pasternak-Rubinstein slowed their numbers down, and Carmen noticed the dancers seemed to enjoy the more leisurely rhythms.

Carmen was making a lot more money than the rest of us, but he never had it in his mind to stay on his own. When we got another prestigious engagement during the summer of 1923 to play in the resort town of Port Stanley, we told him about it and it gave him an opportunity to leave Detroit. "My brothers need me" was the simple explanation he gave Steve Pasternak and Irving Rubinstein, who would find it difficult to replace their talented, young sax player. He showed them a telegram I had sent which said we couldn't take on the Port Stanley job without him. Pasternak and Rubinstein gave him their blessings, saying they understood.

With Port Stanley in the summer and London's Winter Garden in the winter, we now had a guaranteed income and prospects of making more. That income wasn't half of what Carmen had been making in Detroit, but he didn't regret his decision. We had formed a three-way partnership that owned the band and both my brothers and I were beginning to think of getting to the States and the big time.

To get to this point, we owed much to our heroes, the best-known bandleaders of the day. From Whiteman, we had borrowed the symphonic sound and the idea of making Carmen a sax player. From Jean Goldkette, we had personally watched and learned from the great musicians who played in his band. From Pasternak-Rubinstein, Carm, who would become our musical director, had assimilated the idea of a slower rhythm that made dancing easier. From Isham Jones, Lebert got the idea of becoming a trumpet player.

Jones, himself, came to London on the night of June 14, 1923, to play an engagement in the Loew's Theater. It was a big day for our town, because his band, after Whiteman's, was the most popular in America. I remember the day well, because it was my twenty-first birthday and I was waiting at the railroad station for the train that was bringing in the musicians.

I spotted the bandleader, introduced myself as a hero worshiper and the leader of a small London band, and invited him to a birthday party at our house after he finished his last show at Loew's. He seemed reluctant and consented to drop in for a moment only after I promised that there would be a keg of beer from Labatt's brewery in London and good Canadian cheese. We didn't have Prohibition in Canada and maybe it was the idea of real beer that finally convinced him.

He arrived after the show with two of his musicians, immediately fell in love with the local beer and the local cheese, and was soon calling the hotel where the rest of the band was staying to summon them to the party. They came, bringing instruments, and Lebe's eyes grew big as saucers as he finally met his idol, Louis Panico.

Before long both bands were playing together in an improvised jam session that brought neighbors into the street to hear. I remember Panico putting down his trumpet and listening to Lebe. Later he told him, "Lebert, it's fine to copy my style. You should also copy the style of Henry Busse (Paul Whiteman's celebrated trumpeter). Copy all the good ones and then develop a style of your own, so when you pick up your horn, people will immediately know who is playing."

It was advice that stuck. Lebe would develop an identifiable sound on his trumpet as Carmen had on his sax and those two sounds would set the Lombardo style, recognizable the moment it was heard.

We were to get yet another bonus out of that party. I had been experimenting with the idea of transforming our banjoist into a tuba player so that we could develop a richness by using a legato bass in back of the saxes. The Isham Jones band included perhaps the most accomplished tuba player of the time, an Indian named John Koon.

I told him our man was trying to learn the big horn and having difficulty. He said, "Send him along with us for a week or so, maybe I can help him." We did and our banjo player came back a professional with a show-stopping rendition of "Old Black Joe."

I doubt if one single event did more to solidify our style than that party to which Isham Jones came reluctantly. It helped make Lebe a fine trumpet player and it gave us a man on the tuba to give us a rich sound.

It is my conviction that we would later achieve stardom only when listeners began identifying us as soon as they heard us. So it was with other stylists like Tommy Dorsey, Benny Goodman, and Glenn Miller. And with singers like Bing Crosby and Frank Sinatra, Kate Smith and Peggy Lee. The audience would turn on the radio and listen to these artists and know who they were without being helped by an announcer.

The radio we first turned on was the crystal set Lebe had built himself. The first summer we played Port Stanley, we'd gather in his room in the afternoon and listen to Station WTAM from Cleveland. We might hear a half-hour concert and then the announcer would come on to announce there would be an hour standby. What it meant was the station simply had nothing else to offer.

Then early in the morning after we had finished our night session, we could get a station from Kansas City, which was beginning to develop a nationwide reputation for the Coon-Saunders band, the famous "Kansas City Nighthawks." They were becoming better known even than Whiteman and Isham Jones because they were the first band to take advantage of the new medium. Radio would eventually become more popular than phonograph records and the Nighthawks seemed to be the first to realize it.

It occurred to me that if we could only get a job in Cleveland, maybe we could fill in that standby time, playing for nothing if necessary, just so we could achieve recognition.

Cleveland was only 250 miles from London. But the prospects of finding a job in the city across Lake Erie seemed as dim as if it were in a different continent. It took a girl singer to unwillingly point the way.

We had returned to the Winter Garden after Port Stanley, and one snowy afternoon I walked into a matinee vaudeville show and was kicked in the head, and I suppose, the heart, by one of the acts. Female singers were enjoying their own popularity at the time. We had been hearing much of singers like Marion Harris and Margaret Young on records. The one at the Loew's Theater was named Corinne Arbuckle, and I sat entranced as she belted out blues numbers in a big voice that carried to the far reaches of the balcony without the aid of the microphone of the future. She had a face and figure to match the voice and I felt I had to meet her.

Backstage, I knocked on the door of her dressing room without thinking of an approach. When she opened the door, the first thought that came to mind was a rather clumsy question. "How would you like to take on a band?" I asked.

I guess she overlooked what could have been interpreted as classic *double-entendre*. I was seeking to convince her to join our group, feeling that a singer of her ability would make it easier for us to get to the States. She was nice enough to answer:

"I'm sorry. I'm having enough trouble getting bookings on my own." I asked if she'd come over to the Winter Garden between shows that night and listen to our group, suggesting that if she liked our style she might talk to her booker. He might recommend that she join us. I became so taken with the proposition as I outlined it to her that I even promised we'd give her billing over the band. She agreed to listen and I picked her up like a stage-door Johnny that night and drove her to the Winter Garden. She consented to do a song, "I Wish I Could Shimmy like My Sister Kate," and it was a showstopper.

Thoroughly convinced that Corinne was our passport to the States, I renewed the campaign to get her agent's name. She refused to give it to me, saying her next stop was Toronto and forget about her agent, she couldn't afford a band. We only played the Winter Garden, weekends, so I followed her to Toronto on Monday and stayed there three days, continuing the high-pressure campaign. Corinne stood steadfast until the following week, when I took another three days' leave for Buffalo, her next engagement. I guess the persistence paid off; she finally told me her agent was a booker named Mike Shea. She gave me his phone number in Cleveland.

Cleveland! Home of Radio Station WTAM, our immediate goal. It seemed too good to be true. Of course there remained the problem of convincing Mr. Shea that if Cleveland wasn't ready for the Guy Lombardo Band, we were ready for Cleveland.

Mike Shea couldn't have been less impressed the first time I called him. He listened to my story: Corinne Arbuckle had heard us play, liked the band, had sung a number with us and the response had been phenomenal. Couldn't he find us a job in Cleveland with the band playing in back of Corinne?

He listened and his reaction was identical to his singer's. "I'm having enough trouble booking her on her own," he said. "Much less with an orchestra. I'm only a small booker."

Then how about an engagement for the orchestra without Corinne? We'd take anything, just for the chance to work in and around Cleveland. Even a few days would suit us. That tiny wedge he could handle.

"I've got a one-night job for the Elks Club in a couple of weeks. It's an eight-act show. You want to be one of the acts and can get down to Cleveland and back for two hundred bucks, you got a date." I accepted as happily as if I'd just signed a contract for the Palace Theater on Broadway.

We took the day coach to Cleveland, traveled most of the day, and hauled our instruments onto a bus that took us to the Elks clubhouse on 105th and Euclid. We appeared on stage somewhere in the middle of the bill between the trained seals and a comedy

acrobat team, played for fifteen minutes, and listened to a few desultory handclaps when the curtain came down. Shea came backstage, counted out our wages, and I eagerly awaited his reaction.

He continued unimpressed. We hadn't been too bad; the audience had refrained from throwing eggs. But he thought we had a
lot to learn. Final judgment: "Come back in a year or so and I'll
see what I can do for you."

Our debut in the United States had been about as auspicious as
that Guy-Carmen duet for Mama's lawn party almost ten years
ago. And it had put me in a difficult position. Before we left for
the one-night stand, the word had leaked around London that the
Lombardos had a booker and a job in the States. Nobody said anything about the job being of a twenty-four-hour duration; I was
young and optimistic enough to believe that all we needed was
one opportunity for the folks in the States to hear us. They'd
never permit us to go back to London.

But back we went the same night and the London *Free Press*
wanted an interview the next day. I told the reporter that our
booker had high hopes for us, neglecting to impart the information that if we had a commitment it was for a year hence. The reporter assumed we were returning to Cleveland almost immediately and that's the way his story read. They began giving us
farewell parties in London.

Now I was faced with a crisis of my own making. By my being
less than frank, all our relatives, friends, and fans were talking
about the wonderful future that lay ahead for the Lombardo boys.
Carmen and Lebe couldn't have been more wonderful. They
suggested, what the hell, let's go to Cleveland, and if we have to,
we'll walk the streets till we find a job. The boys in the band
agreed. To save face, we gave two weeks' notice at the Winter
Garden and on the Sunday before the Thursday that we were to
leave, the editor of the London *Free Press* gave us another party.
All of London's dignitaries showed up, including the mayor, and
we sat guiltily listening to much extolling of our virtues. Papa and
Mama attended and basked in the adulation heaped on their sons.
I had never felt so low in my life.

The next few days were spent on the telephone. I kept calling
Mike Shea, explaining the embarrassing situation, pleading with

him to dig up anything. His answer remained constant: "Don't blame me, you brought it all on yourself. I don't have a thing and there just aren't any prospects."

We had just about enough money for fare and a week's lodging for the band, but the decision had been made. Thursday we go. And as we were dolefully packing our bags, my sister Elaine came running to my bedroom. Her face radiated excitement. She was carrying a telegram and it said, "Open Akron, Sunday, one week, Mike Shea." I called him immediately and he confirmed it, saying, "One week and after that I don't know what you're going to do." But all I remembered was an old Irish lady saying, "Everything turns out for the best."

I keep thinking back, wondering about the faith the folks in London had in us. We had to make a train at one o'clock Sunday morning and perhaps a hundred people were there to see us off. A bunch of kid musicians who hadn't proved anything yet, but here were friends standing on a bitter-cold railroad platform, losing sleep to reaffirm their confidence in us. It sounds corny in retrospect, but I remember thinking I never would let them down.

2. Cleveland Gave Us Style— and Wives

The die was cast. We were nine young Canadians coming to the United States, like characters out of Horatio Alger, seeking fame and fortune. At twenty-one, I was the oldest. George Gowans, seventeen, was the youngest. Except for Carmen, a mature twenty, teen-agers comprised the rest of the band. Our finances were precarious and all of us knew that, if another job didn't present itself after the week in Akron, we would be going back to London red-faced.

We had traveled most of the night and most of the day to get to Cleveland, and by the time we emerged from a frosty bus in Akron, we had only a few hours to begin our dance-hall date. I had heard somewhere that big-city hotels had what they called sample rooms to accommodate an entourage, and I found one at the Howe. The price was right. For a dollar a day each, they sent up nine cots. The first thing we did was install a clothesline running the length of the room. We had to get the creases out of our new outfits—black tux jackets and crisp white trousers.

We had found dance halls in Canada to be uniformly neat and attractively decorated. Some even had roofs painted to look like the sky, with fake stars and a moon for romantic atmosphere. The Akron dance hall had been born a garage and it looked like one. A tiny bandstand gave us a logistical problem, since it was plainly built for about five musicians. The room was bisected with pillars and there were bouncers in red sweaters leaning on them to see that the dancers behaved.

But the biggest disappointment was the size of the crowd. Perhaps fifty people showed up before the end of the evening. There were even less on Monday and it required no financial genius to figure out that this job, which was to last seven days, would last no longer. I found out, however, that the dance hall was owned by a man named Botson, who also owned a small theater across the street.

I called on him in the theater on Tuesday, told him I was his bandleader, and gave him a proposition. If he could extend our engagement a week, we'd play at his theater for nothing in the daytime.

Mr. Botson hadn't even heard us play, but he liked the proposition. We were only getting $300 for the week and that sounded like fair enough remuneration for playing at his dance hall by night and his theater by day. So now London was at least another week away.

The following week, Mike Shea came to the theater, and Corinne Arbuckle was with him. I asked him if he'd turned up another date for us, and he shook his head, almost in exasperation. "You guys are something," he said. "I didn't have a job for you in the first place and then you make me go out and dig one up because you make me feel it's a matter of life and death. Now I get you a job for a week and you've stretched it out to two weeks. Honestly, Lombardo, I think you've had it. I'll be in Cleveland, so keep in touch. You never know."

So we finished Akron and returned to Cleveland and found another sample room in the Winton Hotel. As we signed the register in the lobby, we heard nice sounds coming out of a small ballroom. The sign in the lobby said "For dancing—Vernon-Owen Band." All of us walked over and peered into the ballroom, watching the nicely dressed dancers, wondering when we'd get the opportunity to play in a hotel dining room one day. We must have looked like poor kids looking into a department store window at Christmas.

And that's the way Larry Owen, the co-leader and saxophonist for the band, remembers seeing us for the first time. "I knew you were musicians," he would say later. "Because you were all carrying instruments. But I couldn't figure out where you came from. You looked like the north country with your caps and knickers and heavy coats."

Larry was to play an important role in the history of the Lombardo band, but for the time being he became our friend and confidant. He was about my age, a home-town boy who had gone to the Cleveland Conservatory of Music and had graduated as a talented saxophonist and arranger. Now he was a partner with Dick Vernon in a five-piece band, and the Winton Hotel job was his start in the business. He had empathy with our band and the problem of finding work.

"Try the Chinese restaurants," he suggested. "We've got loads of them in town and you'll get plenty to eat."

Our dining tastes were not yet that cosmopolitan, but we were about to start the rounds of chop suey joints when Mike Shea came through again. He had a date in two weeks for a private party in a hotel. It would pay $250 and that meant we could stay another two weeks. It gave us time to take a crack at our original target—Radio Station WTAM. It didn't turn out to be a problem. The station manager permitted us to play a couple of half-hour segments, advising us there was no salary attached to it. We played for free gladly and the reward was twenty or thirty complimentary letters from listeners.

For once Mike Shea was impressed. The fan mail and a good review in one of the papers might help him book us for a few weeks with Corinne. He began talking about a name for the band. It ought to identify where we came from; a number of bands had so named themselves. There was Abe Lyman and his Californians, Fred Waring and his Pennsylvanians, the Kansas City Nighthawks, the New Orleans Rhythm Kings.

"Well, we could be the Canadians," I suggested.

"Just doesn't have the impact," Mike said. "The thing Canada is best known for is the Royal Canadian Mounted Police. Maybe we could play with that."

"How about the Royal Canadians."

"That's it. Guy Lombardo and His Royal Canadians."

That's how the band got its name, and shortly after Shea had

lined up a five-week vaudeville tour for us with Corinne Arbuckle.
The billing was to be Corinne Arbuckle and the Royal Canadians.
Somewhere the Lombardo name had gotten lost, but I wasn't
about to make an issue out of it when there was five weeks of
work at stake. Our itinerary would begin on Christmas week in
Portsmouth, Ohio, and the following weeks would be in the
college towns of Ann Arbor, Michigan, and Madison, Wisconsin.
The tour would continue to Detroit and end in Cleveland.

Before we left, Larry Owen came up with a tip that a new night
club might be opening in February. If we could get a job there
after our tour, it would ensure our continued stay in Cleveland.
The place was called the Claremont Tent, on Eighty-sixth and
Euclid, and had been operating as a speakeasy. Larry said it was
owned by one Louis Bleet, who also operated the Carlton Terrace,
a night club at which most of the name acts of the day frequently
appeared. Larry suggested I ask Bleet for an audition.

Armed with a scrapbook of radio fan letters, I took a trolley to
the Claremont and asked to see Mr. Bleet. A waiter took a hasty
look at it and advised me that Mr. Bleet usually spent afternoons
at the Carlton Terrace, in downtown Cleveland, two blocks from
the Winton Hotel.

"But he just don't see everybody," he said encouragingly.

I went back to the hotel to talk it over with Carmen, and my
brother wouldn't let me quit on Bleet. He called downstairs and
asked the manager if the band could use the unoccupied ballroom,
and got an affirmative answer. Carmen said, "Now you go get this
Bleet and bring him back here to listen. Don't come back without
him."

The maître d' at the Carlton Terrace was less approachable than
the waiter at the Claremont. "Mr. Bleet is having lunch," he said.
"He usually does not like to be disturbed. Who shall I say is
calling?"

"Guy Lombardo of London."

Mr. Bleet evidently did not wish to disturb Anglo-American
relations. He came out to the lobby, an impeccably dressed, silver-
haired and handsome man of forty, obviously curious about what
an unknown Englishman wanted of him.

I could see the interest fading when I told him I was from London, Ontario, and that I had a band set up waiting for him to hear at the Winton. If he liked us, perhaps he could hire us for the Claremont or the Carlton Terrace to play for the acts. He wanted to know how big the band was, and when I told him he said, "Too big. The bandstands at both places are only about big enough for five places."

I tried to tell him we'd overcome that problem before, but he turned around and walked back into the dining room.

Dejectedly back at the hotel, I found my usually placable brother unwilling to listen to excuses. During that year, Carmen had acquired a nickname. We called him "Bull" after Luis Firpo, the Argentinian prize fighter known as "The Wild Bull of the Pampas." It wasn't that Carmen resembled this giant; all the Lombardo brothers, unlike Papa, who was six feet, were rather short.

Maybe it was those broad shoulders he had developed as a kid when he was a physical fitness devotee that had earned Carm his sobriquet. But at this moment, he began acting like a matador's prey, almost snorting in exasperation.

"You're supposed to be our leader. You go lead this Bleet back here in a cab, if necessary. But get him. All the guys are sitting in the ballroom waiting and they'll be disappointed as hell if he doesn't come."

Carm always had a buck more than the rest of us, so I appropriated one from him, hailed a cab, went back to the night club, and asked the driver to wait, hoping the dollar would be enough for the four-block round trip. I brushed past the maître d', walked up to Bleet, who was lunching with his wife, and put it to him squarely:

"Look, Mr. Bleet, I got a cab waiting outside. It will only take you ten minutes to hear the band and get back here. You'll make a bunch of young fellows very happy if you just hear them play one number."

Louis Bleet shook his head, came to the hotel, and shook his head again when he saw the waiting band. I asked what he wanted to hear and he said, "Anything."

We had exactly one arrangement where everybody played notes and sounded like an orchestra. It was "Bambalina," from the hit

Broadway musical *Wildflower* and we played it slow in the Pasternak-Rubinstein tempo. Bleet was not exactly enthralled; he said we had a nice kind of Hawaiian sound. But he didn't need a band right now and where could he get in touch with us if he changed his mind. I gave him our itinerary for the next five weeks and watched him depart. If Bleet had nothing for us when we returned to Cleveland in February, we might have to go back to London after all.

The first Christmas Day any of us had ever spent away from home, we opened in Portsmouth. Papa had been fond of saying, "No matter what any of us are doing or wherever we are, we should always be together at Christmas." And now we had finished the last show in a dingy theater and we tramped around in the snow, looking for a phone. There were only two in the small town and we located one in the lobby of the post office. I put a call through and Mom answered. She started crying. I turned away and handed the phone to Carm, and he hurriedly turned it over to Lebe. Papa had tried to talk to them and choked up. Now the three of us were crying. The other boys in the band got on to relay messages to their folks, and all around me all I could see were eight pairs of very wet eyes.

Papa finally came on the phone again, asking for me. Now he was furious. "Families should never be separated on Christmas," he said. "You belong here, not there." I promised we never would be separated again and Carm and Lebe nodded their heads. And that would be the last Christmas that all of us would not be together in London or wherever we were living.

Through that tour of Midwestern vaudeville houses, the band's performance was more akin to the old Lombardo Brothers Concert Company than the sophisticated, symphonic outfit we had hoped to become. Corinne was the star, and when we weren't backing her up we were donning funny hats and acting out novelty tunes. A few short months before, I had almost fallen in love with Miss Arbuckle. Now I was becoming disenchanted; she was acting too much like a prima donna.

In Ann Arbor, the audience was mostly composed of students from the University of Michigan, and it was our first experience with the collegiate crowd that would become our biggest boosters later on. We liked our reception there and in Madison, where the University of Wisconsin collegians were equally enthusiastic. In Madison, the snow was so high it became a tundra trek just to get from the hotel to the theater.

But we didn't mind the weather nearly as much as Corinne's imperious attitude. Plainly she considered herself the star and the bandsmen her underlings to perform her bidding. She traveled with a small bulldog and would often ask me to walk her pet from the hotel to the theater. This would require much stopping for the mutt to find a hydrant buried under the snow and I began to resent the imposition.

She kept the canine in her dressing room, and this led to an embarrassing situation while we were performing. We were doing a number and suddenly the dog came through her door, walked on-stage, and lifted its leg at the piano where Freddie was playing a beautiful solo. Very unprofessional and embarrassing to us and Corinne didn't even apologize for leaving her door ajar. She laughed.

That night she decided to have dinner at the hotel between shows. We ate sandwiches backstage. The dog was curled up in her dressing room, and we decided that if she wanted a performing dog we'd make him up like one. I grabbed the lipstick on Corinne's dressing table; Carm got the powder puff, Lebe handled the rouge. When we got through, Corinne's bulldog could have qualified for a circus act. Corinne got back and didn't appreciate it. I heard her yelling, "You dago bastards, I'll get even with you."

It was the kind of remark that would make me fight as a kid; now I burst into her dressing room, prepared to tell her that if she didn't apologize we didn't want to continue working with her. But I never got a chance to say it. Corinne was sitting there, naked, about to change into her stage clothes. That shut me up effectively.

I stood there unable to speak as she launched into another tirade. She said she was going to tell her husband (I didn't even know she had one) and he'd take care of us when we got to Detroit the next week. I went back to the boys and we decided to stick out the tour, Miss Arbuckle and her husband notwithstanding.

He met us in Detroit as promised, but he was a rather mild-mannered man named Ray Hofhine, who managed the Columbia Burlesque House in Cleveland. He said that Corinne had told him she couldn't get along with us and that we'd have to bust up after the tour was over. I remember him ending that declaration with a slightly menacing "Got that?"

A much more pleasant figure came backstage just after Hofhine left. It was Papa. He was fifty now, still tall and erect and prepossessing. I had just finished telling the boys that we were through if we didn't get a job when we got back to Cleveland, and they were sitting around rather disconsolately.

So rather than have Papa walk in on this gloomy scene, I took him across the street to a restaurant and we sat down over coffee.

"How is it going?"

"Oh, I don't know, Pa. No use lying. It's tough."

He said the man who managed the Port Stanley resort had called to find if we were coming back for the summer. He had to know pretty soon or he'd start looking for another band.

"I guess we will, Pa. We have this week in Detroit and one more in Cleveland and it looks like we'll be coming home. Tell him to save our job."

"Don't worry about it, Son. I know you did your best. The worst that can happen is we'll all be together again. That's the important thing."

We walked back to the theater and all the boys gathered around Papa, embracing him. Carmen pointed to a telegram on the table, saying it had just been delivered before we walked in. I opened it and the signature seemed to jump from the paper. Louis Bleet had sent the wire, which read, "Can you open Claremont, Feb. 18?" Another miracle of unplanned timing. We closed the last week of the Arbuckle tour in Cleveland the night of the seventeenth. I called Bleet and he verified the engagement and I was so excited I forgot to ask him about money. I figured it had to be union scale, $75 a week per man and double for the leader.

The moment we hit Cleveland, Carm and I rushed down to the Claremont Tent. It had been raided as a speakeasy shortly after we went on tour, and now it was reopening as a small night club after being shuttered for thirty days. The door to the club was closed, but there was a small billboard against the wall of the building. It contained the most beautiful prose I had ever read. "Opening Feb. 18, Guy Lombardo and His Royal Canadians."

And we opened, full of hope with a salary larger than any of us had ever received, except Carmen. As I had anticipated, the band's take was about $700 a week. It soon became apparent that our salary was much more than Louis Bleet was taking in. That first week we played to an average audience of about twenty-five people a night. They'd come in with hip flasks and pay for soda and ginger ale setups which cost about what they would pay for the whiskey dispensed in speakeasies.

Louis Bleet did not permit the lack of business to go on permanently. He set about to improve the band, hoping to attract more customers. And he was a man who knew how to improve an attraction. He had been a hoofer and knew the ins and outs of show business and music.

He came in one night and positioned himself directly opposite the bandstand, standing up and listening intently. He had a habit of biting his thumb and I watched him watching us, his thumb rarely leaving his mouth. When the last customer cleared out, he sat down at a table and asked us to continue playing.

During a break, he asked me, "Who's that fellow on the sax?"

"That's my brother, Carmen."

"Well, he's good. Who's that on the trumpet?"

"My brother, Lebert."

"Oh, a family affair. Well he's not bad either. But the trouble with the band is you play too loud. This is a small room, it can't hold all this sound. I noticed a couple of people walk in and they seemed to be deafened. They walked out again. You're just going to have to play softer."

I promised we could do that and he asked another question.

"Now that young man playing the clarinet. When he's doing a solo, why does the rest of the band sit around clapping?"

It was one of the things bands who hadn't yet achieved a Whiteman or Isham Jones symphonic sound did in those days. Somebody would play a solo and the rest of the band would clap as if for moral support or as a means of sustaining the rhythm.

I tried to explain the theory and Bleet said, "Forget about the clapping. Put some notes in there instead and you'll sound more like an orchestra. You fellows need a lot of work."

I realized we did. During the vaudeville tour, we had concentrated more on being vaudevillians than musicians. Just before we left for the five weeks with Corinne, Archie Cunningham, who played the sax behind Carm, had decided to go home. We replaced him with another saxophonist Carmen had trained in London. Fred Higman was all of sixteen. His name spelled backward came out Derf and that's what we called him. He was a tall, good-looking kid with a pleasant voice, and he soon became the band's comedian.

For the vaudeville act, we had worked out such numbers as "Thanks for the Buggy Ride," during which Carm would deck him out with harness and blinkers and drive him around the stage. For "A Cup of Coffee, A Sandwich and You," Derf would eat a sandwich while the band sang the lyrics. Derf would never know what we'd fix up in those sandwiches and without changing expression he would eat combinations that would make ordinary people choke.

But while those antics had seemed sufficient for small-time vaudeville, it was evident now that they would never carry us through to our goal of recognition as a fine orchestra. I welcomed suggestions from a pro like Bleet.

Although we had yet to develop what was later to be referred to as "the Lombardo sound," we had a certain style. Carmen's sweet sax, full and rich, set the tone for the reed instruments and was not too difficult to follow for the other saxes and clarinets. He played with emotion and sincerity and with a vibrato that was almost a simulation of the human voice. It was different from the so-called "legitimate tone" you might hear in a Broadway pit band.

Lebert, whose trumpet set the pattern for the brass section, had his own individual style too. He had learned the instrument without formal instruction and he didn't have a very wide range. Nor could he hit the high notes on the stock arrangements generally purchased by bands. So we practiced on vocal arrangements, and Lebe also began to get that voice-like quality out of his trum-

pet. Those were the key elements of our style—the identifiable
Carmen sax and Lebert trumpet.

And now Louis Bleet was pressing for us to improve. We
worked for two weeks, rehearsing every day, getting the volume
down, softening our sound. We never had used a loud drum and
George Gowans started playing even softer, complementing rather
than dominating.

It had taken work to learn how to play soft, but I noticed it was
beginning to please the Claremont's patrons. They would talk or
whisper to each other as they danced and seemed to like the idea.
It is difficult to offer an endearment if you have to compete with a
loud orchestra.

One night Bleet asked us to troop into the kitchen after we had
finished playing. He wanted us to get to work on eliminating the
clapping. "You guys aren't a minstrel show. You're a band and I
want you to sound like one. Now I've gotten some complaints
from people who say they've made requests for certain numbers
and it took you an awful long time to get around to them."

"That's true," I said. "But what do you do when you get a
dozen requests?"

He saw the problem and he had an answer that was to make
musical history. "Well, why don't you cut down on the length of
the request number. Say you get a request for 'All of Me' and
another one for 'It Had to Be You.' You don't have to give each
one of them the full three-minute orchestration. You can start on
the first request with the saxes and the rest of the band harmoniz-
ing softly behind them. Then in a minute or so, you swing over to
the next number."

"But you can't play one chorus, stop, play a new chorus, stop
again, and go on to another one all night. It would be too jerky."

"I don't mean for you to stop. Keep right on playing, but play a
different song."

"You can't do that. One song might be in a different tempo
from the one before and another might be in a different key."

"Why don't you have your piano player come in with a few
chords to modulate from one key to another and from one tempo
to another?"

I'd never heard of any band doing this before and neither had

Freddie Kreitzer. But he gave it a try. It worked. And thus was the first medley born. It is a form that gave us a new identity, because it was ours alone. Later, bands would begin imitating the Lombardo medley, and by the time of the Big Band era it was an accepted part of virtually every band's repertoire.

I fell in love with the medley idea the moment I saw it would work. It gave us, first, an opportunity to play many more songs during the course of an evening. We could take care of requests, lumping three or four together, smoothly jumping from one chorus to the next. I gave much thought to the composition of the medleys, learning early that they were best when songs in different tempos and different keys followed each other. And I varied the instruments so that different ones were used to punctuate each number.

Through the remainder of that winter and the following spring of 1924, we were beginning to mesh as a band. Bleet had taught us other things I think we inherently believed in. Like Papa, he was a stickler for good grooming. In the Claremont Tent, I began to lay down rules for the band that would last our lifetime. Each musician would be required to look like he just got out of the tub; there would be no spots on his outfit, the trousers would be knife-creased, the shoes highly polished. Papa had given me a flair for fashion and new uniforms were picked with care and taste.

Bleet had experience with musicians who would wander around the room between sets, accepting drinks, cigarettes dangling from their mouths. He thought it gave neither his room nor the musicians character. I agreed and it became band policy for each member to look and behave like gentlemen. The policy that developed under Bleet's tutelage we maintain today, and I consider it the reason that we are so frequently asked to play the same engagements year after year.

And as we began to mesh and improve, business improved at the Claremont. We weren't turning people away, but it was evident we were earning our keep. One night in May, Bleet informed me that a special guest would be coming to hear us. "It could mean a summer job, if she likes you."

The guest turned out to be Sophie Tucker, the best-known songstress of the day, who headed the bill at Cleveland's Palace.

She was Bleet's partner in the Lake Road Inn, a swank roadhouse twenty miles outside Cleveland. She came in with a large party, listened and watched intently, and at the end of the evening Bleet gave us the word.

"She liked the band. You've got the summer job at the Lake Road Inn."

Everything was beginning to fall into place that summer of 1924. The band lived in two tents and we all felt like we were on vacation and being paid for it. The beautiful lakeside setting attracted the Cleveland society set, and the inn was crowded every night with attractively dressed couples—the girls in the new flapper style with bobbed hair and short skirts, the men in blazers belted in the back and white flannel trousers.

I had time to indulge myself in a hobby carried over from London, where Papa had introduced me to motorboats. There were new friends to take me on rides and I was spending as much time as I could either in borrowed or rented craft.

But I realized that the euphoric conditions of that engagement might make us feel fat-cat. We were living as if we had already arrived, which I knew was not yet the case.

Louis Bleet knew it too. He kept working with us. We rehearsed every day, working on new arrangements and stockpiling medleys in various combinations. We made the tuba the big fat sound in back of the horns, and that added another dimension to the identifiable sound that would be exclusively ours. I think by the end of the summer, we had progressed to the point that if we were not quite ready for the major leagues, at least we were playing in Triple-A.

Bleet booked us back to the Claremont in the fall, and we had begun to feel like young men about town. The specter of returning to London as failures had vanished, as had the financial uncertainties of the year before. There were pretty girls to engage our off time and the business of learning how to drink in a society where liquor was forbidden to be sold.

There was a bootlegger in town known to most musicians because he was their exclusive supplier. He was rather aptly named Earl Nipper and he had bargain rates for the bands around town. His bathtub gin cost two dollars a pint, but for an entire band he would supply eight pints for twelve dollars. At those rates, we could hardly neglect our drinking education. Eddie Mashurette, our tuba player, introduced that rotgut to Larry Owen, who had never taken a drink before, and he remembers that the first time he made the noble experiment, it gave him the nerve to stand up and lead the band in which he was a partner.

That doesn't mean we became a band of alcoholics. Early on, I had introduced another regulation, like the one about good grooming. No member of the band or its brotherly triumvirate of owners was to take a drink before coming to work. Our job usually began at night and there was to be total abstinence until we finished our last set. It's another rule that remains today.

It was time to meet head-on the *raison d'être* for our being in Cleveland in the first place. We had all felt that if we were ever to become known we ought to get on radio. We had listened to all those unused time gaps on WTAM and the situation hadn't changed much, although in New York and Chicago bands were coming on the air with more frequency, usually through wires in hotels or night clubs.

The management at WTAM did not look with favor on the proposal I gave them that they put a wire in the Claremont and have us broadcast directly. Their opposition stemmed from the fact that the Claremont had once been a speakeasy and that the attendant publicity about the federal raid had cheapened its reputation to the point WTAM did not want to associate with it.

But the station was magnanimous about permitting us to play—from the studio and for free. Actually there were numerous bands in Cleveland that could have availed themselves of the same opportunity. But in none of them were the personnel willing to work without remuneration. Musicians expected scale pay for every job. Of course, our crew had a different make-up. We weren't just a bunch of assorted union musicians pulled together to make up a band. We were a family that went beyond the Lombardo brothers. Every member of the band had grown up together in London and all of them had the same desire to be part of an operation that could succeed only through a family effort.

So I got not a single dissent when I asked the boys if they were willing to give up an hour a day for the needed exposure radio would give us. Every night the nine of us would pile into a Checker cab and head for the studio, where we kept an alternate set of instruments. We'd play a concert from six to seven and then head back for the Claremont for the nightly stint that began at 8:30 and lasted until 2 A.M. It left us little time during the day to enjoy the pleasures of Cleveland and the company of our growing number of friends.

But I don't suppose we ever made a more important investment in time or effort than that gratuitous engagement on radio. We rehearsed daily for each concert and for the program that would follow at the Claremont. And I knew we were sounding more like a fine orchestra every day. The radio listeners confirmed it. We got batches of mail daily. They said they liked our slow tempo, the soft tones, the lovely reed and brass sounds. And they loved the way we filled all the requests through the new medley technique.

We were now repaying Louis Bleet for his confidence in hiring us and for his very important efforts to improve us. The Claremont was doing capacity business as more and more people who had heard us on radio came to see the band in person. I knew radio was making us known, but at the time never realized how much.

It took a man from Lorain, Ohio, to confirm, once and for all, how well known we had become in the area through the airwaves. He represented the Lorain Fife and Drum Society, and he wanted to know if we had an open Monday in April to play at a dance under the society's auspices. Monday was our night off, so I told him we could make it. Since we were paid about $100 a night at the Claremont, I figured the trip was worth $300.

He said he wasn't authorized to pay that kind of money, but he could offer us $200 and 50 per cent of the gate. We finally settled for $250 and turned down the percentage.

The date was for the night of Easter Monday and it rained all day. On the trip, Carm and I were congratulating each other on taking that extra fifty bucks and eschewing any percentage deal. It didn't look like many people would brave that downpour for a group of musicians from Cleveland.

The roads were almost awash as we got to Lorain. But the street leading into the small town looked like a futuristic drawing of a Long Island parkway on a July Fourth weekend forty years later. We were in the middle of a traffic jam. It took us more than an hour to traverse the few blocks to the barnlike structure we were to play in.

The place, which could accommodate about 1,500 people, was a wall-to-wall sea of humanity, numbering nearly 4,000. They had paid a dollar apiece to see the band they'd heard over that Cleveland station. The man from the fife and drum society happily turned over a $250 check and Carm and I looked at each other ruefully. Had we gambled on the percentage, we'd have been almost $2,000 richer. But now we were sure of one thing. Our gamble on free radio had paid off.

That first radio show also helped us name a sister. We had received a wire from Papa that Mama had just delivered a new baby girl and they hadn't decided on her name. I called back immediately. I asked if the folks would mind if their three oldest sons made that decision. I heard Papa laughing and giving the news to the new mother. They both agreed to let us do it, but how and when would we let them know?

I told them to listen to our show very carefully that night. We would announce our new sister's name on the air. The choice wasn't too difficult. Everybody in Cleveland was humming the title song of the musical comedy that was playing at the Hanna Theater. It was named "Rose Marie." So was our baby sister when we delivered the radio message to our waiting parents.

By the time of our second summer engagement at the Lake Road Inn, we had become well enough known to get feelers from entrepreneurs whose livelihood was show business. It was a good feeling. We no longer had to go hat in hand, virtually begging for work. The approaches were coming from owners of night clubs, booking agents, artist's representatives, and song pluggers. I listened to the feelers with extreme caution.

We were happy with Louis Bleet and grateful for all he had done. I wasn't going to leave him unless somebody offered us a much more attractive proposition. The first such offer came from Sam Stecker, who had taken over Bleet's Carlton Terrace and renamed it the Music Box. Bleet had been paying us from $750 to

$800 a week for two years, now, and Stecker offered us $1,300. He also said that WTAM would put a wire in the room, because the Music Box had never been raided as a speak.

I told Bleet about the offer and he received it coldly. I said we'd be willing to stick with him if he'd give us some kind of raise; we'd settle for $950 a week and were willing to sacrifice the radio wire. We'd just continue playing at the studio. Like he had done once before, Louis Bleet turned around and walked away from me. This time it got me mad enough to accept the Music Box job.

We opened to a packed house in September, and I felt much better about Louis Bleet when he paid us the compliment of showing up with a party at a front-row table.

Although the new job paid more and enabled us to move into better quarters at the Westlake Hotel, it was much more demanding than the one at the Claremont Tent. We played six days a week, starting with luncheon music from 12:30 to 2. The dinner show was from 6 to 9 and the late show from 10 to 2. But we had an hour program that was broadcast live during the late show and it began attracting the song pluggers looking to get their numbers on the air.

Tin Pan Alley, domiciled in New York, had pluggers in all the major cities. If they could get a bandleader, especially one who was on radio, to play the songs their firms published, it would enhance the sale of sheet music and recordings. I looked at the business in a different way. I'd play a song if I liked it, but I wanted first rights in our area so the song could be identified with the band.

We might not have become quite that big to make such a demand, but a representative from the Irving Berlin Music Company listened attentively as I made it. His name was Phil Julius and I had welcomed his overtures because Irving Berlin songs were bread and butter for an orchestra.

The master songwriter had such hits that year as "Always" and "Remember" and they were part of every band's repertoire. I was more interested in the fourth song on Julius' plug list, "Give Me a Little Kiss, Will Ya, Huh?" Julius said it wasn't an important song, but I asked him if we could have it alone for six weeks. I said I'd have an arrangement made and put it on the air. The song plugger didn't know what I had in mind.

My motive, naturally, was to establish the song in the mind of listeners as a Lombardo number. Julius gave us the okay and we made it an important hit around Cleveland. It became a major policy of the band as the years went on. We'd take a song we liked and ask to introduce it. The songs that became hits invariably were identified with our band.

So now most of the steps that we used to reach for the top rung of that ladder had been set in place. We had a style the people liked; it was individual and our own; we were getting constant exposure on radio; and we were playing songs people would remember both for their quality and the fact they first heard it on a Royal Canadians' Program.

We didn't have to go looking for a summer job in 1926. It came to us. The old Cleveland Yacht Club on Lake Erie had been converted into the most luxurious roadhouse in the Cleveland area. The new Blossom Heath was the kind of place that attracted the members of the country clubs that were springing up with the prosperity of the times. We were offered the engagement and found it even more attractive than the Lake Road Inn. Again we set ourselves up in tents, luxuriated in the water sports, and found no end of female company.

I was twenty-four and having the time of my life, careerwise and socially. But all the adulation and success must have been too heady for me to handle wisely that summer. Every member of the band was a bachelor and none of them had difficulty getting dates. It began to worry me that if several of them should decide to marry we now would be faced with problems we never had before. Like what to do with wives and babies when we went on tour or did a series of one-nighters.

I made the most arrogant and selfish decision of my life. Any member of the band who wanted to get married, I announced one day without consulting Carm or Lebe, would have to find another job. I didn't know it at the time, but actually the only one who was even comtemplating such an idea was Carm.

He had met the lovely and wealthy Florence Haas in a rather unlikely setting. He was sitting in the inn's kitchen with several other members of the band, munching sandwiches during a break. Florence walked into the kitchen, a refugee from a large party that had come to the Blossom Heath after a day of golf. She knew the owner and had asked for scraps to feed her chow dog, and he had directed her to the chef. Carmen smiled at her and she smiled back and I guess they both knew something I wasn't aware of.

Florence kept coming back to the inn and Carmen would arrange to meet her for quick chats between sets. It is not easy to carry on a romance when you're a musician working nights; it was one of the reasons I'd put in the no-marriage rule to ensure everybody's being on the bandstand when they were supposed to. But *l'affaire* Florence-Carmen began assuming serious proportions, although both of them knew they had roadblocks to consider.

Florence had been brought up to wealth and she had to worry about how she could adjust to life as a musician's wife. Carmen had to worry about that stupid big-brother embargo on marriage.

So Florence decided she better get away to think it over. That fall she went to Florida. And Carmen sent her a portable phonograph in a leather case. A record was on the turntable—Irving Berlin's "Remember."

Florence came back from Miami with an assist from Irving Berlin. They eloped the following May and I got the announcement of the marriage by telegram. I read it with mixed emotions—happiness for my brother and disgust for myself for trying to alter the laws of nature. Naturally, I welcomed back the newlyweds with all the grace I could muster.

Florence even became a member of our organization. I made her the paymaster of the band. It was a job I had never been comfortable with. I just don't have an accountant's mentality or heart. I could never turn down one of the boys when he'd ask for an advance. And both he and I were often forgetful about the loan, which meant that there were many times when we got paid that I found there was no money left for me. I'd advanced it all. So Florence, who added a hell of a lot better than I did, took over the payroll and handled that chore for years.

Carmen got back just in time to participate in another milestone for the band. One of the prestige engagements for all successful aggregations were the big summer proms in the leading colleges. Those engagements had made Fred Waring's reputation and he became a favorite with the collegians, who, like today, buy the records and set the pattern in the music market.

Benny Friedman, the all-American quarterback at the University of Michigan, had heard us play when he was a freshman and we were on the bill with Corinne Arbuckle at the Ann Arbor vaudeville house. He had liked the band, and now that he was a big man on campus he invited us to play at Michigan's famous Jay Hop. It was the first of hundreds of college proms at which we would appear and it gave us a built-in coterie of fans who started with us when they were young and remained our supporters through their lifetimes.

We followed the Jay Hop with one-nighters around Ohio—in ballrooms in Dayton, Columbus, Erie, and Toledo. And wherever we went the reputation we had built on radio preceded us. We broke each ballroom's attendance record. The thrilling part of it was that the records had been held by the Kansas City Night-hawks, the Coon-Saunders band that had kept us up listening on our crystal set in London. Coon-Saunders had given us the impetus to set our sights on Cleveland and Station WTAM. Now we were breaking their records.

We proceeded triumphantly to our second season at the Blossom Heath, where the climate continued conducive to romance. Like Carmen, I fell in love at the roadhouse kitchen with my own version of the most beautiful girl in the world. He had met Florence hunting scraps for a dog. I met Lilliebell Glenn with the assistance of a litter of kittens.

The restaurant's resident cat had become a mother and the band had adopted her offspring. They were domiciled in a cardboard carton in the kitchen, and between sets all of us would come and visit. I remember stopping by and picking up a sandwich from the chef before paying my respects to the family. I had the sandwich in one hand and a kitten in the other when the most gorgeous girl I had ever seen walked in, knelt, and began petting the occupants of the box.

Lilliebell was then and is now the complete animalarian. No species escaped her attention or failed to touch her heart. She had grown up on an estate abounding in horses, dogs, and cats and childhood pets had included a descented skunk and a baby lamb. It was natural that when she heard about the kittens in the kitchen, after sitting down at her table in the Blossom Heath, her first impulse was to visit them.

But all I knew about the girl who knelt next to me, stroking the tiny bundles of fluff, was that she was beautiful. Tall and willowy, blond and cream-complexioned, she lit up the room for me when she smiled her departure. I was to see that winning smile a little while later when she danced by the bandstand in the arms of a handsome young man. I remember two sensations: a pang of jealousy and the warmth engendered by the smile that was obviously directed at me.

It developed that the young man was her husband, Chet Caldwell, the heir to a printing fortune. In the weeks that followed I got to know both of them quite well. They were steady customers and would invite me to their table between sets. Ironically they were still dating, though they had separated and were on the verge of a divorce. Chet was a likable only son who had never wanted for anything and admitted he had been spoiled both by his father and uncle. "I don't blame Lilliebell for refusing to put up with me," he told me candidly.

The three of us would often go out together after I finished work, and Lilliebell (named for two of her mother's friends, Lillie and Belle) began coming to the lake in the mornings and afternoons. She was a low handicap golfer but she also loved the water, and I began to look forward to sharing the swimming and boating with her.

Our first date alone after her divorce was not a memorable one. I had been invited to a late house party honoring the celebrated vaudeville team of Clayton, Jackson and Durante, which had opened that night at Cleveland's Palace Theater. Carm was taking Florence and I asked Lilliebell to come.

Jimmy Durante, who was to become a lifelong friend, was warm, likable, and as funny offstage as on. It was a great party up to the point that I heard Carm involved in a shouting match with Jimmy's partner, Lou Clayton. The remarks were getting nasty and both of them were beginning to square off when I interceded for the home team. Nobody was going to take a punch at my brother while I was an onlooker. So I punched first and Lou Clayton came up from the floor with something sharp in his hand and I was bleeding from a cut on the face, all over my clothes and in front of a very agitated first date. She was obviously appalled at the way show business people behaved at parties and I didn't see her again for several weeks.

I'm afraid I did not quite live up to her picture of an impeccable young gentleman the next time we met, either. Since boyhood when Papa had purchased his first motorboat and then that 1915 Studebaker, I had always been fascinated by motors and what made them tick. And now at twenty-five, with money in the bank and all prospects pointing to more, I had purchased a big new Marmon car with a powerful engine.

I was engaged in unraveling the mysteries of the motor when Lilliebell drove up with a girl friend. She had come to say hello and I guess to forgive me for the fight episode. When I emerged from under the hood, she must have had second thoughts. My overalls were decked with grease, and so was a skullcap I had worn to protect my hair. My face and hands were black.

But they were temporary obstacles after all. We were married in September, four months after Carmen and Florence. And shortly after that, Lebert met and married a beautiful girl named Carol Williams, who would be tragically taken from him by illness before too many years.

The band, meanwhile, had undergone a few changes of its own. Both Carm and I felt we needed another sax to complement his and Derf Higman's, and it took us some time to decide between two applicants for the job.

The choice was between an extremely talented young musician named Freddy Martin and Larry Owen, our closest friend in Cleveland. Larry had decided to leave his own band if he could go to work for us because he believed in our potential. He also liked the idea of the family atmosphere under which we worked, with every member contributing ideas and none being unwilling to talk up for fear of offending the leader.

We owed Larry a lot for heading us in Louis Bleet's direction and giving us support when we most needed it upon our arrival in Cleveland. But it wasn't friendship that finally made me decide on Larry. It was simply that he had an added talent, besides being a fine saxophonist. He was also an arranger and we now needed somebody to assume the arranging chores. Freddy Martin, of course, would go on to become one of the top orchestra leaders in the country. Larry Owen is still with the band today.

The other change had occurred before Larry joined us. We regretfully had to part company with Eddie Mashurette, our tuba player. Young Eddie had learned to drink with the rest of us in Cleveland, but he couldn't handle it. And that was one cardinal rule I would never abandon. The rule was no drinking until after work, and Eddie wouldn't abide by it. I forgave him two trespasses and the third time he was out.

It posed a problem. The tuba is an important element of our sound. Most orchestras had replaced it with the string bass, but we retained the bass horn to accentuate the faster numbers with its oompah sound and to augment the brass and reed sections in the slower numbers. The brass horn's long, slurring notes gave us an organ effect we never wanted to lose.

In a phone call to Papa, I had mentioned that we were losing Eddie and asked if he knew of another young man in London good enough to replace him. Papa came up with another Carmen Lombardo student. He reminded me of Bernard Davies, who had learned to play the bass sax under Carmen. "Shouldn't take much work to convert him to the tuba," Papa said, reminding me that we had already converted Carmen from clarinet to sax and Lebe from the drums to the trumpet. I told Papa to lay out the money to buy Bern a tuba if he was interested, and have him practice on it until he thought he was ready. Two weeks later, Bern Davies reported for work in Cleveland. It didn't take him long to become accomplished on the big horn and he blended in perfectly with the rest of the young Londoners.

I was beginning to feel that we had smoothed over most of the rough edges, that the band had arrived professionally. Cleveland and its suburbs might not have been the music capital of the world, but it was a large metropolitan area in which all manner of musical outfits were playing. And all indications were that the Royal Canadians comprised the chief musical attraction in town.

Radio had brought us prominence and now everywhere we went we were confronted by fans and flattery.

My judgment about our professional arrival was confirmed by a flattering review in *Variety*, the show business bible. Abel Green was a young roving correspondent at the time and had come to Cleveland to review the city's attractions and been directed to the Blossom Heath. Later, of course, he became editor of the weekly Broadway paper and was considered the most knowledgeable authority of every aspect of the entertainment industry. Green began his review by lamenting the general ennui that had set in at Cleveland's places of entertainment. Then he told about the Blossom Heath Inn:

> . . . The band attraction is Guy Lombardo's Royal Canadians, so named because of their Canuck derivation, and shaping up as a musical find that should inspire a "rave" in these dog days of dreary dansapators and so-so entertainment. Under Lombardo's direction, this combination of 10 which includes two other Lombardo brothers (Carmen, sax, and Lebert, trumpet) socks out dance music that would make the jaded New Yorkers, for instance, sit up with startling alacrity. Only every so often does a dance unit come along that possesses a gifted knack of presenting smooth syncopations of inspirational proportions. A tonic for sluggish feet, the double quintet delivers a brand of dansapation that places them head and shoulders above a general run of standard units.
>
> Whether it was Emerson or Noah Webster, as has been debated, the parable of the world beating a pathway to the doorstep of the man who makes the best mousetrap in the world, or does anything better than his neighbor, is aptly illustrated in the Lombardo engagement. With the heart of the city places doing nothing, here's a band that averages $1,000 in minimum trade on weekdays and $1,500 on weekends . . .

That review and the dance hall records we had broken in Ohio now introduced us to a pair of brothers with whom I was not particularly anxious to get involved. A man named Billy Stein called one night and said he represented a Chicago booking agency called the Music Corporation of America. His brother, Jules, ran the operation and they wanted to represent the band. I had never heard of MCA, was rather suspicious of bookers, and felt that we were now doing well enough so that we could book our own dates. I turned him down.

Billy Stein reminded me of the Guy Lombardo of only a few years before, trying desperately to win over Mike Shea and refusing to take no for an answer. He kept calling the Blossom Heath from Chicago every night. It got so I wouldn't answer the phone; all that useless conversation was interfering with my between-sets courtship of Lilliebell. Finally, Stein walked into the Blossom Heath one night, carrying a brief case.

He opened it and showed me the press clippings of the bands he and his brother represented. They were all doing well. He only began to perk my interest when he mentioned the Coon-Saunders band. Jules Stein had taken the Nighthawks out of Kansas City and put them on a nationwide tour of ballrooms. They were breaking attendance records with every appearance.

"Now the reason Jules is so interested in you fellows," said Billy, "is that you have the only band that ever beat the Nighthawks anywhere. We've been reading about how well you did in northern Ohio. I'll tell you one thing, we can get you three times as much as you get for one-night stands now."

They were an interesting pair, the brothers Stein. Sons of Lithuanian immigrants who owned a dry-goods store in Chicago, they had been pushed by their parents toward careers in law and medicine. Billy had become the lawyer in the family at the time Jules was studying ophthalmology in Chicago's Rush Medical College, the year we arrived in Cleveland. To help pay his tuition, the medical student, who had taken violin lessons as a boy, would play what he later termed "a schmaltzy fiddle" with makeshift combos at school functions.

Jules found out about the tremendous demand for musical groups around the Chicago area in that era when the jazz age was busting its seams with an ever-increasing number of people who wanted to dance. So he opened a one-man booking agency in Chicago the year he became a resident eye doctor at the college. He told me once that he used to do his bookings through an attachment on his telephone called a Hushaphone. "I'd have a patient in front of me, fitting him for eyeglasses," he said, "and I'd get a call, and while I was putting on the glasses I'd whisper into the Hushaphone, 'Book the band in Lafayette.'"

Jules had become so successful by the time he started seeking out the Lombardos that he had given up his budding career as an eye doctor and had taken Billy in with him.

It was Jules Stein who innovated the lucrative and killing one-night stand. His milieu was basically the Midwest and he would take a band and book it for weeks, playing a different town every night. With Coon-Saunders, he had expanded the operation, nationwide, and the commissions were piling up. In fact business was so good the gang leaders in Chicago began sending emissaries to his office. They wanted a piece of his piece of the action. Jules Stein turned them down, not neglecting to take out a $75,000 insurance policy on himself, to be paid if he were kidnapped or otherwise physically manhandled.

I learned all this after telling Billy Stein I would give his offer consideration. Of course, what I could never visualize at the time was that Jules Stein and his Music Corporation of America would become the most powerful empire in show business, a corporation that would gross $224,000,000 a year, own motion picture companies, and represent Hollywood's biggest stars and Broadway's highest-paid performers.

When we had booked ourselves through northern Ohio, our asking price was about $200 a night for the band. Sometimes we'd take $150 to fill in between one town and the next. Billy Stein said he could get us $450 a night and Carm and Lebe agreed we ought to take a crack at it between closing the Blossom Heath and reopening the Music Box that fall.

During the last part of our engagement at the Blossom Heath, Jules Stein called me for the first time. He was in Cleveland on several matters and he had something important to discuss. Could I please come over to the Statler, where he was staying. I had now become fascinated with the man's operation and I consented.

He was an elegant young man, poised and self-confident, and he told me he was about to open an office in New York. "We're just starting and it's going to take me a while to get the lay of the land. But the thing I have uppermost in my mind is that I'm going to bring Guy Lombardo and His Royal Canadians to New

York as my big attraction. I think you guys are so good you're going to make it big and the other bands are going to line up to be represented by MCA."

It was almost too much to contemplate, but I had to get my suspicions off my chest. What did we need MCA for? We'd booked ourselves and broken Coon-Saunders' records. Why did he want us, particularly, when there were so many good musicians looking for work? Why didn't he make up his own band?

"Guy, I want you to know one thing. Bands aren't made. Bands just happen. And you have happened. Look, let's sign a contract for us to represent you. You can eliminate northern Ohio, where you've proved yourself. We'll represent you everywhere else."

That's the way it eventually happened. We signed the contract and MCA would represent us for almost thirty-five years, up to the time an antitrust suit against the corporation would force it to break up its artists representative division. But the contract permitted us to represent ourselves in northern Ohio.

Back at the Blossom Heath, we now began talking about not going back to the Music Box for the fall and winter. For one thing, the hours were too confining and Billy and Jules Stein had promised they could get us much more than the $1,300 a week we were receiving from Stecker. I decided to take a night off and visit Jules in his new office in the Paramount Building in New York. Maybe he could book us in England, where American bands weren't permitted long engagements. We were still British subjects; that rule wouldn't apply to us.

Jules welcomed the visit, he began buzzing around with plans; he'd get in touch with people in England right away. If England wasn't immediately possible, how about the Muehlbach Hotel in Kansas City, where the Nighthawks had received their start? That sounded good to me, too.

But when I got back to the Blossom Heath, it developed that Billy Stein had a prospect Jules didn't even know about. He introduced me to a giant of a man, named Al Quodbach, owner of the Granada Cafe in Chicago. "Al wants to hear the band," Billy said.

Quodbach did not appear to have the class of the two night-club proprietors for whom we had worked, Louis Bleet and Sam

Stecker. He wore patent leather shoes and gave off sparks from all the diamonds he was wearing in his shirt studs, cuff links, and rings. His face was craggy and reminded me of Jack Dempsey's. And he was very, very loud.

We could hear him above the music as he watched the band. Every few minutes, he would shout, "Great, wunnerful," and people at other tables would turn around, looking for the noisemaker. When we finished, he was waiting in the band room with Billy Stein. "You got the greatest band I ever heard," he said. "I want you for my joint." I looked at Billy and he said quietly, "He's offering $1,600 a week and you only play nights."

I asked Quodbach and Stein to wait outside and went into a huddle with Carm and Lebe. We all agreed it was time to make a move beyond Cleveland. Chicago was the second biggest city in the States. We knew it was a rough town and big Al Quodbach looked like the kind of citizen who belonged in it. But we all decided to take the plunge; the pay was $300 a week more than we'd been earning, and Chicago was only a step away from the top of the ladder in New York. Stein and Quodbach came back into the room and I told them we wanted to go, but I'd better check with Jules Stein in New York; he might have come up with another proposition by now.

Jules was aghast at the idea of going to Chicago. "Billy ought to know," he said, "that an out-of-town band can't go to work there without an okay from the union. And Jimmy Petrillo doesn't give that kind of okay unless the guy that owns the place is a friend of his."

Al Quodbach reassured him. Jimmy Petrillo was an old friend. Jules needn't worry. Our new agent in New York finally said go ahead. We would open on September 12. That gave me time enough to get married. We left Cleveland, with the feeling that if we failed in Chicago we had made enough friends that we could always come back. And we could always tour northern Ohio without having to pay a commission to MCA.

3. That Wonderful Town—Chicago

It was a lighthearted caravan that set out for Chicago early in September of 1927. We were living in the best of all times and prosperity went hand in hand with peace. People were working and buying radios with fancy cabinets and cars to get around in and stocks to become rich. We had become the best-known band in Cleveland. What was there to stop us from taking over Chicago?

I drove the big Marmon with Lilliebell at my side. Carmen followed in his car with Florence, and Lebe in his with Carol. Enemy Kreitzer was the chauffeur for the band's bachelors. We were heading for the Oglesby Arms, an apartment house on the south side of town, where Billy Stein had rented an entire floor for the band.

I had no illusions about finding Chicago a pastoral refuge. But I was taken aback when we stopped for a snack at a roadside lunch wagon outside Chicago. I picked up a newspaper idly and the first word I saw in headline type was "Lombardo." The second word said "Killed." Reading further, I got an inkling of the kind of town we were heading for. The story said that the deceased Anthony Lombardo had recently been installed by Al Capone as president of the Unione Siciliana, Chicago's most dreaded mob. He and his bodyguard had been cut down by a hail of bullets on the busy intersection of State and Madison streets. Police suspected that members of the Bugs Moran gang had fired the fusillade.

Left to right: Carm, 3, Guy, 4, Mrs. Lombardo holding Lebe, 18 months, in front of first home in London, Ontario.

uy, at 7, a "Huck Finn" who hadn't arted music lessons yet.

Guy (sitting) and Carm, ready for debut at strawberry festival, 1914.

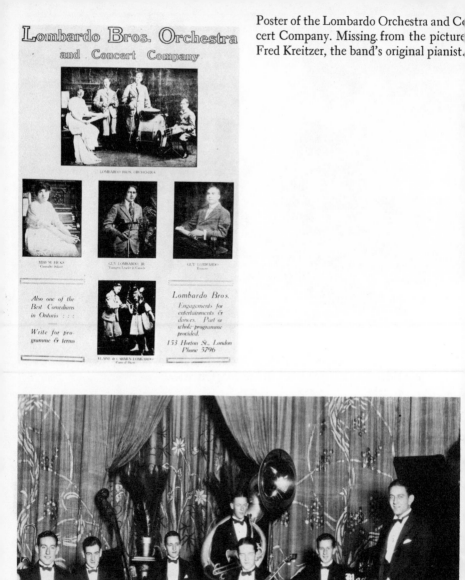

Poster of the Lombardo Orchestra and Concert Company. Missing from the picture is Fred Kreitzer, the band's original pianist.

The original Lombardo band, London, 1921.

The band in Port Stanley, Ontario, before leaving for Cleveland.

First recording session in Indianapolis, 1924. Carm (second from left, standing), Guy holding violin, Lebe (sitting, second from right).

Guy and Al Quodbach in a recent picture. Quodbach gave the Lombardos their start in Chicago at his Granada Cafe. *(Photo by Michael Nagro, Las Vegas.)*

First season at the Roosevelt Grill, 1930. Guy with two of the three-man sax section and original Lombardo saxophone trio. Missing is third man, Carmen. Left to right: "Derf" Higman and Larry Owen.

The Royal Canadians' first live broadcasts from the Roosevelt Grill in 1929 were set up by William S. Paley, the young president of CBS, over his radio station WABC. *(Photo by CBS.)*

Typical Lombardo engagement during the thirties. Steel Pier, Atlantic City. The boardwalk in the Depression year of 1931. *(Photo by Central Studios, Atlantic City, N. J.)*

The Lombardo brothers stroll the boardwalk after a performance. Atlantic City, 1931.

The Gaetano Lombardo family in London, Ontario, 1929. Standing: Joseph, Elaine, Mrs. Lombardo, Rose Marie, Mr. Lombardo, Guy. Sitting: Victor, Lebe, Carm.

Benny Goodman, who authored the new sound called "swing."

Guy and Jules Stein at Universal Studios in 1974. Jules Stein founded the Music Corporation of America and represented the Royal Canadians for many years. He brought them to New York in 1929. In the background, Elaine Lombardo.

The Lombardos on Guy's first yacht, *Tempo*, in 1934. Left to right: Carmen, Victor, Guy, and Lebert. *(Photo by CBS.)*

Phil Harris, who urged the Lombardos to go to Hollywood.

Jean Harlow joins Guy at Cocoanut Grove table, 1934.

Guy sits on Paramount lot during the filming of *Many Happy Returns*. He is surrounded by a bevy of starlets. In the center of the photo is Jack Oakie. 1934. *(Photo by Paramount, courtesy of Universal Pictures.)*

Lilliebell laughed at the idea of a Lombardo headline on our first day in Chicago. "I hope nobody gets the idea he's a relative of yours."

I assured her that the only Lombardos I knew were in London and that I had been reassured that our new boss wasn't a gangster. Billy Stein had told me that Al Quodbach knew "a lot of the boys" but that he wasn't in the rackets himself. "You got to learn to live with them when you run a joint in Chicago," he had told us.

I learned on opening night at the Granada Cafe how Al Quodbach kept on the good side of the gangsters. He ran a small gambling room upstairs for their accommodation. But the first thing he told me after reaffirming how great he thought the band played was that the upstairs room was off-limits for the musicians. "I don't want to see you or the other fellas come up there. Don't forget one thing. You can never beat a house game, too much percentage comes off the top. And I don't want you guys working for nothing."

It was nice to know that our boss had our interests at heart. It would have been even more welcome to find ourselves in the middle of the city's entertainment district, near the big hotels, night clubs, and theaters. Instead the Granada Cafe was a small club on the South Side, directly opposite a cemetery and a most unlikely location for a big-time band earning a big-time $1,600 a week.

Our Chicago premiere was no more successful than our debut in Cleveland. Nobody was beating down the doors to get in. Al Quodbach had a front-row table for his wife and family, and several others at ringside were occupied by people who were obviously the boss's close friends. There was much table-hopping up front and very little happening elsewhere. All I could see from the bandstand was a sea of white tablecloths with hardly anybody using them. I don't think there were fifty people in the room.

It didn't bother Al Quodbach. He kept shouting in our direction, "Great, great, wunnerful. You kids are great."

The next night was a duplicate of the first, except the customers had dwindled by half. At eleven o'clock, Quodbach chased the occupants of the last table and sat there alone, a one-man audience. And he kept shouting those flattering encomiums, "Great, great."

During a break, I walked over to him and asked, "Where's all the business, Al?"

"Whatta you worried about? They'll come. Lissen, play me 'Melancholy Baby' and after that 'What Can I Say After I Say I'm Sorry?'"

He called us "my kids," and every night for more than a week, we performed almost exclusively for Al. You had to like the guy, he never complained about the tariff he was laying out for his personal concerts. He'd say, "You worry too much, Guy. Someday we're gonna fill up this place and make 'em wait out in the street to hear the band."

If there was any solace to playing in a deserted house, it was that we had more than enough time to rehearse and rehearse and build up a sizable repertoire of arrangements. But we couldn't continue performing for ourselves and our one fan. I finally told Al we wanted a wire in the room. It had worked in Cleveland, where we had become overnight sensations. It ought to work in Chicago too, I told him.

It was a device that did not appeal to Mr. Quodbach. "I don't want to get involved in no radio. That's what's killing the nightclub business. People ain't goin' out. They're stayin' home listening to the goddam radio." Soon after, I had to give him an ultimatum. Get us a wire or we'll go back to Cleveland. Not even our relatives know where we are. We are beginning to feel like we belong in the cemetery across the street.

He shook his head incredulously. "I don't understand you guys. You got the softest touch in town, a boss that loves you like his own family. I don't work you hard and you get the paycheck every week. But if it's gonna take a radio wire to keep you here, I'll go out and find out what's available."

The only radio station to evince even the slightest interest was the city's newest, WBBM. The station had been launched only a few months before in the Wrigley Building and hadn't officially received its license. It was owned by two brothers named Atlass and one of them, Les, had heard us in Cleveland. He was willing to put us on for fifteen minutes a night from the Granada, but someone would have to assume the $75-a-week line charges. Quodbach and MCA agreed to share the expenses with the band and it cost us $25 a week each to finally get the Lombardo sound into Chicago radio sets.

Our first broadcast was set for nine o'clock on a blustery night in November. A man from the station had installed a small box under the piano and told me to turn on a switch at the stroke of nine. When the light went on, we were on the air. Five minutes before, surveying the completely barren house, I had asked the waiters and kitchen help to congregate near the mike and applaud loudly when I gave them the signal. I flicked the switch, approached the standing mike, and said, "This is Guy Lombardo in the Granada Cafe on the south side of Chicago."

We played for fifteen minutes, the waiters and busboys and even the chef clapping between numbers, and I flicked the off switch, wondering if there would be a reaction and how long it would take to find out whether we had generated even the tiniest spark among the music lovers of Chicago. I got the answer in exactly thirty seconds.

The headwaiter came running over. "The station just called," he said. "They want you to keep playing." So we played another fifteen minutes and another call came in to keep the wire open. I asked for a five-minute break at ten o'clock so we could prepare new numbers. And the word came back, keep playing all night until the club closes.

By eleven o'clock the waiters and busboys weren't standing around clapping anymore. People had begun trickling in. They said they wanted to see that band they'd been hearing on the radio. We kept the wire open and I was thankful we'd had those two months to prepare all that music and new arrangements. We played until one o'clock with five-minute breaks, and between midnight and our last number Al Quodbach was hustling around the room setting up tables. There wasn't a vacant seat in the club.

I went back to the Oglesby Arms, happy for the first time in two months. Lilliebell and Florence had fixed up a spread for the band and we went from one room to another, celebrating through most of the night.

I didn't mind it a bit when a call awakened me early in the morning. It was from Les Atlass at the station. He said, "Come on down to the studio. I just got a call from Mr. Wrigley of the chewing gum people, who own this building. He's very excited. He heard your program and he wants to sign you up for a half-hour commercial program every Saturday night."

I walked into the station and found myself a celebrity. The switchboard had been choked with calls since early morning and they were still coming in from people who had heard the concert from the Granada. And while I was there, a call also came in from Harold Florsheim of the shoe company. He wanted a half hour of the Royal Canadians, too. Could we do a commercial program from the Granada on Thursday night? I was dumfounded. Two commercial programs in one day after we had been virtual ghosts near a cemetery for two months!

The new programs did not make us overnight fortunes. We would be getting paid only slightly over union scale for the appearances. But in a few weeks, the combination of our unpaid broadcasts from the Granada and the Florsheim and Wrigley programs made us not only the most celebrated band in Chicago, but probably in the whole country.

The Atlass brothers had ample proof of the tremendous audience we attracted. When they appeared before the Federal Communications Commission at a hearing to determine whether they had enough listeners to make them eligible for a license, they submitted one enlightening piece of evidence. It was a letter the station had received from the Bell Telephone Company and it was in the nature of a complaint. The phone company was put out by the fact that they were doing virtually no business in Chicago between 9 and 9:30 P.M. on Saturday night. "Everybody in the city must be listening to the Lombardo program," the letter said. "Because almost nobody is making phone calls at that time." WBBM got its franchise.

I think I was mature enough by now as a married man of twenty-five to better handle the fruits of success than I had been two years before in Cleveland when I had gotten a first taste of it. There were no new rules to promulgate since they had already been set up and we had learned to live with them. I had also learned you couldn't dictate things like a man's desire to get married. What I needed to know was exactly what people liked about our band.

It wasn't a matter of arguing with success; rather I wanted to solidify the ingredients that had overnight turned us into Chicago's
best-known band and the Granada Cafe into the busiest night
club in town. Customers began pouring into Quodbach's club like
a deluge. Big Al no longer could afford the luxury of sitting around
while we played for his exclusive entertainment. He was too busy
sawing away at tables so he could accommodate more people.

The best illustration of the Granada's new popularity came
from Karl Kramer, who had recently been hired by Jules Stein to
handle our affairs in Chicago. One snowy night he had to come to
the cafe so we could sign some contracts. He had brought the contracts home with him in the afternoon and by the time he ventured out of his apartment, a couple of miles from the Granada,
the snow had drifted and virtually paralyzed the city's traffic.

Neither cabs nor trolley cars were moving, but it was important
that Karl get the contracts to us immediately. So he put on
snowshoes and laboriously reached the club. He remembers it
must have taken him three hours and was "expecting it to be entirely empty when I got there. However, when I opened the doors
and walked in, there was the room jam-packed as usual, with an
enthusiastic crowd of dancers. How they got there—by foot, auto
or streetcar,—I will never know, but it taught us a lesson that if
the attraction is big enough, no weather will keep people away,
and that's how big the Lombardo orchestra was in Chicago in
those days."

Which all meant that we never lacked for people to ask exactly
what it was that drew them to the band. Most of them repeated
what we had heard in Cleveland: they liked the slow tempo which
enabled them to dance; the soft sound that permitted a swain to
whisper endearments his girl could hear; the sweet, rich tones of
Carmen's sax and Lebe's trumpet, which sounded like the human
voice; the medleys that allowed us to fill virtually every request.
But almost all of them added a new dimension we hadn't heard
before. They were unanimous in their praise of our new vocalist—
Carmen Lombardo.

Carmen sang like he played. You may recall that he had started
as a flutist and that even before he reached adolescence he was
able to get a full, rich, sweet sound with a vibrato unique among

musicians of the day. When he taught himself the sax, he sought to get exactly the same sound he had mastered on the flute. He learned that the way to do it was to use a hard reed, which eliminated the wind and reed sounds.

So his sax sound was distinctive, uniquely his, unmistakably Lombardo. When it fell his lot to become a singer, a task he abhorred and resisted, he did it the only way he knew. He sang with the same vibrato, the same emotion he milked out of his flute and sax. He crisply enunciated the lyrics, making each word recognizable; that, of course, was an outgrowth of Mama's diction lessons. And he sang only songs he believed in and his listeners believed his sincerity. As mentioned before, when he sang, "I love you," every girl in the audience felt he was delivering a personal message.

Carmen became our vocalist only on a temporary basis. He had been one of the original members of the Lombardo trio, a feature we installed when Larry Owen joined the band in Cleveland. The trio consisted simply of our saxophone section—Carm, Larry, and Derf Higman. None were possessed of great voices, but they sang pleasantly, remained on key, and blended together perfectly just as they did when they were playing their instruments.

In Cleveland, we occasionally permitted our banjo player, Wes Vaughn, to do a solo chorus. But Wes left to join another band, and when we arrived in Chicago I tapped Carm to become our vocalist until we could find somebody else. He wanted to know why I didn't do it, and I reminded him that I had a lousy memory for lyrics.

I had really made a diligent search for a vocalist before we left Cleveland, because singers were becoming an important part of every big band. They would usually sit with the musicians, holding an instrument they couldn't play, but when the time came for a vocal, they'd step up before the mike and earn their keep. Paul Whiteman even had two such singers. A young man named Bing Crosby sat with the sax section and Morton Downey hid behind a French horn.

Shortly after my marriage I heard about a good singer who could play the banjo and was possessed of great charm. I heard he was appearing in Toledo, and Lilliebell and I made the trip from

Cleveland to hear him; if we liked what we heard, we'd offer him
the job. It turned out he'd closed the night before and moved on
to another town. I narrowly missed him several other times.

In the second week of our engagement at the Granada, he
walked in, a blond and handsome young man. He said he'd heard
I'd been looking for him and if it was about a job he was interested. I told him the situation; we weren't doing any business at
the cafe and we weren't likely to stay around much longer if conditions remained the way they were.

It just seemed too chancy to take him on at that time, I told
the young man. He agreed. He said he had an offer to be a singer-
emcee in a Pittsburgh theater. He'd try us again in a few months.

The young man's name was Dick Powell, and of such circumstances are careers made and lost. Had I hired him that depressing
night in Chicago, he might never have gone on to become a
Hollywood superstar and later one of television's most celebrated
actor-producers. And Carmen Lombardo would never have become one of the most imitated vocalists in the band business.
Once the people in Chicago heard the few numbers he did on
radio, they wanted more. Carmen Lombardo's voice was now as
much a part of our identity as his sax and Lebe's trumpet. He
knew it as well as I did and for the next twenty-three years he continued as our vocalist, besides singing with the trio, playing the
sax, flute, and clarinet, acting as our musical director, and working
on the side as one of the most prolific songwriters in the business.
But all the time, he thoroughly detested his role as a singer.

Meanwhile at the Granada, Al Quodbach was not enchanted
with the boom in business. "I hardly get to hear my kids play
anymore," he would say.

The boom had also attracted the patronage of various members
of Chicago's warring factions. It was a matter of status. The
mobsters were always seeking out the hottest attraction in town,
and in the winter of 1927 that happened to be the Granada Cafe.
Quodbach knew them all and had to prove himself a master of
protocol in determining who sat at his best ringside tables.

Up on the bandstand, it wasn't always easy to distinguish the
gangsters from other customers. Generally they were well behaved,
but after a while there were telltale clues that helped to identify

them. Most of them sat up front and sought to impress their dates by summoning Quodbach to the table. "Meet Al," they would say. "He owns this joint." Or "If you're good, I'll letcha meet Guy Lombardo."

The gangsters were the first to subvert a corny idea introduced by Station WBBM during our Sunday night remote broadcasts from the Granada. It was something called the "Nutty Club" and the way it worked, listeners would send telegrams to the station for the privilege of hearing their names announced over the air by Guy Lombardo.

I went along with the idea because Les Atlass of the radio station thought it would develop even a larger audience than the one we had. The idea of hearing one's name mentioned on the air obviously titillated a good segment of the Chicago population. But I never felt quite comfortable holding a telegram and announcing into a mike, "Cuckoo, so and so, you're a member of the Nutty Club."

The town's hoods had no such compunctions about using the Nutty Club as a communications device. We weren't to learn until much later that they were signing phony names to telegrams and adding meaningful postscripts. "Give my regards to Benny" might be suggesting that Benny get out of town or that he was wanted at a council of war. Apprised of the situation, the radio station had to hire additional help to screen the messages.

About all Al Quodbach could do to make sure that his gangster clientele kept in line was to insist on certain rules of etiquette. No loud or abusive language. No profanity. And, most important, no hardware on the premises. Al would stand at the door, and if he saw a suspicious bulge he would courteously ask the offender to dispose of it outside. In the main, they respected his wishes.

But the furthest thought from my mind was the problem of how to live in the company of gangsters the night they told us Al Jolson was coming to the Granada to hear the band. He was the most celebrated name in show business and riding high on the phenomenal success of the first talking picture. Warner Brothers had starred him in *The Jazz Singer* and Jolson had come to Chicago for personal appearances in conjunction with the opening of the picture in the Loop. The Comedy Club, an organization of performers, had decided to give the star a night and had selected the Granada as the locale because they wanted Jolson to catch the most popular act in town.

He hadn't arrived yet when I flicked the on switch to begin our radio show. Instead of opening the show as I usually did by launching immediately into music, I let the listeners know that we were expecting Jolson as a guest and I told about this remarkable innovation in the movies, where you could actually hear the actors talking and singing. I explained we were dedicating the entire broadcast to Al Jolson and that when he arrived perhaps we could get him to the mike to do a number from the movie.

And in a trice, I was not speaking into the microphone any longer. A man about my size had ascended from the dance floor without my noticing him, had grabbed the mike out of my hands, and was about to burst into song. I reacted immediately, grabbed him by the collar and tie, and walked him off the bandstand. To emphasize my outrage, I gave him a push and he slid across the slippery dance floor, ending up at the foot of the table reserved for Al Jolson.

I walked back to the mike and continued talking as if nothing had happened. The band began playing and I left the stage for a drink of water. As I passed one of the ringside tables, usually reserved for consequential characters, one of them said to me, "Don't worry, Guy, everything's been fixed up. We took care of everything."

The full import of the remark did not sink in until Al Quodbach arose from the next table and accompanied me to the water cooler. "Yeah, everything's been taken care of," he said. "You don't have to worry anymore."

And then he filled me in on why I had anything to worry about in the first place. The man who had grabbed the mike, it turned out, was one George Maloney, a fiery member of an Irish gang that was seeking to end the domination of the Italian troops led by Capone.

"He just got himself a little too liquored up and decided he wanted to sing an Irish ballad," Al explained. "Luckily he followed my rule and left his piece outside in the car or he mighta used it on you when you grabbed his collar. But some of the other boys and me, we explained he shouldn't have behaved that way and he shouldn't blame you for protecting your mike. He cooled down when I said he couldn't come in here anymore acting like that and he promised he'd be good from now on."

That didn't quite end *l'affaire* Maloney, but I didn't know it at the time, and besides there were happier events in store as Christmas week approached. Papa had called. He'd be coming down with the family to spend the holidays with us. It would be the first trip for Rose Marie, who was two years old. And Mama would bring a turkey and Elaine and Victor and Joseph would come too.

We all sat down to Mama's turkey in the hotel suite we had rented for the family, and none of us ever partook of a more memorable Christmas dinner. Elaine took me aside and mentioned that on the drive to Chicago they had passed a house and farm for sale in Glendale, just four miles outside London. In the last few years, Papa had been mentioning that he'd like to own a farm someday, raise some cows, and putter in a big garden.

"This place has twenty acres and a lovely old house," Elaine said. "Papa almost interrupted the journey to drive in and look it over. But he decided he'd wait until the return trip. He said if the for-sale sign was still up, he'd buy it."

I called Carm and Lebe into a bedroom and told them what Elaine had said. All of us reacted the same way. We'd buy the farm for Papa. It would be the first time we could ever give him a Christmas present that would really tell him how much we loved him and how much we appreciated his struggle to make us musicians. We sprang the news during dessert and our father sat there stunned. He protested; he said he could afford to buy the place himself; he would rather we kept our money to raise our own families. But the odds were three to one against him and the postcript is that the house was still for sale when he returned home and he permitted us to make the down payment.

The Sunday night after Christmas, Papa came to the club with Elaine, who still remembers the occasion because her Christmas present was a first fur coat to wear in the big city. Mama stayed in the suite with Rose Marie and the boys. And Papa and Elaine and the rest of us will never forget that night, for a reason other than the fur coat.

At midnight, we would go on with the weekly rendition of the Nutty Club. It had become so popular that we now had a Western Union teletype printer near the bandstand, from which I would snip off the telegrams to be read on the air. On this Sunday night, I guess we had a record attendance to date. There were at least five hundred people in a room that defied you to get in more than three hundred.

I had just read my first "Cuckoo, you're a member" when I heard two pops. They sounded like two waiters opening champagne bottles simultaneously. And all of a sudden people began disappearing from the room. At the table in front I could see my father's head under the tablecloth and his fanny sticking up in the air. Elaine had vanished and only her fur coat hung draped on the chair. In back of me, my band had disappeared. Only Freddie Kreitzer sat at the piano, apparently too terrified to move.

I was still unaware of what had happened, but I was on the air and I kept reading wires. It came time for me to announce that after a moment's notice, "We will return you to the Wrigley Building," where an organist would play while we took our break between the wire-reading and the dance numbers. I put my hand over the mike and shouted to Freddie to play something so I could lead into the return to the studio.

Freddie began playing "I've Got a Woman Crazy for Me, She's Funny That Way," a song we had rehearsed that very afternoon. Now I had never sung a note in my life, but I was so nervous and frustrated I began singing. I didn't even know I knew the lyric, but the words came and I didn't miss a line. I finished the song and gave the air back to the Wrigley Building, gratefully, just as Al Quodbach approached.

He was not his usually imperturbable self. His face was white and my knees began shaking when he said, "Oh, God. Two guys is been shot dead. And you know who shot 'em. George Maloney, the character you chased off the stage the other night."

Painfully, he pieced together the story as he now knew it.

Maloney had come in with a girl thirty minutes earlier. He had passed Al's inspection at the front door, acting rather subdued and obviously carrying no munitions. He sat down and then asked his girl to excuse him so he could wash up. As he was washing, two members of a rival gang entered the lavatory and began frisking him. They walked out when they found him clean.

Back at his table, the two men sat down uninvited and began ribbing Maloney about the incident in the Granada the previous week. "Big, tough George Maloney," they sneered. "Getting himself kicked off a stage by a bandleader." They then turned their attention to his girl and were equally uncomplimentary about Maloney's taste in women. They left and Maloney whispered to his date to make believe she was going to the ladies' room and slip outside, instead, to get his gun underneath the front seat of his car.

She complied and brought it back in her bag. Maloney slipped the revolver into his pocket and approached his tormentors, who were sitting at a table against a wall. He sat down opposite them and asked if they wanted to repeat those slurs to his manhood. They did. Maloney tipped over the table and fired five shots. Each man got a bullet in the head and one in the heart. The fifth bullet buried itself in the wall behind their table.

A shaken Quodbach expressed himself as repentant. "I guess it's my fault. I should never have let that crazy Maloney in here again. But you're drawing so many people I can't keep tabs on everybody. All I can do is ask them to behave and hope for the best."

More upset than Quodbach were Lebe and Papa. The youngest partner in the band had broached the subject of gangsters before. He hated violence of any kind, had been terrified at my encounter with Maloney, and had wondered to Carm and me if maybe we oughtn't to move on to another city that was not so obviously tenanted by hoodlums. And now, back in the family hotel suite, Papa was expressing himself along the same lines. We sat up for hours discussing the situation, with Papa voting that we go back to Cleveland. "This town is too rough for nice boys," he said.

At about four o'clock Al Quodbach walked into the suite, obviously relieved. The police had finally captured Maloney, who had fled the club after the shooting, leaving his girl behind. He was safely ensconced behind bars and had been booked for murder. "At least I don't have to worry about that nut for a long time," said Al. Then he wanted to know, "What's this meeting all about?"

I told him. "It looks like this is the end of the Granada and we're thinking about going back to Cleveland."

That horrified him even more than the shooting. "Don't even think about that, Guy. Let's all go to bed and talk it over tomorrow."

The papers had a field day with the story the next day. They billed it as the first murder ever to be committed live on radio. Several accounts had "thousands of people" in the room. One of the dead men remained unidentified; the other was determined to be a member of the Bugs Moran gang. I was not unhappy that none of the stories mentioned the fact that Guy Lombardo had made his singing debut during the height of the excitement.

Lebe reluctantly went along with our decision to stick it out at the Granada until Jules Stein found a way to get us to New York. Stein was spending most of his time in his Manhattan offices in the Paramount Building working on plans toward that end. The Guy Lombardo band, he told his associates, was going to be his "icebreaker" into New York. When that was accomplished, Jules Stein envisioned even bigger things for his Music Corporation of America.

The shooting in no way diminished the popularity of the Granada. Rather than scare away patrons, it seemed to attract more. In addition to all the ingredients that had made the band successful we now had morbid curiosity working for us. Almost everybody who came into the place wanted a look at the bullet hole in the wall. For our part, we just hoped that Al Quodbach would screen his customers more carefully in the future.

There were other matters to occupy our attention than the antics of Chicago's underworld. Carmen, for instance, had become deeply involved in a budding extracurricular career as a songwriter. That career would mean almost as much to the band as his vocalizing, giving us original numbers that became yet another identifying mark of the Royal Canadians.

Carmen's compulsion to write songs was rooted in his personality. He was without pretension or sham and his sincerity showed in the way he played and the way he sang. He was also brutally frank and never bowed to the decisions I made as leader if he thought they were wrong. One of the reasons he wanted to write songs was a desire to put into music what he felt in his heart.

The other reason was curiosity. He was interested in each new trend that came along, and would read everything he could get his hands on relating to the subject. Perhaps the best illustration of his motivation is found in the very first song he wrote and the very last.

The first was written shortly after we came to Cleveland during the height of a new mania that was sweeping the country. Crossword puzzles had become almost a national obsession in 1925, when Carm wrote words and music to "Crossword Puzzle Crazy."

And shortly before he died in 1971, Carmen's last song also reflected what had become a major preoccupation across the country. It was called, "Look What We've Done to Our World." The theme, naturally, was ecology.

The crossword puzzle song, a classic in rhyming, never became a big hit, but Carmen now knew he could write both lyrics and music and in his spare time he began writing other songs. Before we left Cleveland, he had written two more: "Mama's Gone Goodbye," a blues number, and "A Lane in Spain." Both were passably received and we included them in our repertoire. "A Lane in Spain," published by Harms Music Company, was recorded by Paul Whiteman, got a fair play around the country, and Carm was on his way.

But he did not become a major factor in Tin Pan Alley until he met Johnny Green, who had recently graduated from Harvard and had come to Cleveland to visit relatives with whom we were acquainted. They took him to the Blossom Heath to hear the band and he and Carm hit it off immediately. John was heading for law school, but he had studied music and Carm had him work out an arrangement of *Rhapsody in Blue* that we would feature that summer. It turned out to be a classic for a nine-piece band.

Then he showed Carm one of the songs he had written. He called it "I Want You All to Myself." My brother thought the lyric was trite and the melody too reminiscent of a recent hit, "La Rosita." His reaction was typical Carmen. He might as easily have told Johnny Green, who was later to become one of the biggest names in the business as musical director at Metro-Goldwyn-Mayer, that he liked the song and let it go at that.

Instead, with Johnny's permission, Carmen went to work on the melody. Just before we left for Chicago, he had revised it into a haunting tune that was infinitely less complicated, more professional, and with a commercial potential. Carm thought it was so good he got Green's approval to seek out the best possible lyricist to put words to the song.

In Chicago that man was Gus Kahn, a boyhood idol of Carmen's who had collaborated on such standards as "Carolina in the Morning," "Yes Sir, That's My Baby," and "Memories." He specialized in lyrics, and composers came to him from all over the country to put words to their music. He had written perhaps sixty hits, a number of them to melodies composed by Isham Jones, who had so strongly influenced the progress of our band. Two of the biggest Kahn-Jones successes were "I'll See You in My Dreams" and "It Had to Be You."

Carm was more than just an admirer of Gus Kahn. You could even call him a disciple. He believed in his understandable approach to a lyric. I remember when we received the sheet music for "I'll See You in My Dreams" and played it for the first time in Cleveland. Carm's enthusiasm for the song knew no bounds. Between sets, he expounded at length on his admiration for the lyricist.

"What a master that Gus Kahn is," he said. "He makes everything sound so simple. You hear the words and you think a child could have written them. I just read a magazine article he wrote in which he explains the secret of a real song hit. He says when a boy and girl are dancing together and they hear a perfect lyric, the boy wonders why he didn't think of that line and the girl believes the line was written exclusively for her. That's the kind of lyric I have to learn to write."

Carm began seeking out Gus Kahn immediately after we arrived in Chicago. He hoped he could get him to listen to the tune he had written with Johnny Green. If he liked it, maybe he'd offer to put words to it. Finding Kahn wasn't easy. Carm finally got his home phone from a music publishing company and Kahn was gracious. He knew of our band and was grateful that we included several of his songs on our music list.

He made a date for the next morning at his home. This posed a problem. We worked at the Granada until 3 A.M. We lived on the South Side and Kahn on the North. It was about an hour away by train and bus. But Carm got up at seven o'clock to keep the date. He should have brought along an instrument, because he didn't play the piano and neither did Kahn.

So Carm hummed the tune and Gus Kahn's wife played it on the piano as the lyricist reclined on a sofa, jotting down notes on a pad. Then he got a phone call. Ted Fiorito wanted to play golf. "Come along," Gus said to Carm, "we'll discuss it while I'm playing." For the next week or so, Carm followed the same routine, getting up after a few hours' sleep, transferring from train to bus, and getting in just enough time with Kahn to be invited along to a golf game with another bandleader. Carmen didn't play and after that introduction to the game he never wanted to. He hated golf for the rest of his life.

But one night at the cafe, he got a call from Kahn, who had recently seen the Broadway success of the season, *Coquette*, starring Helen Hayes. He hadn't been able to get the title out of his head.

"Carm," he said. "I think I have a lyric for that tune. Take it down: 'Tell Me, Why You Keep Fooling, Little Coquette . . .'"

Two hours after Carm had transcribed the lyrics over the phone, we made an arrangement of the song and put it on the air. Carm did the vocal. The lights began flashing on the radio switchboard like they had for our debut; the listeners were calling to say how much they loved the song. In a few weeks it was the best-selling song in the nation. It has remained since a classic standard. During the Big Band era, "Little Coquette" was featured in virtually every bandleader's repertoire, no matter his musical style. I even heard it on radio, recently, mangled but still identifiable as played by a rock-and-roll combo.

The song would earn Carmen an annual income for life in ASCAP royalties. More immediately, he turned to writing another one with Kahn. The routine didn't vary. Carmen would always end up on the golf course, trying to hum a tune for Kahn's ears, while the other members of the foursome complained he was distracting their attention from the little white ball. One day as Carm was seriously considering ending his collaboration with Kahn, the lyricist grabbed his arm. It was 4:30 in the afternoon and Carm had to make that long return trip, shower, shave, eat, and get dressed so he could reach the bandstand in time.

"Let's try doing our next song in reverse," Kahn suggested. "Last night, I was dreaming about hitting a ball 250 yards. I love that title: 'Last Night I Was Dreaming.' Why don't you come up with a melody for it and then we'll finish it off."

Carm hastened to his bus and took out the note pad he always carried. He started putting down notes to go along with that title, using it as the first line of the song. He had a melody by the time he was on the train, and when he got home he skipped dinner and began to pick one-finger notes on the little Japanese piano that decorated his apartment. He worked out a three-part harmony for the sax section and gave the original copy of the melody to Fred Kreitzer. At the same time he hummed the tune to Bern Davies so he could fake it on the bass. What he had was one chorus of "Last Night I Was Dreaming," and he asked me to include it with a medley for the radio broadcast.

When I agreed, he called Gus Kahn and told him to listen to the broadcast that began at nine o'clock. And, he said, listen particularly for the second tune in the first medley. That would be "Last Night I Was Dreaming" sans lyric. The chorus sounded good, and by the time we stopped for a break Kahn was back on the phone with a full set of lyrics.

It started off: "Last night I was dreaming, I dreamed that you kissed me, while bright stars were gleaming . . ." Carmen took down the full lyric and in the hour before the band went back on the air, he had worked out a complete arrangement with Larry Owen, including his own vocal. I told the story on the air and we played the song in its entirety, only a few hours after Carmen had first put a note on paper. "Last Night I Was Dreaming," while it never reached the best-selling proportions of "Little Coquette," was an immensely popular country-type song. I always called it an example of instant song-writing by two people who knew what they were doing.

And now every aspiring lyricist in the vicinity of Chicago and beyond began approaching Carmen to write melodies for their poetry. One day Carm and Florence were strolling in a park and sat down on a bench while she opened the morning mail. She handed him a note from a lyricist friend, Charlie Newman. The note contained a brief lyric and the title "Sweethearts on Parade." Into his mind flashed the sounds of a parade, the bugle call, the pounding of drums. Almost instantaneously, he had an entire melody in his head. In a couple of minutes, he had written it down, and when we introduced it a few weeks later, it again became a No. 1 bestseller and would add to the royalties that through the years matched Carm's profits from the band.

In little more than a year's time as the band was moving ahead meteorically, so was Carmen's career as a composer. Now not only were songwriters by the dozen approaching him for collaboration, so were song publishers. Their overtures may have been flattering but they did not appeal to Carm's sense of values. Most of them simply wanted to put his name on songs—lyrics and music—that had already been written. The idea was that if Carmen Lombardo was mentioned as a co-writer in the title the song was bound to take off. There was the added hope that most of the big bands, including Guy Lombardo, would play it. Carm was being offered a piece of each song for what his name meant to it.

It was not an uncommon practice, but my brother would have none of it. He was incensed at the idea and had a standard answer for every publisher's representative who tried to cajole him with the thought that it was being done every day, even by well-known bandleaders.

"I don't want to hear about it," he would bellow. "How can I put my name on something I didn't write? How can I take it to Guy and ask him to play my song when it isn't my song? I wouldn't lie to my brother and I wouldn't lie to my wife. And I'll be damned if I'm going to lie to myself."

I admired Carm's stand and agreed with it. I was less enchanted by his willingness to listen to the ever-increasing number of aspiring writers who came to him with lyrics and expected him to produce melodies. Carm could turn down important people in the business who simply wanted the use of his name. He found it more difficult to say no to novices who sought out his help. He found himself so immersed in work he barely had time for the band, although he never missed a rehearsal or turn on the band-stand.

I felt he was spreading his talent too thin and told him so frequently. One night during a road engagement, the issue came to a head. I put it to him bluntly: "Carm, you've just got to stop writing for every jerk who comes along and butters you up."

The remark infuriated him. "You're just jealous," he said, "be-cause nobody ever asks you to help them with a song. I'll write for anybody I want to."

And before we knew it, my brother and I stopped shouting at each other and began trading punches. It wasn't exactly a battle of the century and only feelings were injured. Choked with emo-tion, I started walking out of the room. Carm stopped me.

He put his arm around my shoulder and said, 'Forget it, Guy. I don't know what the hell we're fighting about. I've known all along you were right, but I couldn't get myself to admit it. I'll just have to be a bastard and only work on songs with pro-fessionals."

He did from that moment, was more discriminating about how he utilized his time, and ended up a prolific producer of song hits. More about that later.

My shy brother, Lebe, was having different problems in adjust-ing to success. The band was so much the craze of Chicago that the Granada was attracting more than just the normal comple-ment of gangsters who came to see and be seen. All of a sudden, we were noticing band leaders and bandsmen coming in to find out the secret of the Lombardos' success. And Lebert, a hero-worshiper, began doubting his ability. Without my knowledge he started taking trumpet lessons to impress the knowledgeable visi-tors.

He should have known better. His most faithful admirer at the time (and I know this will raise eyebrows among the *cognoscenti* of jazz) was to become the best-known trumpet player in the world, Louis Armstrong. Louis had recently come to Chicago from New Orleans and was playing trumpet with the Carrol Dickerson band at the Savoy Ballroom, which was also on the South Side.

I'll let him carry on the story as he told it in a special edition
of *Variety* honoring the Royal Canadians, many years later:

"I can remember as far back as 1927 and 1928 when the Guy
was playing in Chi at the Granada Cafe and we (Zutty Singleton
and myself) we were playing in Carroll Dickerson's band at the
Savoy Ballroom on the Southside of Chicago also . . . And the Guy
would come on—on Sunday nights and play real late . . . It seemed
as though they were playing late so's we could get off from the Savoy
and make a Bee-Line to the Ranch—(That's an apartment flat the
boys in our band rented to have our private sessions, etc.) . . . And
we would turn on the radio as we were coming in the door . . .
Yass Lawd! . . .

"There we would listen to the sweetest music this side of heaven
. . . With the lights down real low—and no one would say a word
while they would play . . . Guy Lombardo had us spellbound . . .
'Sweethearts on Parade,' 'Among My Souvenirs,' 'Coquette.' . . .
Guy Lombardo inspired us so much with their sense of timing—
their beautiful tones (the most essential thing in music), their
beautiful way of phrasing—we stepped right into their footsteps
with our big band at the Savoy. . . . We phrased so much like 'em
until the patrons of the Savoy . . . they all went for 'the sweetest
music.'

"Meantime, Carroll Dickerson's band (featuring Louis Satchmo
Armstrong) played THE HOTTEST MUSIC THIS SIDE OF
HELL . . . HA, HA, HA . . . Cute?

"Guy Lombardo and his band has always been my favorite
band. . . . His trumpet playing brother has always been in my mind
as my first chair man in my dream band if he ever leaves the Guy
. . . Over in Europe (where I'm about to make another trip real
soon) they all can tell you—I've always had the greatest respect
and admiration for Guy and his brothers—personally as well as
musically."

It was Lebe who first introduced us to Satchmo. Lebe was
always seeking out the best musicians in town, trying to learn
from them, wondering how to make himself a complete and com-
posite trumpet player. The first time he ever heard Louis at the
Savoy, he came rushing back, unable to contain his enthusiasm. "I

always thought Panico was the greatest," he said. "But Armstrong is so good it scares me." And on a Monday night off, he pushed Carm and me to the Savoy to hear his new hero. Both of us were as thrilled as Lebe, who introduced us proudly to the grinning master.

And the next Sunday night Satch and Zutty reciprocated. They came down to the Granada to hear us in person. It was a visit that first made me aware of the shame of America—the blind prejudice that was the lot of the black man. Al Quodbach unwittingly spelled it out for me.

I say unwittingly, because Al was no different from all the other night-club owners of the day. Their places of business were simply off-limits to blacks. It was an unwritten law promulgated by profit motive. Black customers would chase away white customers and you couldn't exist on the patronage of the mostly impoverished "coloreds."

So it was just as we finished our last radio number and broke for intermission, Quodbach came into the band room with a scowl on his face. He went up to Lebe and said. "There's two coons outside, call themselves Satch and Zutty, say they want to see you. I told them we don't allow Negroes in here."

The Lombardo brother with the least amount of temper flew into a frenzy. He raced out of the room, out the back entrance, and caught up with Satch and Zutty just as they were hailing a cab. He practically dragged them back into the club, sat them down at the bandstand, and stormed into Quodbach's office, Carm and I hard on his heels.

And gentle Lebe vented his outrage on the burly and speechless man who paid our salaries. "Don't you ever dare pull a stunt like that again," he shouted. "You let the worst scum in the world into your club and try to kick out the best musicians in Chicago. They welcomed us at their place and you're trying to tell them the Lombardos can't welcome them here. I don't know about my brothers, but if you don't go out there and apologize to those men, I'm walking out of here for good."

Quodbach looked at Carm and me. We nodded our heads, proud of our brother. Al shook his head resignedly. "I ain't got nothing against them," he said. "It's just something you take for granted.

Most colored people stay with their own." He went out and apologized to Louis and Zutty, who were chatting amiably with the rest of the band. And I will permit Mr. Armstrong to finish the story as it appeared in that special edition of *Variety*.

> . . . I shall never forget the night Zutty and I paid the Lombardo band a visit out at the Granada in Chicago. They treated us so swell I'd be here all night explaining how thrilled Zutty and I were . . . They introduced us, we sat in, sang and just felt at home . . . I've never forgotten . . . I said to myself, "My, my, here I am sitting in with my favorite band—the band we've broken our necks to get to the Ranch to hear."
> So there you go folks . . . Another highlight in my life . . .
> Red Beans and Ricely Yours,
Louis Armstrong.

Louis would often in later years shock interviewers with his gratuitous compliments for the Lombardo band. He compared our style to his in very simple terms: "I can't play anything I can't sing and I can't sing anything I can't play. That's Guy Lombardo's philosophy and I learned it from him."

But if Satch knew even at that time what had propelled us to the very top of the Chicago entertainment scene, few other musicians, bandleaders or performers could fathom the secret. They'd come into the Granada and Quodbach would report back what they were saying: "What have they got for crying out loud? What's their secret? Simple arrangements, simple beat, everything goes so easy."

And that was about it as far as I was concerned. The major part of our success was that what we did was easy for us. Our listeners recognized the melody because we didn't dress it up with fancy embellishments. We weren't playing for musicians even if it flattered the hell out of us that a genius like Louis Armstrong appreciated what we were doing. We were playing for the people who demanded the melody of their favorite songs and the beat that encouraged them to dance.

And that was the time that Lebert began having self-doubts. He always had been the most sensitive and impressionable member of the band, and he began to worry that he just wasn't good enough, especially for the ears of the name musicians who came to the Granada to doubt us. He had first evinced that self-doubt in Cleveland when Vincent Lopez came to hear the band and he sweated through the performance, so tightened up he began missing notes.

And now that the Granada had become a cynosure for other musicians, it got worse for poor Lebe. One night Paul Whiteman came in. Here was the man who had first influenced us in our choice of a career. I could see Lebe perspiring, wishing he could run away somewhere and hide. Often, it would be Louis Panico who would visit, and I guess the great side man had the most deleterious effect of all on Lebe. It was Panico's trumpet and then his advice that had made a trumpeter out of Lebe.

And here was Lebe, now, a third owner in an orchestra even more celebrated than the one in which Panico was still just a member of the band. He was wretchedly uncomfortable, concerned more about his mentor's reaction to his playing than about doing what came naturally—playing that muted trumpet with his identifying vibrato. Another traumatic night, Bix Beiderbecke came in and again Lebe failed to sound like himself. Bix was a new member of the Whiteman band and had been receiving ecstatic reviews for his trumpet playing.

And so it happened that Lebe, the sole trumpet player of Chicago's best-known band, began taking lessons on the sly. He wanted to develop a legitimate tone and sound like every other trumpet player. He had forgotten Louis Panico's advice the night Isham Jones visited us in London. You remember Panico had told him to imitate all the great ones and then develop a style of his own. Lebe had done that and his style was one of the band's greatest attributes. A few days after he began taking lessons, I noticed that his vibrato was fading away.

I was not a gifted instrumentalist like my brothers, but what I had going for me was an ear that could detect the slightest difference in the sound coming out of every instrument in the band. Lebe had been playing a Conn Model 22-B trumpet, the kind used by most members of his fraternity. Now with his changing sound, I suspected he was trying out a new instrument.

He denied it. My next thought was that he might be using a

different mouthpiece. I said he sounded like he was blowing through a lead pipe. No, he wasn't using a different mouthpiece. "Honest, Guy," he said, looking injured, "I'm not doing anything different."

But Lebe doesn't know how to fib. I kept at him until he finally admitted, "The only thing I've been doing is taking lessons. Everybody tells me I don't have a legitimate tone."

I could have killed him, except for that forlorn look that reminded me of his expression as a boy when he was bringing up his porcupine defense to turn away Papa's wrath. I gave him a lecture out of Gaetano Lombardo, Sr. "You dope, if you had a legitimate tone, you'd be like every other trumpet player looking for a job in a pit band. You've got your own tone and it's one of the big reasons your band and mine is the hottest outfit in Chicago. If I ever catch you fooling around with that teacher again, I'll wrap the horn around your neck."

I should have paid more heed to my own advice as we began our second year in Chicago. We had reached unparalleled heights. Jules Stein was in New York, keeping in constant touch. He would bring us to the big city, but not before he had found the perfect spot. We were big on radio and big on records. Carm's new songs were being played all over the country, but the Royal Canadians had them first and our name had spread across the land.

It was the worst of all times to change policy in midstream. All the boys in the band, including my brothers, were beginning to talk about improving themselves, getting fancy arrangements, improvising—in short, fighting with success. Even I began to feel that maybe we had reached the heights too easily, that to stay there we had to learn new tricks. The first few weeks of the new season we worked hard on new arrangements.

I just never had the time to sit down by myself and do some soul-searching. If I had, I would have stuck with all those Papa precepts, rejected the innovations that might make us sound like other bands, but would erase the identifying marks on which we had built our popularity. We began denigrating our famous saxes and replaced them in large part with straight clarinets. Lebe's celebrated mute, which only a few months before I had so steadfastly sought to retain, went out in favor of the standard open tone. We started the new season at the Granada and on radio and sat back complacently, awaiting the flood of fan mail to tell us how happy our listeners felt about our efforts at self-improvement.

The deluge was a trickle. I could feel that we were doing something wrong, but it never occurred to me that what we thought of as improvement had eradicated what our fans liked in the first place. I was finally shown the light by, of all people, my barber.

Lou had a shop near the Oglesby Arms and probably was our most enthusiastic fan. Whenever Carm, Lebe, or I paid him a visit, he was quick to give us an instant review of the radio program the night before. Both he and his wife listened every night and Lou would tell us what they liked about the program. I had to suspect that the adulation had something to do with his business acumen, for it always earned him a generous tip.

He changed my mind the morning I came in, despondent at learning that nobody had phoned the station with bravos for the Lombardos. Lou put the bib around my neck and did not go into his usual paean of praise. Instead he asked a question. "You change some of the boys in the band, Mr. Lombardo?"

I sensed immediately he was onto something, asked what was on his mind. "Well," he said, "don't get me wrong, but me and my wife, we listened like we always do last night and we both had the same feeling the band doesn't sound the same anymore."

The remark had the honest feeling of a breath of fresh air and I didn't resent it. I asked him, "What do you think sounds different about it."

He was afraid he had hurt my feelings. "Maybe I shouldn't have said anything. I ain't no musician."

That was precisely what was the matter, I thought. We'd been listening to musicians instead of the people who liked our music. Lou couldn't put his finger on exactly what had changed, but I knew by the tone of his voice that he preferred the band the way it used to be. I thanked him and hurried over to Les Atlass' office at Station WBBM. I asked to look at the logs of last year's programs to compare them with what we were playing now. Les wanted to know why and I told him that people were saying we sounded different this year and I wanted to understand why.

Les had an opinion of his own. He said, "You're not going bump-bah, bump-bah like you used to with a number like 'Button Up Your Overcoat.' You know, bump-bah, bump-bah."

I spent the whole day checking on those logs which listed every number we had ever played on the station. With Atlass' complaint about our lack of bump-bah, I noticed that this year we had discarded almost every schottische number that had been such a distinctive part of our repertoire. We'd played schottische numbers from the time we had a concert company in London and we had been using the rhythm as a transition from a slow number to a fast one. Now we had discarded that rhythm as too simple and Les Atlass was missing the bump-bah.

Lou the barber and Les the station owner had given me clues as to why the band's popularity had seemed to diminish in a matter of weeks. Now, as I traced last year's programs, it hit me that more was missing than bump-bah. I could almost hear last year's sound, the one we had worked on for years to perfect. How the hell had I permitted myself to lose Carm's golden sax with its inimitable vibrato and Lebe's muted trumpet in these new arrangements we had made in the name of improvement?

Everything people liked about our music had been thrown away unconsciously as we sought out new things. I rushed back to Carm and Lebe and they saw what had happened immediately. We took those new smarty-pants arrangements and dumped them and in a few days we were back playing as we always had. The switchboard began lighting up again at WBBM. And the next time I went to see Lou, the first thing he said was: "That's more like it."

I look back on that episode with a sense of thanks that we were able to correct a grievous mistake before it proved fatal. I've seen it happen to so many other bands that never fully recovered from experimenting with formulas foreign to the ones that had won them acclaim.

It had happened, of course, to the master himself, Paul Whiteman. When he introduced the symphonic sound into dance music, his crew became the No. 1 dance band in the country for most of the decade known as the Roaring Twenties. The lovable and genial Whiteman was not content. He decided to exploit the symphony sound and slowly began to lose his dance audience. His orchestra would become prestigious as a concert aggregation but it would not survive the Big Band era that followed.

I remember the case of Shep Fields, too. Shep was a good friend of mine in the thirties when he burst on the national scene with a distinctive sound he called "Rippling Rhythm." I can recall the night he told me he was abandoning that sound at the height of his success. I tried to change his mind to no avail and Shep's popularity plummeted from that point on.

As I say I should have known better. I had already behind me in Chicago one clear-cut example of the danger of changing a tried and true product. That had occurred in January of 1928 while we were enjoying the fruits of instant success. Jules Stein had been quick to capitalize on our radio popularity and had signed us for a week's engagement in the the Palace Theater in Chicago. The theater played two-a-day and featured headliners like Al Jolson and Sophie Tucker and Eddie Cantor.

Always an innovator, Jules wanted to prove he could ask and get a higher fee for a band than the Palace had previously paid its most celebrated act. The maximum rate had been $3,500 per week and Stein said the Lombardos would play the Palace for nothing less than $4,000. He got the figure with a minimum of haggling.

So now we were returning to a vaudeville theater, but one that was a far cry from the tank-town houses in which we served our apprenticeship with Corinne Arbuckle. The Palace, like its namesake in New York, was the highest point to which an act could aspire. We immediately began thinking about all our old vaudeville routines, discarding the kind of numbers the radio listeners and Granada customers had come to expect.

We resurrected the props; the funny hats; the sandwich makings for "A Cup of Coffee, a Sandwich and You"; harness and blinders for Derf Higman to wear for "Thanks for the Buggy Ride"; no end of corny accouterments for the other novelty numbers. We were going to kill them with novelties, forgetting that novelty numbers had hardly been responsible for the Lombardo success story.

We were to play two shows a day, a matinee and evening performance, and on that wintry day of our opening, we were well prepared to prove that the band was comedic as well as musical.

We knocked ourselves out to prove the point and when the curtain came down were well pleased with ourselves.

The theater manager was less satisfied. He was apoplectic. He was bellowing, "Who told you guys you were comedians? Comedians we can get a dime a dozen not for four grand a week. We're paying you that kind of money for music, not jokes." He stalked off grimly and we got the message. For the next show, we would go back to what we knew, the same numbers and medleys that were our trademark.

Fortunately for us, the reviewers had missed our attempt at comedy. They came to cover the night show. One of the them was Ashton Stevens of the Chicago *Herald Examiner*, who was regarded as the city's leading critic. I shudder to think of how his review would have read had he caught the afternoon show. His critique of the night performance was to include a phrase that has stayed with us ever since. He referred to the band as "the softest and sweetest jazzmen on any stage this side of heaven."

That phrase, slightly changed in context, is the origin of the slogan that was forever after attached to the band: "The sweetest music this side of heaven."

The experience at the Palace and at the start of our second season in Chicago made an indelible impression upon me. Only on rare occasions, in later years, would we ever stray from our own formula—and those experiences wouldn't be happy, either.

But once we got over the foolishness and experimentation, Chicago became a wonderful town during the 1928–29 season. We were frenetically busy, of course. There were the rehearsals, the nightly Granada appearances, the radio remotes, and the commercial programs. We were getting into recordings, of which I will treat more fully in a later chapter. And we were enjoying prosperity. If the income of the band wasn't making millionaires out of us, we seemed to be on the road through stock investments.

I had an uncle in Chicago who told us how to invest in the stock market. He was sold on Cities Service and sold us. Carm's royalties from his songs permitted him to invest more than Lebe and I could, and after each of us put up a few thousand for the stock, suddenly Carm was worth about $150,000 on paper and Lebe and I about $100,000 each. The other members of the band went along too, and each of them enjoyed a sizable amount of shares.

We were enjoying life and every night was a party at the Granada. Chicago was jumping to the tune of a decade in which everybody seemed able to afford a good time. The speaks flourished, the entertainers entertained, and the gangsters mowed each other down in relentless pursuit of all the money that was lying around. After work, the Oglesby Arms was the band's after-hours club, and we entertained nightly for most of the name performers and musical people who came to town.

Chicago was the kind of town in which the young Royal Canadians could not stop at a mere $4,000 for a week's work at the Palace. A year later, Jules Stein booked us into the Chicago Theater, owned by Barney Balaban, who would in time head Paramount Pictures. Stein's asking price for us was an unheard-of $7,000 a week and he got it for a two-week engagement. We played seven shows a day, seven days a week, and every show was packed. I ran into Balaban only a few years ago, and he told me that to this day our attendance record for an engagement at the Chicago Theater has never been broken.

We opened on St. Valentine's Day, 1929, and I remember the day not so much for what happened onstage as off. After our first show in the morning we all walked out of the theater for breakfast, and newsboys were on both sides of the street yelling, "Extra." The story they were hawking concerned the gangland execution of seven hoods in a garage. We shrugged it off as typical Chicago. A few days later the story struck home.

The papers printed a picture of the suspected executioner, an Al Capone lieutenant known as Machine Gun Jack McGurn. We knew him as one of the band's favorite fans, who came in almost every night and sat at a table near the saxophone section. He always brought with him a younger brother, a quiet teen-ager, and a beautiful blond girl.

Not knowing McGurn's name or reputation, we had christened him Rudolph Valentino for his resemblance to the dominant lover of the silent screen. He was darkly handsome and his hair was patent leather. Whenever a number pleased him, he would toast the band, raising his glass, which contained nothing stronger than ginger ale. Now I looked at a newspaper and staring at me was "Rudolph Valentino," mastermind of the St. Valentine's Day Massacre, the bloodiest incident in gangland history.

Once again we began thinking of leaving town. But this time, it had nothing to do with our aversion to the gangster element of Chicago. The time was ripe to move on to New York. For one thing, a young crooner named Rudy Vallee recently had made a tremendous impact in the world's entertainment capital by bringing in a band that played in the same slow tempo as the Royal Canadians. He was also being heard on radio. We wanted to get to New York before other bands caught on to the tempo and diminished one of our trademarks.

Perhaps the most important reason was that Jules Stein had finally come to the conclusion that New York was now ready for us. From William S. Paley, the new young president of the Columbia Broadcasting System, he had received assurances that the band would be given a radio program sponsored by Robert Burns Panatella, the cigar people. And there were four or five hotels competing to book us.

Jules Stein came to Chicago to help win us what I hoped would be an amicable divorce from Al Quodbach. Our contract was about to expire, but I didn't want to just pack up and leave. I had become genuinely fond of the boisterous roughneck who had brought us to Chicago, and was grateful for his efforts in getting us on radio, a move he had first resisted. I hoped Jules Stein could make him see that the move to New York was just a matter of natural progression, rather than a desire to get away from the Granada.

We had the meeting in Al's office while the band was performing. I broke the news to him quickly: we would be leaving for New York when our contract was up; we had a job waiting in one of the big town's busiest hotels and a sponsored radio program on a national hookup. "We hate to leave you, Al, but I feel it's in the best interests of the band," I said.

His face took on the expression of a wounded elephant. "You can't do that to me, Guy. You can't leave me. You boys are like my own sons."

I told him we'd be back; we'd arrange to play at the Granada whenever we were booked in Chicago. He had to understand.

He didn't. The hurt turned into anger. He pointed his finger at Stein, shouting, "What kind of agent are you? Don't you know, I have an option to renew on these boys?"

He rummaged through his desk drawer, finally held aloft the contract that Billy Stein had originally negotiated. Al Quodbach must have realized that "his boys" might want to leave someday. At the bottom of the contract he had penned in a line, giving him the option of renewing the band on termination of the present contract.

Jules Stein reached into his brief case and produced his copy. "Nothing here about a renewal option, Al," he said. "And yours doesn't show Guy's signature on any addendum to the contract. It won't work, Al, the boys have a perfect right to leave."

Quodbach admitted he had put in the renewal clause only a few days before. "I was frantic. I just couldn't see losing my boys."

He had cooled down somewhat and now he was pleading. "Maybe they won't even like New York. Here they got a home and friends without no wolves trying to eat them up."

Jules then made a remark he instantly regretted. "They may like New York even better than Chicago," he said. "And they might never want to come back."

The rage and frustration in Al Quodbach boiled over. He went back to his desk drawer and this time he pulled out a nickel-plated revolver and started shooting at a picture of Stein that hung on the wall. "You took away my band," he shouted.

I couldn't stand it. I told Al to put the gun down. "We're going to New York, Jules Stein or no and Al Quodbach or no. You'll have to excuse me. I've got to get back on the bandstand." And I walked out the door, with Quodbach still holding the gun. As I ascended the bandstand Carm gave me a queer look. "You're white," he said. "What happened in there?"

I found out from Jules Stein later, asking him what had happened after I left. "Nothing much," Jules said. "Al put the gun back in the drawer. And then he started crying."

4. New York Was Big-Time

Jules Stein was the best-known band booker in the country in 1929, when he brought us east in an ice-breaking expedition to establish a foothold in New York. His reputation had been made in Chicago and extended throughout the Midwest, representing dozens of bands that included such nationally known names as Art Hickman, Abe Lyman, and Coon-Saunders. Yet none of them had been able to get successful bookings in New York. But now Stein was convinced he had a winner as three of New York's leading hotels competed for the services of the Royal Canadians.

He also had going for him and for us the formula that had gained us recognition in Cleveland and Chicago. No longer would we have to go begging, hat in hand, for the radio exposure that had given us instant recognition. Bill Paley had also learned from that formula, and since taking over CBS he was anxious to put live music on his New York station, WABC. He assured Stein that he would install a wire remote in whatever hotel we chose as our New York base of operations. The promise from the General Cigar Company to sponsor a commercial program featuring the Royal Canadians was icing on the cake.

I may be getting ahead of myself, but the fact is Jules Stein did break the New York market with our band. Once the radio exposure worked for us again in New York, the best-known bands in the nation came to Stein to represent them, and his Music Corporation of America would become a talent empire handling the biggest names in show business.

The immediate concern was to choose the best possible location for the band. I made numerous trips from Chicago to Stein's new offices in the Paramount Building, poring over blueprints and layouts of hotels we might play in. Billy Stein visited us frequently in Chicago, too, discussing strategy for the New York invasion.

Two hotels, particularly, were making overtures for our services. The St. Regis, uptown and a favorite spot for the social register crowd, approached MCA first. Even more interested was an old friend, Ralph Hitz, the former manager of the Winton Hotel in Cleveland, who had just been appointed managing director of the recently built New Yorker Hotel in the garment district. Ralph wanted to open the new hotel with our band; he had watched us take over Cleveland and he felt responsible in small part. It was Hitz who had given Larry Owen permission to leave the Vernon-Owen band, which was playing the Winton. And Larry had joined us as third sax and arranger. Hitz believed we owed him something for that and was sure we would make our debut in New York in his hotel.

Showing an interest, too, was the Roosevelt Hotel on Madison Avenue at Forty-fifth Street. Ben Bernie had become a fixture there, having played the Roosevelt Grill for four years. Now the "old maestro" was seeking to get around the country more, and had accepted an engagement in Chicago. The Roosevelt management asked if we would be interested in replacing him.

The two Stein brothers and the three Lombardo brothers finally agreed on the Roosevelt. We dismissed the St. Regis because we felt the social clientele might be too restrictive in their musical demands. And we thought the New Yorker would not attract the collegiate crowd, which was among our biggest boosters. Ralph Hitz was furious when we turned down his offer; he vowed he would never book an MCA Band in a hotel with which he was associated. And that left the Roosevelt, the most centrally situated hotel for our purposes, with our kind of following—the general public.

The Roosevelt's offer was less than the others; the contract called for $2,000 a week for the fall and winter seasons. We had been offered almost twice that much to stay in Chicago. But we were convinced we had made the right choice and that once we became known in New York there was no limit to our future. Money, at the moment, was the least of our worries. All of us were loaded with that Cities Service stock.

We left Chicago in the middle of September for a two-week engagement in Washington preparatory to opening at the Roosevelt. Most of the band had never been farther east than Cleveland and the date in the nation's capital would give us a feeling for the eastern seaboard and a chance to brush up on new tunes so we would come in to New York with our best arrangements.

We were like touring school kids taken by their teachers to the capital at cherry-blossom time. Our engagement was at the fine Wardman Park Hotel, but most of our time was spent visiting the federal buildings, savoring the monuments. None of us could guess how many times we would be back to play Inaugural Balls, to meet every President from Roosevelt to Nixon.

On October 2, the night before our opening at the Roosevelt, we were a caravan of cars again, finding our way into New York through the just-completed Holland Tunnel, losing ourselves in the confusion of overhead trains and trolleys and double-decker busses, stopping again and again to find out which way was crosstown and which way uptown. We checked in at the Roosevelt, a happy crew, paper-rich with stocks, confident of our ability to take over the big time.

I can imagine how smug the young Guy Lombardo was feeling when I remember the next morning in Jules Stein's office. He asked if we had made preparations for opening night. I laughed. Who needed rehearsals? They'd loved us in Washington, and with the market the way it was we'd be millionaires in no time. We had purchased Cities Service at 30 and now it was 80. Carmen had almost 2,000 shares, I had about 1,500, and Lebe, about 1,000. Every member of the band was worth at least $25,000 on the current market.

I walked around the theater district, thinking how fortunate we were, remembering how but a few short years before we had almost given up and returned to London. I took in the names on the marquees. Clayton, Jackson, and Durante were at the Winter

Garden. The Chateau Madrid featured Jack White. Libby Hol-
man was singing torch songs at the Club Lido. Eddie Cantor was
starring in *Whoopee*, and the season's first hit musical was *Sweet
Adeline*, with Helen Morgan and a Jerome Kern score. George
White's Scandals was playing on Forty-second Street, and on
Forty-fourth Earl Carroll's *Sketch Book* was advertising "the
prettiest girls in town." The top plays were *Journey's End*, *Street
Scene*, and *Strictly Dishonorable*.

I looked through the newspapers to acquaint myself with the
bands that would be our competition. Surprisingly, New York did
not seem to be crowded with as many orchestras as we had found
in Cleveland and Chicago. Rudy Vallee was about to open at
Villa Vallee, a new club; Leo Reisman was at the Central Park
Casino; and Emil Coleman at the Club Montmartre. There was
only one hotel ad which listed a band and that was the St. Regis'
Seaglade Room, which featured Vincent Lopez and the dance
team of Veloz and Yolanda. The room requested patrons to wear
formal clothes.

We had survived disappointing debuts in Cleveland and Chicago. Our opening night in New York on October 3, 1929, was
overwhelming. I don't suppose I expected more than a smattering
of the regular patrons of the Roosevelt Grill to come out of curiosity. Instead the room was sold out hours before we appeared on
the bandstand. All the heads of the music publishing firms had
reserved tables. So had, it seemed, the entire segment of New
York's show business community. Wall Street had sent a large representation of stock brokers, most of them in white ties and tails
and with what looked to me like the most beautiful women in the
world in minks and ermines.

In attendance, too, was Bill Paley, who had come to work. We
would be doing two or three sustaining remotes a week from the
Grill over WABC and he was there opening night to see that the
program ran smoothly, that the mikes were properly placed, the
band balanced, and the cues understood between his announcer,
David Ross, and myself. This was a network president who early
in his career did not leave details to subordinates.

Paley, who was my age, was the son of a Russian-born cigar
maker. The elder Paley and a brother had made a fortune in and

around Philadelphia, and Bill had learned the business early. He had also convinced his father of the advertising benefits to be derived from the new medium of radio by sponsoring a program over a Philadelphia station. The Paleys spent $50 a week for their La Palina hour, which huckstered the cigar named for the family, and it proved so successful that when a family friend purchased CBS they were among the network's first sponsors.

And the year before we arrived in New York, Bill Paley had become so enamored of radio's future he purchased the network with a million dollars advanced by his father. Paley's network hardly could be considered competition to David Sarnoff's National Broadcasting Company with its blue and red networks and two New York stations, WEAF and WJZ.

But Paley did not take long in establishing himself as a healthy Sarnoff competitor. One of his first moves was to bring live music to his affiliated stations, which were obligated to play whatever programs emanated from New York if he so ordered. He had decided that the Royal Canadians broadcasts from the Roosevelt, although nonsponsored, would be carried by the eastern stations in the network.

And so Bill Paley was working with us on opening night, leaving nothing to chance. Like Jules Stein, he had a stake in the band. The Royal Canadians would test the interest of listeners in dance music. We would get better than passing marks on the test, and the airwaves would be opened for all the great bands that would follow.

But Paley was not entirely happy with the debut. His displeasure was not with the band, but with David Ross, the announcer he had assigned to introduce us to the New York public. Ross was too professional. As the moment arrived for us to go on the air, he was sitting at a small table set up in back of the bandstand, intoning, "Five, four, three, two, one . . . you're on."

We played our theme song, "Coming Through the Rye," and Ross took over. He sure was articulate. He kept talking and we kept repeating the theme. He described the glamour of the opening, the physical dimensions of the room, the young musicians on the bandstand who had hit the big time on a route from London, Ontario, to Cleveland to Chicago to New York. At the end of five minutes, we had only played one number. Then Ross professionally cupped his ear and spoke for another few minutes. The people in the room began getting fidgety and Paley was pacing up and down, livid. By the time we finished the half hour, we had put five numbers on the air, but the audience certainly had received detailed histories of the songs and the composers.

Paley did not mince words once he had a chance to talk to Ross. He told him bluntly, "The people didn't come to hear you announce. They came to hear Guy Lombardo's music."

The next day there were auditions for a new announcer. The one who could say fastest, "And now Guy Lombardo, playing 'Heartaches,'" would get the job. That man turned out to be Frank Knight, with his beautifully cultivated British accent.

And in time the short introduction would become another trademark of our band. No speeches, no flowery descriptions by me or the announcer, whose job was simply to say, "Guy Lombardo playing . . ." And we used that style away from radio, too. Wherever we played and in whatever milieu—dances, concerts, theater appearances—I never found it necessary to do other than announce the song before putting the baton in motion.

One of the unsuccessful candidates at the audition was Andre Baruch, who was to become one of radio's best-known voices. I ran into him recently and he still remembered that test. "You broke my heart, Guy," he said. "I put a lot of preparation into that audition. I spent all that morning researching the band and its history and had made notations on almost every popular song of the day you might be playing. Then they told us all we had to say was the name of the band and the number. I just couldn't do that as fast as Frank Knight."

Meanwhile, we had apparently left a lasting impression on New York. We would continue playing the Roosevelt Grill every fall and winter but one until 1963, but Ben Gross, the long-time radio editor for the New York *Daily News*, would always remember our opening night. Writing in *Variety* on the occasion of our twentieth anniversary at the Roosevelt, he said:

The night of Oct. 3, 1929 was a historic one but I didn't know it.

That was the evening Guy Lombardo and his Royal Canadians opened in the Grill of the Hotel Roosevelt. At first, it seemed much like any other opening of those hectic days. After all, there were some other pretty good bands at the time, Whiteman and Lopez to name just two; and so those of us who were present at Madison and 45th had no reason to suspect that this occasion would be a memorable one . . .

Anyway I was there. And probably no other practicing radio editor of today can make that claim.

I shall always recall the effect Guy's first number had on the audience. It was rhythmic, it was gay, but it had a soothing quality. There was talk about the band playing "off pitch," an assertion that Lombardo firmly denies. But most of those present had one comment: "This outfit's music is distinctive; it's unlike any other."

And that's why I regard Lombardo as one of the smartest men in show business. Since his beginning, he has recognized that a trademark is a precious asset. . . . I have heard thousands of bands since beginning to listen to radio professionally in 1925, but Lombardo's has been one of the few I could ever identify without the help of an announcer.

Back in 1929, crowds used to gather around a bandstand merely to watch the orchestra or certain soloists perform. But it didn't happen that night at the Roosevelt. And it still doesn't because Guy always has had the notion that the people on the floor are out there because they want to dance. So he sees no reason for spot-lighting an instrumentalist or vocalist for the sake of pleasing those who merely want to stare . . .

We learned how firmly we had established ourselves in the big time at the rehearsal following opening night. We walked into the Grill and there must have been fifty song pluggers waiting to peddle their wares. It was flattering that Tin Pan Alley was making overtures to the Royal Canadians, but it wasn't exactly welcome. We had long since established a rule that rehearsals were secret.

The reason was that we wanted to keep the practice sessions uninhibited. We didn't have anything to hide, but a feature of the rehearsals was the open forum presented to every member of the band. They could get up and disagree with a particular orchestration or arrangement, make suggestions, voice opinions. Many times the forums got heated, especially when they became debates among the Lombardo brothers. We might even shout and scream at each other, but it was a matter that would be kept within the family, which meant the entire band.

A more important reason for keeping the sessions closed was the knowledge that, if we followed the permissive policy of other name bands, we would find ourselves with no time to do anything but listen to the songs the pluggers wanted us to hear. I had been all through that in Chicago and learned to be selective about the material we chose and the manner in which we made the selections. The time for choosing material was not at a rehearsal. Carm and I had developed a system where we spent many hours a week together going over new songs, picking out what we liked without pressure, and fitting them into our style.

I had made it clear in Chicago that we would not lean toward material that was strictly a matter of *quid pro quo* between a publishing company and a bandleader. The companies, through their pluggers, were always coming up with theater tickets, admissions to sporting events, suits of clothing, and other gifts designed to make a bandleader look with favor on their product. The biggest inducement was to offer the leader a "piece" of a song. And many leaders allowed themselves to be romanced that way. They felt they could make money by promoting a song in which they had been given a financial interest.

It wasn't that I was a complete idealist. The plain fact of the matter was that I knew that, if I was pressured into mediocre material, the band would suffer. If we played anything but first-class numbers, our band's reputation could not remain first-class.

It came, therefore, as a surprise to the assemblage of pluggers when I asked them what they were doing at the rehearsal. They told me they were simply following an old New York custom. They had always had free access to the rehearsals of the best bands in town—Whiteman, Lopez, and Bernie—and the leaders had always been willing to listen to their tunes.

I have never fancied myself an orator, but I made a speech that day. "Boys," I said, "I appreciate the compliment you showed us in turning up. But as far as that New York custom you were talking about, I can't go along with it. Our rehearsals are private and they're going to continue that way. You simply won't be admitted and we're not going to play whatever you have at a rehearsal. As a matter of fact I'm calling off today's rehearsal right now and we might as well all go home.

"First let me put you straight on one thing. Neither my brothers nor I want tickets to anything. We don't want free booze and we don't want dates with chorus girls. Most important, we don't want to be cut in on any song. We welcome your material, but don't bring it into rehearsals. We'll look over everything you submit and we'll accept whatever we think is for us. And then we'll make a hit out of it. When we do, don't thank us or try to show your appreciation. We're doing it for ourselves, not for you."

It was another policy we would stick with throughout the life-time of the band. A few months later when we began the weekly radio show for Robert Burns Panatella, we would introduce a "hit of the week." The song would be the result of careful attention, selected only after Carm and I had screened virtually every new tune on the market, finally narrowing them down to three. Then we would submit our finalists to the band for a vote and the winner would be introduced on the program. In that manner and without high pressure salesmanship, we would be able to in-troduce hundreds of hit songs to the public in ensuing years.

For the moment, however, the commercial show that Bill Paley had promised us was not forthcoming. We were stymied by a union regulation that neither Stein nor Paley had anticipated. The rule was that a band coming into a new city had to play for a year before it was entitled to double up on a sponsored radio pro-gram. I resigned myself to waiting out the year, content in our popularity at the Roosevelt, the increasing demand on us to make records, and the sheer pleasure of being a recognized part of the New York entertainment scene in its most golden era.

We quickly fell into the pattern of New York living. We were still living in hotels but were looking for apartments close to each other. We discovered Lindy's and Reuben's and became ac-quainted with the songwriters, song pluggers, and show business personalities who frequented the restaurants. One day Eddie Can-tor might come over to the table; another day Harry Richman or Jimmy Durante. In those three weeks of October that were closing out an era, we sat on top of the world.

But we did not occupy that celestial space long enough to

become accustomed to it. On October 24, the day that would forevermore be remembered as Black Thursday, we had spent all of the morning and part of the afternoon in a recording studio. One of the songs we put on wax was "My Fate Is in Your Hands."

The irony of the title was not brought home until we finally broke for a late lunch. In Lindy's, the diners weren't eating or telling jokes. They had their eyes glued to the black headlines in the newspapers. The stock market had crashed. I rushed to a phone and called a broker. Cities Service had been quoted at 80 that morning. Now it was 14 and I had lost more than $60,000 in a few hours. Carm had lost even more. We had a job but suddenly little more security than when we were struggling in Cleveland.

But the full extent of the crash did not strike us until we went to work that night. The Roosevelt Grill was no longer filled with gay, happy, paper-rich patrons. Even those without money in the market hardly felt like dancing. I saw a panorama of white tablecloths, reminding me of another time and another place when we were struggling for recognition in the early weeks at Al Quodbach's Granada Cafe. Only Carm, with his usual talent for picking out the most topical songs of the day, saved us from wallowing in self-pity. For the first song on our sustaining program that night, he selected, "I Can't Give You Anything but Love, Baby."

Business continued horrible right through Thanksgiving. Carm, Lebe, and I hadn't worried about the minimal $2,000 a week the Roosevelt was paying the band. We didn't have to worry as long as Cities Service had made us rich and we had the prospect of the sponsored radio show. Now there was hardly anything left after we paid the members of the band and we would have to abandon our search for fancy apartments. We could just about pay our hotel expenses.

I confronted Jules Stein with the idea of going back to Chicago, where we had been offered double what we were making in New York. He was shocked; he said he was working with Paley on an idea that might clear up the obstacle that was keeping us off commercial radio.

"I just found out," he said, "that Ben Bernie signed up for an engagement in Chicago. But he has the same trouble about getting on radio there as you have here. Jimmy Petrillo, the Musicians' Union boss in Chicago, is an old friend of my brother Billy. I think I can get him to waive the regulation for Bernie in Chicago if the New York union does the same thing here for the Royal Canadians. Hold on, Guy, it won't take long before it comes through."

I did, but not before an occurrence that perfectly matched the depressing atmosphere of those days. Carm and Florence had finally rented an apartment on Amsterdam Avenue near Seventy-second Street. You may remember that I had made Florence the band's paymaster in Cleveland and she was still performing that function in New York. The Friday before Thanksgiving, I got the $2,000 paycheck from the Roosevelt and turned it over to her. She couldn't cash it at the banks, which were closed, but got the cash from the manager of the Roosevelt and took it to her apartment and filled out pay envelopes for the members of the band, who would stop by to pick them up.

She had just finished when the doorman called from downstairs and said, "Some of the boys are down here and they're coming up to see you."

The doorman could hardly have been blamed for assuming "the boys" were in the band. They were carrying instrument cases. When Carmen opened the door, he faced a battery of high-powered weapons carried by three men. They proceeded to tie him up, repeated the procedure on Florence, scooped up the payroll from a dresser, and helped themselves to my sister-in-law's jewelry. The value of the gems was about $50,000.

Nothing like that had ever happened to us in the more notorious city of Chicago and it couldn't have come at a worse time. The newspapers played the story on Page One. The headline in the *Daily Mirror* read: "Lombardos robbed; Grover Whalen Hints Inside Job."

That night New York's fashionable police commissioner came to the Roosevelt to take personal charge of the investigation. He came, wearing a tuxedo, putting his best foot forward for the photographers who had been apprised in advance that he would be there to interrogate each member of the band on the theory that one of them had to be the "inside" man. Who else would have known about the payroll?

That theory led nowhere. After many pictures and many questions, Whalen convinced himself that the Royal Canadians were hardly the types to go planning armed robberies. The robbery was never solved and the assumption was that the intruders had simply known that Carmen and Florence lived there and had jewelry in the apartment. The payroll was an unlooked-for bonus.

It all added up to an unappetizing Thanksgiving. I hadn't yet reached a stage where I could accept reverses with equanimity. Lilliebell served turkey in our cramped hotel room and I couldn't get myself to eat it. There were people in New York waiting in line for holiday dinners in soup kitchens, but all I could think about was how quickly our fortunes had been reversed. I remember putting the petulant question to Lilliebell: "What in hell have we got to be thankful for?"

Through the month that was left of 1929, we could find only one bright note. Weekdays, the Roosevelt Grill hardly did any business at all. Weekends, the room showed signs of life. If our following had fallen off among patrons who no longer had the money or desire to go out evenings, it remained constant with the collegians who still came to the city for a good time on Friday and Saturday nights. The students of the eastern colleges regarded us as their band, the one they listened to on the remote broadcasts, and they came to see us in person.

Among those who came were some who were to become lifelong friends. I remember the seventeen-year-old Dan Topping, later to become the owner of the New York Yankees. At the time he was a preppie at the Lawrenceville School. And there was a sweet girl named Barbara Hutton, and another we called Rocky. She was Veronica Balfe, who would later marry an actor named Gary Cooper.

The presence of the young crowd kept us going through December, and we were further heartened when not only CBS but NBC asked us to broadcast from the Roosevelt Grill on New Year's Eve. We rang out the old year for Bill Paley and ushered in the new one for David Sarnoff. We would never miss a New Year's Eve on the air again. But it hardly seemed at the time that the broadcasts would make us a national rite, almost as closely identified with New Year's Eve as Santa Claus with Christmas.

The New Year of 1930 also ushered in the decade of the Depression. It was a time to test the mettle of a nation. The workingman would abandon his dream of riding the stock market to fortune. He would struggle, instead, to merely bring food to the table. Curiously, the Depression would bring a paradox of plenty to the Royal Canadians.

We had staked our future on radio—in Cleveland, in Chicago, and now in New York. But we never anticipated that a terrible recession would make the medium the dominant force in the entertainment business. How could we know that the day would come that few people could afford a speakeasy, a night club, a night of dining and dancing in a hotel? Americans, however, never abandoned their quest for entertainment. They turned now to the cheapest way they could get it—in their own living rooms. Radio had progressed from the crystal set and earphone era. It came now as furniture, in handsome cabinets and with an ever-increasing variety of stations and programs.

In the early months of the new year, Jules Stein made good on his promise. He persuaded Jimmy Petrillo to waive the Musicians' Union regulation and permit Ben Bernie to play on Chicago radio without waiting out the required year. Petrillo, who would become a virtual union czar in the music business, persuaded the New York local to do the same for Guy Lombardo and the Royal Canadians.

That was all Bill Paley needed to sign us up for the weekly Robert Burns Panatella program to be broadcast coast to coast. And that put us on the ground floor of radio. At the start of the Depression, it was all we needed to become one of the major show business attractions in the nation.

The half-hour network show, broadcast every Monday night from 9 to 9:30, transformed the Roosevelt Grill into a popular mecca for out-of-towners. Tourism may have suffered greatly from the economy, but apparently there were still some prosperous citizens who came to the big city on business trips and for honeymoons and special occasions. Invariably they headed for the Roosevelt Grill to see in person the band they had heard on radio. By that spring the Roosevelt Grill was filling up, even on weekdays.

The impact of the band's popularity was appreciated by the management of the hotel. When our engagement ended in early April, we were offered a contract for a flat 25 per cent of the Grill's total receipts. We signed and for the more than thirty years we would play the room, every fall and winter, the band's take would average $7,500 a week. That was big money, especially during the Depression, and I would never complain again that I had nothing to be thankful for.

The radio program also reaffirmed our popularity with collegians. We began getting offers from campuses all over the country, asking us to play college functions during Easter and commencement weeks. We opted, finally, for the University of Virginia at Easter, happy to leave behind those sidewalks of New York that had become progressively gloomier during a hard winter.

But now I had a permanent home to come back to. Lilliebell had found a fine apartment on Riverside Drive and Seventy-fifth Street. She had been tipped off to it by a couple we knew from Chicago, songwriter Sammy Stept and his wife. The Stepts lived there, as did a number of other people in the music industry, including George Gershwin, who occupied the building's penthouse.

Before we left, Lilliebell put all her energies into decorating the apartment in the style she thought a successful bandleader was entitled to. The income from the Robert Burns show helped. So did the fifth Lombardo brother, Joe, who was in New York studying interior design. The job he did on that apartment was the first of many for which we would call on his expertise. He would become one of the city's leading designers and antique dealers specializing in the Louis XIV period.

Joe and Victor were the little brothers we had left at home in London. Papa had not been as rigid in forcing a musical education upon them as he had with his oldest sons, the band owners. In the first place, Joe just couldn't carry a tune. And he wasn't interested in learning an instrument. His creative ability lay in drawing pictures and producing harmonious blendings of colors. Papa sent him to New York to study, and Joe later went abroad to finish his education in a field that would prove even more lucrative than the band business.

Victor was another matter. My second youngest brother, even without Papa's prodding, decided to follow in Carmen's footsteps. On his own, he learned the saxophone and clarinet. At seventeen, he had put together a small band that played a summer engagement in Cleveland. The following autumn, he joined an orchestra in Toronto.

One day, after Victor came home from Toronto, Mama called me in New York, a few weeks before we were to go on tour, and asked if I could take him on with the band. Naturally we were interested but we didn't want to hurt the band. We'd never really had a chance to hear Victor since he started to play professionally. I wasn't about to hand over a chair on the bandstand to an unproven musician, even if his name was Lombardo.

But Mama was confident. "He's good, Guy," she said. "You'll see. And if he isn't good enough, it won't take long for the three of you to teach him."

I told her to put Victor on a train and he arrived at the hotel in time for a rehearsal. He also arrived rather sheepishly, complaining it was colder in New York than in Canada. It seemed he had hocked his overcoat. And he wasn't prepared for the rehearsal because his saxophone had followed the same route to a pawnshop.

Carmen loaned him one of his and Vic sat down and played, amazing all of us. Where ten years before Carm had developed his own sax style listening to Paul Whiteman records, Victor had taught himself on Guy Lombardo records, with special attention to Carm's lead sax. He had the same rich obbligato and we found no difficulty at all fitting him into the band, playing the baritone sax and sharing the lead with Carm, but in a lower key. We now had a complement of eleven instrumentalists if you include my own violin, which I had phased out as far back as Cleveland.

I had continued, however, to carry the fiddle under my left arm, using the bow as a leader's baton. It was not a satisfactory arrangement; it invariably left that side of my jacket shiny. After nineteen-year-old Vic joined the band, I decided to get rid of it altogether. But it took some doing and I let the matter lie as we took off for the week in Virginia.

It's funny how that college date remains in my memory. We had played on other campuses before and we would again, almost for the lifetime of the band. Probably the first thing that struck me when we arrived at the university in Charlottesville was the lift in spirits we received from the change in scenery. We had undergone, after all, some traumatic experiences in that first winter in New York, and here we were under warmer skies and in a pastoral setting where students not much younger than the members of the band regarded us as their heroes and offered us hospitality.

We got to know many of them personally and some we would count as our dearest friends years later and many miles removed from the campus. I remember, for instance, one handsome lad everybody called Teentsie. We met him at a house party to which we were invited after playing a formal dance. The U. of Virginia students weren't permitted to drink during the dance and neither did we as a matter of band policy. But at the nightly frat parties to which we brought our instruments, libations flowed freely and we got to know a considerable number of undergrads by their nicknames.

Twenty-five years later, when the band was playing the Waldorf, I noticed a party of white-tied gentlemen enter the room with their ball-gowned ladies, and shouted from the bandstand to the dignified man who led the party, "Hey, Teentsie, good to see you again."

Nobody else in the party looked up; they had apparently never heard of "Teentsie." But T. H. Daugherty remembered. He was now president of the Metropolitan Life Insurance Company and more likely to be addressed as T.H. He came up to the bandstand, shook hands warmly, and I wondered how many other Chucks and Hanks and Pudges were now initials that were big names in the world of business.

"An awful lot of them, Guy," said Teentsie Daugherty. "And they all remember that first Easter week you came to Virginia."

What was even more memorable and lasting about that week was that it put into place for us the song that would forever be identified with the Lombardo band and New Year's Eve. It is a story that started off with a concession to commercialism and ended up as a tradition.

I refer, of course, to "Auld Lang Syne." The song had been in our book since we were the Lombardo Brothers Concert Company, touring the hamlets of Ontario, playing a largely Scottish population. The verse had been written by the revered Scottish poet Robert Burns, as had "Comin' Thro' the Rye." Music had been written for both songs in the nineteenth century and they still enjoy great popularity among the Scots everywhere.

We hadn't been playing the songs much in Cleveland and Chicago, but there seemed to be the best of all reasons for bringing them back when we got to New York. Bill Paley, of course, had promised us that Robert Burns radio show. When we opened the Roosevelt, it seemed fitting to use the Robert Burns verses—"Comin' Thro' the Rye" as an opener, and "Auld Lang Syne" as a sign-off. We expected to do that when we finally got on the air for the cigar company.

And now during one of those fraternity parties at Virginia, we ended the evening with "Auld Lang Syne" and were amazed at the reception it got from the students. They demanded one encore after another. I leaned down from the bandstand and asked one of the committee chairmen, "What's so great about 'Auld Lang Syne.'"

"That's the school's marching song," he said, "same tune, different lyrics."

We would always keep Auld Lang Syne after that, especially on New Year's Eve. The boys at Virginia had given us a reason to retain it. Robert Burns's words would always remind us of that wonderful Easter week in Virginia. ". . . Should Auld Acquaintance be Forgot . . . and the days of Auld Lang Syne." Of such beginnings are traditions born.

We had so enjoyed the week in Virginia that I was surprised at the sad faces among the dance committee as we said our farewells. It may have been Teentsie Daugherty who summed up the reason for all the melancholy. The committee had met the night before and decided to invite us back again for commencement week in June. The problem was their budget couldn't stand it.

Many Happy Returns, Guy's first picture. Gracie Allen holds the confused attention of Franklin Pangborn and George Barbier as George Burns listens. Behind George Burns is Ray Milland (this was his first leading role in pictures).

ank Sinatra, Vaughn Monroe, and Guy, the mid-forties.

At the end of the thirties (1939), a Lombardo billing on Broadway.

A new Lombardo is added to the band. The four brothers (Vic standing, left) hold up their new vocalist, Rose Marie Lombardo. 1943. *(Photo by CBS.)*

Kenny Gardner, the vocalist who replaced Carm in 1940. During the war Kenny married Elaine Lombardo, who had first brought him to Guy's attention when she heard him on the radio. *(Photo by James J. Kriegsmann.)*

Rose Marie, Carm, and Guy going over a piece of music.

Irving Berlin, whose songs the Lombardo have played since before World War I.

Walter Donaldson, who wrote such favorites as "Mammy," "My Blue Heaven," and "My Buddy." To Guy, he epitomized Tin Pan Alley.

Fellow bandleaders drop in for a visit at the Roosevelt Grill. Left to right: Benny Strong, Tommy Dorsey, Sammy Kaye, Guy, Shep Fields, and Vincent Lopez.

Carm and Guy. *(Photo by Maurice Seymour.)*

Louis Prima, whom Guy first heard in N
Orleans in 1934. He brought Prima to N
York soon afterward, where he was an
stant sensation. *(Photo by the Las Ve*
Review Journal.

The personnel of the band had changed in
the late forties. Newcomers included Don
Rodney and Rose Marie (between Guy
and Carmen) and Cliff Grass (between
Carmen and Derf Higman).

Most of the Lombardo clan gathers for t
twentieth anniversary of Carm and Fl
ence at the Capitol Theater. Members
the family include, on the left, Ha
Becker and Rose Marie, Joseph, Mr. Lo
bardo, Elaine, Mrs. Lombardo, and Ken
Gardner, and, beside Florence, Guy, Lill
bell, Helen, and Lebert. *(Photo by J
Sharp.)*

Guy as a cowboy and Lilliebell as a cowgirl at the masquerade party they gave to celebrate the opening of their new home in Freeport. On the mantel is a model of *Tempo*.

Guy relaxes with a soft drink after winning the 1946 Gold Cup and breaking a world record for the ninety-mile race. (*Photo Don Walsh, Steve Hannagan Associates*

Guy breaks another world's record in the Salton Sea, California, 1948, with a time of 119.7 mph, a new record for the single-engine hydro. (*Photo by Ralph Forney.*)

Carm and Lebe agreed with me that we loved the place so much we'd come back in two months and play for nothing. We would not wait a year to renew auld acquaintances. And we would play at the Virginia campus for the next four years.

We had one more week to play at the Roosevelt before the expiration of our six-month contract, and before we went out on a tour of one-nighters. One afternoon during that week I was accosted outside the hotel by a character out of Damon Runyon and via Chicago. His name was Benny and he had been a hanger-on in the Granada Cafe, one of the inevitable troupe selling bootleg whiskey, feminine company and watches at 100-per-cent-discount prices. Benny I remembered as the pitchman who had once put me on to a bargain fur coat for Lilliebell.

"All you gotta do," he had said, "is go up to Marshall Field's and pick out a coat and put a pin in it. You'll have it the next day, practically for nuthin'."

I had resisted the temptation and I think that was the last time I had seen Benny to this moment, when, looking to the right and the left and with a hand cupped over his mouth, he whispered to me, "Come around the side of the building, I got some rocks I want to show you."

Why the sudden interest in geology, I thought, as he pushed me into the side entrance of the hotel and escorted me to the men's room, where in complete privacy he opened a chamois bag sparkling with diamonds.

"What the hell are you showing me these for?" I asked, perspiring. "Don't you know the hotel is crowded with cops. They're still looking for the thief who stole Carmen's diamonds. Is that what you're showing me, the haul from his apartment?"

Benny drew himself up to full height, about even with my shoulders, and looked offended. "I never thought you'd think I was a thief," he said. "Would I do that to you, steal your brother's stuff and then try and sell it back to you? I never thought Guy Lombardo would insult me like that."

So saying, he marched off huffily, and that was the last I heard of illegal rocks. Carm never did find those taken from Florence.

Our first season at the Roosevelt finished, we embarked now on the initial leg of a tour that would last a lifetime. The one-nighters. Overnight bus rides from town to town, from dance hall to theater to country club to college campuses to indoor and outdoor auditoriums. The tour was originally booked by MCA. It has lasted until the present day and we now spend ten out of every twelve months a year on the road.

Jules Stein would make sure, however, that he never booked us in a town that had no broadcasting facilities. Especially on a Monday night, when we were heard coast to coast on the Robert Burns show. He had mapped out an itinerary that would remain virtually unchanged until 1933. We would play the Roosevelt from October to April, including two remote broadcasts a week and the commercial program on Monday. From April to June we were on the road with a large number of dates on campuses. For the summer we played a Long Island roadhouse, the sumptuous Pavillon Royal in Valley Stream. In September we usually played theater dates and then back to the Roosevelt.

I think it was the second year of the tour that Stein decided we needed a band boy. A young man to make the travel arrangements, pick up our fees from the various entrepreneurs who booked us, see that the bandstand was properly set up. A detail man to handle the details.

He might have solved the problem of what to do with my fiddle the year before. I had decided to get rid of it once and for all on our first tour. One night in an Ohio dance hall, I simply left it, bow and all, behind the piano. The next night in a town a hundred miles away, I stepped out on the bandstand for the first time in my life carrying only a baton. I felt pounds lighter. But I never got a chance to wave that baton to lead off the program.

A man came pushing through the dancers. He held aloft my fiddle. It had been given to him by the owner of the hall we had played the previous night. The man was a cabdriver and he wanted fifty dollars for the trip. He handed me the fiddle and I gave him his money. I never got rid of the damn thing until one New Year's Eve, when a group of bandleaders came to the Roosevelt after we had all finished working and sat down for a jam session.

Abe Lyman was at the drums, Russ Morgan at the trombone, Little Jack Little at the piano, and Freddy Martin at the sax.

They had the few customers who hadn't gone home yet literally stomping, and Lyman, carried away by it all, reached over and picked up my fiddle lying on the piano. He splintered it over Jack Little's head. And that was the last time I ever saw the violin my father had purchased for me as a boy, the one that had replaced the fiddle he busted over my own head.

Getting back to our band boy, the first thing we knew about him was that he was addressed as Sonny and didn't seem to mind. His real name was David Werblin and he had just graduated from Rutgers and been hired by MCA. He sat down next to me on the bus and started impressing me with how much he knew. I would never have to worry while he was aboard. He had everything programmed. The operation was going to run like clockwork.

The main thing, he assured me, was that he'd make sure we were never cheated by an unscrupulous promoter. He seemed to be very knowing about the thieves who might be waiting for us en route. He personally was going to count every ticket in every house we played. He showed me the hand clicker that was going to count the tickets. He was a brash young man, Sonny Werblin, but you had to like him and the way he inspired confidence.

It turned out that college had not taught Sonny the bitter lessons you can only learn by experience. It took only one stop to resume his education. We were booked into a giant dance hall in Berwyn, Pennsylvania, and we were to receive $1,000 plus 60 per cent of the gate. Sonny had it worked out so that he would receive $500 at intermission and the other $500 plus our percentage after we finished playing.

The admission charge was a dollar and, depression or no, I would guess there must have been four thousand customers in the hall, attracted by the band they had heard on radio. We literally had to fight our way to the bandstand. Sonny was clicking his hand clicker and wringing his hands. "We're really going to take some money out of this place tonight," he told me.

And just after we returned to the stand after intermission, I heard for the first time a phrase that was later to be the name of a popular radio program. I heard somebody shouting over and over, "Stop the music . . . Stop the music!" I finally identified the voice as Sonny's, and when he eventually made his way to the bandstand he had tears in his eyes.

"Guy," he said, "I can't find the people with the money."

The dance-hall manager had simply taken a powder before intermission. While Sonny was counting the house, he was counting the money. When our collector came around for the first installment, the door to the manager's office was closed, and Sonny learned from an usher that he had left in a car half an hour ago. Rutgers had never prepared Sonny for this and he was so humble, chastened, and apologetic on the bus that took us to our next date I almost felt sorrier about his feelings than the vanished payday.

It was not the only lesson that Sonny learned on his first tour. He was determined he would never be rooked again, and his natural vitality returned after a few more stops at which nothing untoward happened. He was bubbling with confidence again by the time we hit Massillon, Ohio, a town we had played before when we were booking our own one-nighters after the summer roadhouse job outside Cleveland.

This was one town I could warn Sonny about. The first time we played there, virtually unknown, there were 1,200 people in the dance hall, according to the operator's count. The next year after we had made a name on Chicago radio, we returned to the same place and the man said the audience was 1,200. It seemed to us there were three times as many customers as on our previous engagement. "You watch for this guy, Sonny," I told him. "Now that we're the top dance band in the country, he'll probably give you the same 1,200 count."

Sonny told me not to worry. He took out his hand clicker. "This thing will give us an accurate count," he said. "I'm going to stand by the door and count everybody that comes in."

Sonny stationed himself at the front entrance, which narrowed into a single door that led into the ballroom just in back of the bandstand. He stood there and clicked the clicker. And I stood there waving my baton and noticing that people were coming in through two other doors.

The trouble was I couldn't get Sonny's attention. He was too busy clicking and counting and the only view he had of the band was from the back.

I asked him at intermission how many he'd counted. He said 1,200. I shook my head wearily. "And how about the 1,200 that came through that door?" I asked, pointing. "And the 1,200 through that other door?" Sonny looked and blanched. Later he learned that the owner's wife was at one door, collecting dollars, not tickets, and his daughter at the other one. But he had to take the owner's word about the 1,200 total, and in the future he would count doors as well as tickets.

Sonny was to work with MCA from 1932 to 1965. The lessons he was to learn on his first Lombardo tour would help earn him a vice-presidency of the company in 1951. With Jules Stein, he would become one of the most powerful men in show business; he would be summoned by David Sarnoff to provide television programs for the NBC network; he would finally leave the business after MCA was broken up as a monopoly and ordered not to represent talent any longer. Yet Sonny Werblin would probably be better known as the owner of the New York Jets, who signed Joe Namath, than as one of the most astute minds in the entertainment industry. He remains today one of my closest friends.

We would make other enduring friendships in those early New York days. We were uplifted by our acceptance into the ranks of the bandleaders who had been our boyhood heroes and who now regarded us as friends and equals. We would entertain and be entertained by such old pros as Paul Whiteman, Vincent Lopez, and Abe Lyman.

Rudy Vallee and Fred Waring, who made national reputations about the same time we did, were competitors with whom we jockeyed for attention, and often we would rib each other on radio, in the manner later adopted by Jack Benny and Fred Allen. But we considered them our friends.

The younger bandleaders who would follow us into radio after Bill Paley had proved the entertainment value of the Royal Canadians were frequent visitors at the Roosevelt Grill. They came to listen and often they came to find out what had made us successful. Those who asked received the same advice Louis Panico had given Lebe when he decided to become a trumpet player: "Copy the best . . . then develop your own style . . . when people can identify you just by listening to the style and the sound, that's when you can consider yourself a success."

Those young bandleaders who became our friends would later join us as the mainsprings of the Big Band era, which was just beginning and would last for almost a quarter of a century. Each had an individual style and sound, an individual trademark— Tommy and Jimmy Dorsey, Benny Goodman, Glenn Miller, Phil Harris, Harry James, Russ Morgan, and Kay Kyser.

And virtually all the friends we made in those days would represent some part of show business. We got to know intimately the two top song producers of the day, Irving Berlin and Walter Donaldson. We became friendly with the song pluggers and publishers, not so much for what they could do for the band as the sheer pleasure of their company. Three who would become almost as close to me as my brothers were Harry Link, Rocco Vocco, and Sammy Stept.

We knew Russ Columbo and Bing Crosby, who were emerging as the top singers in the country. We renewed our friendship with Jimmy Durante and became close to George Burns and Gracie Allen, who joined our radio program in 1933. Jack Benny would come to our Riverside Drive apartment and wonder if his career was coming to a premature end now that vaudeville was being victimized by the new talking pictures and radio had yet to show an interest in comedians.

Many of the friendships were cemented during those summer seasons we played at the Pavillon Royal from 1930 until 1933. The Pavillon was a roadhouse on Merrick Road in Valley Stream, just over the county line from New York. It was in Nassau County, a Long Island suburb that would later become our home, that would expand and grow after World War II and pioneer the movement out of the cities and into suburbia.

But in 1930 as the Great Depression started, Long Island was a bucolic sandspit stretching a hundred miles between the Atlantic Ocean and Long Island Sound to its tip at Montauk Point. The Great Gatsby age was coming to an end, although the baronial estates maintained by armies of servants still dotted the North Shore.

On the South Shore, which was the location of the Pavillon

Royal, a sizable segment of show business occupied summer residences, taking advantage of the unparalleled facilities for swimming, boating, and fishing provided by the ocean, the Great South Bay, and innumerable inlets, canals, and creeks. A veritable colony of show folk had built homes in Freeport and converted a lighthouse into the Lights Club, an organization that included in its membership George M. Cohan, Victor Moore, Billy Gaxton, Leo Carrillo, Marion Davies, the Dolly Sisters, and assorted vaudevillians who took time off in the summer.

Even more noted as a summer playground for vacationing members of the show business fraternity was the nearby city of Long Beach, with a row of hotels facing the ocean on its mile-long boardwalk. East of the boardwalk was the recently built Lido Beach Hotel, a magnificent resort that included a golf course, its own beach, and the most up-to-date vacation facilities for people like Flo Ziegfeld and William Fox, the movie magnate.

And on summer evenings, many of the vacationers and seasonal residents would descend on the Pavillon for dinner and dancing. Roadhouses were in their heyday at the time. All the big cities had them—just outside the city limits. We had got a first big break at the Lake Road Inn outside Cleveland, and the Blossom Heath, near Detroit, was even better known. In Valley Stream, a miniature Broadway had grown up on Merrick Road. A block from the Pavillon, Texas Guinan maintained a club, and nearby was the Bird Cage, one of the first night clubs to feature female impersonators. Nearby, too, were numerous speakeasies and joints headlining jazz combos.

To these, and especially to the more prestigious Pavillon, headed the performers, the booking agents, the producers on their way back to New York after a day in the sun. William Fox was almost a nightly visitor, and name entertainers could be spotted at the ringside tables, frequently coming onto the bandstand to perform.

The customers came not only to dine and dance but to view at firsthand both tried and untried performers. The Pavillon became a showcase for talent. One night Tony and Renee DeMarco would surprise with numbers from their ballroom dance act. Another night, a young girl named Ethel Merman would come on and sing one of her first numbers in public. I remember the song, "Body and Soul," and the tremendous reception she got from the sophisticated listeners. The next season she would appear in her first Broadway musical.

I think the best account of a night at the Pavillon was written by Jerry Wald, later to become a top movie producer, for *Radio Stars* magazine in 1933. Excerpts follow:

". . . What a Junior League affair is to Gotham's socially prominent, what a Sid Gauman premiere is to Hollywood, and what the Washington Inaugural Ball is to the politically famous, a Lombardo opening at the Pavillon Royal is to the radio world. Everyone in radio attends. Come along and take a peek at the celebrities who come to pay homage to the sweetest band this side of heaven. . . .

"Sleek limousines, their occupants dressed in latest summer toggery, glide to a stop before the Pavillon, disgorging beautiful women and their escorts. There's James Dunn, the movie star, and Claire Windsor, the blond film favorite alighting from Jimmy's roadster . . . and Arthur Tracy, 'The Street Singer,' and his wife coming out of their special-bodied Marmon . . . Little Jack Little and his wife . . . Let's go inside.

"Ted Husing, the Columbia Broadcasting System's top-notch word deliverer, is occupying the center of the floor, as a volunteer master of ceremonies. Husing is immaculately clad in a white gabardine suit, with matching shirt and shoes. A crimson tie flashes between the coat and lapels. Ted is asking for a round of applause for Guy Lombardo and the boys. He gets it and then the Lombardo music plays.

". . . Soft rhythms flow from each instrument and blend into a dance-compelling tempo. Guy turns his back on the assemblage to coax a crescendo from brother Lebert's trumpet; wheels again, smiling, as the musical trick finds a response from the dancers. Carmen Lombardo temporarily forsakes his sax to lend a dulcet vocal interlude to 'Stormy Weather.'

"As their respective wives dance by, Carmen, Lebert and Victor rise from their chairs, interpolating solo passages meant for only one pair of ears. Flashing smiles from Florence, Carol and Virginia Lombardo acknowledge the musical courtship. Guy, alone, makes no melody, but his happy smile is directed at the ringside table where his wife, Lilliebell, sits, her long fingers caressing a cocktail glass, her eyes riveted on him.

". . . But there's so much to see here. That sylph-like figure in the corner belongs to the re-built Paul Whiteman; there's Belle Baker, sitting with Paul Yawitz, the Sunday Mirror gossip writer . . . Now Husing is taking the center of the floor again and introducing the celebrities . . .

"Donald Novis, the tenor, first. Next Ethel Shutta and George Olson, one of radio's best-loved couples. They later confide to us that their children, Charlie, 5, and George Jr., 3, are swimming the length of the pool at the Lido Hotel. You'd never take them for an orchestra leader and a famous comedienne. They're more like next-door neighbors.

". . . Husing continues to direct the spotlight. On Rudy Wiedhoeft, from whom Hubert Prior Vallee, borrowed his first name. He obliges with a solo on his famous sax. Lou Alter and Harold Arlen, the songwriters are next. Alter plays his 'Manhattan Serenade' and Arlen draws tumultuous applause with the first chord of his 'Stormy Weather.'

". . . And many more. Jane Froman, the song stylist who came out of Chicago to capture the hearts of eastern radio fans, her husband, Don Ross, the tenor; Lennie Hayton, erstwhile Whiteman pianist-arranger, who has in the past six months carved a niche in radio's hall of fame.

"Husing now relinquishes the floor and Guy Lombardo raises his baton as Long Island's social set rubs elbows with radio royalty."

Royalty may have been a rather too regal description of those early radio names, but they were in fact full-blown celebrities of the day and numerous radio fan magazines would chronicle their lives, careers, and idiosyncrasies as fully as the movie fan magazines.

Our first summer on the island, Carm, Lebe, and I rented a three-bedroom house near the Lido Beach Hotel and with our wives became enamored with the area. I loved boating, Carm loved swimming, and Lebe was an ardent fisherman. It was the beginning of our roots on Long Island, where we were all later to have homes, to operate a restaurant in Freeport, to take over the summer musical productions at Jones Beach, and where I would get so wrapped up in a new-found speedboating hobby that it would become almost another career.

That first summer, too, I first met and got friendly with Walter Donaldson, a prolific, picaresque songwriter who had almost as many hits as Irving Berlin. It was at the Pavillon that Walter gave us a song called "Little White Lies," which would become one of our earliest hits in New York. We introduced it on radio and it still remains on the all-time list of standards that would be included in every band repertoire.

We were in the big time, now, and it had taken less than a year to capture New York. It would take another forty years to be referred to as an institution.

5.   Tin Pan Alley

We had never heard of Tin Pan Alley in London when we were growing out of adolescence and into musicians. We could buy sheet music, band arrangements, and phonograph records at the music store, but we had no idea of the size and diversity of the industry that was supplying them.

Without knowing it, Lebe was the first to be exposed to that mythical street that began in New York and would later stretch to Hollywood. While Carm and I were busy taking lessons at Papa's tailor shop, Lebe was getting his musical education at the Loew's Theater, doubling as helper to the film projectionist and as back-up man on the drums to the piano player in the pit. The pianist also had two jobs. He followed the cue cards distributed by the film companies as mood music for the silent picture, and during intermission he entertained the audience with the most popular songs of the day.

Tin Pan Alley, of course, supplied the music. The song publishers had found a new medium to push the sale of sheet music, which was a chief source of income during the World War I decade. Before radio and in the infancy of the phonograph industry, people sat down at the pianos in their living rooms and played and sang the songs that Tin Pan Alley was producing.

The movie houses were beginning to spring up throughout the United States and Canada just before World War I erupted. And Tin Pan Alley was sending emissaries far and wide to get exposure for the newest hits of the day. The emissaries, better known as song pluggers, were in effect distributing free samples where they could do the most good.

It had always been this way since the music industry was born about the time of the Civil War. Stephen Foster was writing ballads that are still being played today, and the publishers would send the pluggers to the minstrel shows to popularize his songs ("My Old Kentucky Home," "Camptown Races," "Jeannie with the Light-Brown Hair," "When Johnny Comes Marching Home").

By the turn of the century, the industry was headquartered in a row of buildings along Twenty-third Street, Manhattan. The top composer of the day was Harry Von Tilzer, a onetime circus roustabout, who had joined the well-known music firm of Shapiro and Bernstein. He is credited with having coined the phrase "Tin Pan Alley."

The story goes that Von Tilzer was sitting at his piano in the firm's office one day in 1902. He had already written such hits as "Bird in a Gilded Cage," "Down Where the Wurzburger Flows" —a tune that made Nora Bayes a star—"On a Sunday Afternoon," and "Sweet Bye and Bye."

Into his office came a down-on-his-luck songwriter who sometimes moonlighted as a feature writer for various newspapers. Von Tilzer's piano was stuffed in the back with newspapers to mute the strings.

"What kind of tin pan do you call that?" the visitor asked, referring to the tinny sounds coming from adjoining offices.

"You name it," Von Tilzer responded. "But this street must sound like Tin Pan Alley with all the pianos making such a din."

The writer hurried out and sold a Sunday piece about New York's music industry. He called it Tin Pan Alley and the name stuck when the publishers moved uptown to the area of Broadway and Forty-ninth Street. For years, the Brill Building at that location would be the heart of Tin Pan Alley, its offices dominated by the music firms, the agents, the performers who would audition their songs.

At about the same time Von Tilzer was naming Tin Pan Alley, another major facet of the industry was evolving that would later replace the player pianos in the living rooms. Thomas Edison had invented the phonograph years before, primarily as a business-office piece of equipment to aid in dictation. But in 1901 the new Victor Company had developed a more commercial use for it. The company began to produce flat disc recordings of songs and replaced the phonograph's earphones with speaking horns to simultaneously entertain larger groups of people.

The Victor Company would later affiliate itself with the Radio Corporation of America and be known as RCA Victor. Its competitor, the Columbia Phonograph Company, which started shortly after, would also become a broadcasting affiliate and become part of the Columbia Broadcasting System.

Meanwhile in London, we were becoming more and more aware of Tin Pan Alley, strictly by identifying with the songwriters. It was after World War I had ended and we knew such names as Irving Berlin and George Gershwin, both of whom had written songs for Shapiro, Bernstein and Von Tilzer. Berlin, with his "Alexander's Ragtime Band," published in 1911, had adapted well to the change in musical tastes. They had progressed from the ballads of Stephen Foster's day to the waltzes of Von Tilzer's, aided and abetted by the light operettas of Victor Herbert. Now Berlin and others had brought a syncopated, foot-tapping rhythm into the business and it was identified as ragtime. Vernon and Irene Castle would make the Turkey Trot popular in the cadence of ragtime and one of George Gershwin's first hits, "Swanee," as sung by Al Jolson, also had the same beat. "Tiger Rag" was another.

It always fascinated me that somebody could put a few notes on paper and make it a national craze. Small wonder that I hero-worshiped the composers and lyricists who were writing the music we played even as tempos and styles continued to change while our band expanded beyond its original four-man crew. I would go to sleep at night fantasizing a meeting with Irving Berlin. In my dreams, he always appeared as a giant of a man.

The fantasy almost became reality when we first arrived in Cleveland and were approached at the railroad station by a dapper man who recognized us as musicians by our instrument cases. He wanted to know where we were playing and when I told him we were looking for a job, he put it to me bluntly. "When you get one, I hope you play our music."

The man was Phil Julius, the first song plugger I ever met, and it turned out he worked for Berlin's new music publishing firm. Irving Berlin, through an intermediary, was asking us to play his music!

The song plugger in the early twenties worked a territory. His home office was New York, headquarters for such firms as Berlin, Harms, Shapiro, Bernstein and Von Tilzer, Leo Feist, Robbins, Remick, Mills. There were fifteen or twenty large firms operating around Broadway, exploiting the hit songs—many from the musical comedies—and sending them around the country to the vaudeville houses. The top pluggers remained in New York, the nation's most fertile territory.

The band business was just starting. The musical combos of four and five men had expanded into double that size with the emergence of dance music as popularized by Paul Whiteman, Isham Jones, and other pioneers. Hotels were just beginning to engage the orchestras, but vaudeville and the silent movie houses were still the main targets for the pluggers, who worked the big cities of Chicago, Detroit, Cleveland, and Los Angeles.

On that first vaudeville tour with Corinne Arbuckle we learned how important Tin Pan Alley was to the performer. Not only the big names like Al Jolson, Sophie Tucker, Van and Schenck, who had long since graduated from the small-town theaters we played on the tour. Every singer, every dancer got his music from Tin Pan Alley, most without paying for it. The more performers who used a song in their routines, the more exposure it got and the more sales it would bring at the sheet music counters in the department stores and five-and-dimes.

Some acts would work forty-five weeks a year, using those songs all around the country, coming back the next year to refill their musical material in New York before embarking on next year's tour. If a new hit had been born back on Broadway, the song plugger was on the road in the circuit cities to offer the act up-to-date numbers.

Song pluggers did not come looking for Guy Lombardo and his newly named Royal Canadians when we were playing vaudeville dates in towns like Portsmouth, Ohio; Madison, Wisconsin; and Ann Arbor, Michigan. But we felt the presence of Tin Pan Alley, especially as it related to some of the other acts on the bill.

One was a husband-and-wife song-and-dance team that had seen better days. However, the team had a certain status and they proudly displayed it every time a visitor came to their tiny dressing room. Taking up most of the cubicle was a gigantic Hartman trunk, out of which they lived on their annual hegira. The Hartman trunk had been a gift of a music publishing firm years ago when the team was at the height of its popularity. If you had a Hartman trunk, it meant you were or had been somebody in show business.

Tin Pan Alley's largesse to this rather sad pair of vaudevillians was not an isolated incident. Hartman trunks were given by the music houses to all noteworthy vaudeville acts in exchange for exclusively using the firm's songs. The trunks were worth as much as $400 and were cumbersome affairs in which one could fit an entire wardrobe and all the act's props. In later days, the Hartman trunk song routine would have been called payola. In the days we were learning about vaudeville and Tin Pan Alley, it was simply another way songs got around the country.

And then in the middle twenties along came radio, unshackled finally from headsets with earphones and bursting into America's living rooms to provide Tin Pan Alley with its biggest market. Lebe's self-built crystal set in London had brought the outside world of music to our ears; we had heard the Coon-Saunders band on late-night pickups from Kansas City, and we had heard dance bands playing on Station WTAM in Cleveland. We had noticed all that empty time on the Cleveland station; it seemed to be begging for other dance bands to fill it.

And that had given me the idea that was to change our lives. Somehow we had to get to Cleveland to offer our services to the radio station, to get on the air even if we had to play for nothing. That we did and that was the making of the Royal Canadians. It would work again in Chicago and it would bring us to New York, where the CBS network would carry our programs nationwide.

But before Tin Pan Alley had the dance bands playing its music on the air, it had to develop initially another method of plugging songs. The networks were still a few years away and radio was a matter of small local stations primarily located in the cities. The music publishers reached them as they had the vaudeville houses and the silent movie theaters. They sent out teams of singers and piano players to the stations, performing for nothing, but performing the songs of the companies they represented.

Little Jack Little, who later fronted a big band, started that way. He was part of the team of Little and Small, traveling from city to city, with the songs his publisher was selling. One of the first big hits manufactured on radio by Jack Little and Mary Small was "Jealous."

From this beginning, the music publishers began contacting the best-known bands around the country, pressuring the leaders to play their music. At about the time we were playing for nothing at WTAM, Tin Pan Alley had developed the idea of remotes from the hotel rooms in which the bands were playing. Among the early bands that were producing song hits on radio were Vincent Lopez from New York's Pennsylvania Hotel and Ben Bernie from the Roosevelt; Hal Kemp in Chicago and Gus Arnheim in Los Angeles.

The song pluggers began hounding us during our last year in Cleveland, and after we had become an overnight success in Chicago when we first were heard over Station WBBM. They offered us everything to play their music—from pieces of a song to tickets to the theater and ball games. Instinctively, I resisted the overtures, especially the part about accepting financial interest in a tune. I felt it was stupid because for the one song you would play that might make money, you were playing ten dogs. I felt we had to have at all times songs that had hit potential, and I knew they were not easy to come by.

Carm, who was writing his own songs, felt the same way. We would congratulate ourselves on our policy, watching as other leaders jumped at the opportunity of airing songs under their own names, hoping to add to their incomes but never succeeding. All they did was establish reputations for playing bad music. Abe Lyman, with whom I later became friendly, probably would have become a giant in the band business if he had just played his fine music and stopped looking for those pieces of songs. He had his name on almost as many titles as Irving Berlin, but the difference was that few of them became hits. Phil Spitalny was another.

Of course when we got to New York, the procedure started all over again. In the big town we were dealing with the best, Tin Pan Alley's smartest, most gregarious, most endearing high-pressure salesmen of music. They would sell us songs, but on our own terms and with payola never a factor in what we would choose to play.

The publishers thought we were crazy. They couldn't understand a bandleader who seemed to have an aversion for money. After Carmen had come to town with hits like "Little Coquette" and "Sweethearts on Parade" behind him, the least they figured was that brother Guy and the band would play any number he wrote.

They'd overwhelm him with flattery. They'd send their top lyricists after him. "Write us a couple of songs," the publishers would tell him. "You're the best in the business." Carm obliged; it was heady stuff to be pursued by the big names of Tin Pan Alley. He immersed himself in writing and almost every week I would be confronted by a new Carmen Lombardo song presented to me by a plugger.

Again they were astounded by my reaction. I told them there was no guarantee that we would play the song just because Carm had written it. It had to be a gem or they could peddle it to another band. Quality determined the selection of a song for the Royal Canadians, not authorship, even by one of the band's owners. The only exception I made in that regard was that I was always looking for songs by Irving Berlin or Walter Donaldson, both of whom hardly ever came up with a loser.

This time there was no big emotional confrontation between my brother and me. I reminded him that he had made the same mistake in Chicago, wearing himself thin trying to write for almost any lyricist with an idea. Now Tin Pan Alley was trying to make a factory out of his talent and leaving him little time for all the demands his duties with the band required. Carm saw the danger. Now he would continue writing songs only when an inspiration struck. He would form a partnership with a young man named Johnny Loeb, and when they thought they had a good idea for a song, they would write it.

Johnny Loeb had come out of college to Chicago, seeking out Carmen, hoping to form a song-writing partnership. He had written the words and music for several songs as an undergraduate and he had heard that Carm could do both, too. We liked Johnny but weren't impressed with his songs. We considered them smarty-pants, full of impressive chords, but too involved to become popular. They might have been considered clever from a musician's standpoint, but they were difficult to remember. I couldn't see people humming or singing those tunes while they were driving cars or doing housework. Johnny's lyrics were in the same mold.

Carm agreed and Johnny was a disappointed young man the night we told him he ought to go to New York and get a job with a publishing firm to learn the song-writing trade. The trick was to learn what was marketable. If he could get a job, he would be around songs and he would learn what the publishing houses were turning down at the rate of fifty a day, songs I had to tell him were better than the ones he had submitted to us.

He would learn what to write by finding out what not to write. I told him the story I had heard about George Gershwin and how he had learned his trade under Jack Dreyfus, who worked for Harms Music. Harms was the leading publisher of songs from the Broadway musical hits in the first two decades of the twentieth century. Dreyfus was the man who saw the latent talent in Gershwin's earliest offering, and he persuaded the brilliant young composer to do odd jobs around the office until he learned the mechanics of his craft. The rest is history.

Johnny took the advice, landed a job as parcel boy for the Santly Brothers firm, and by the time we got to New York he had obviously learned what kinds of songs were salable. Two of his songs, "Masquerade" and "Reflections in the Water," were already on the market.

Carmen had one moderate hit when he started writing in New York, "Snuggle on Your Shoulder." Then, when he decided to write only when he was inspired by an idea, he teamed up with Johnny Loeb. The first song they wrote together was one of their best known and the story of its conception illustrates the hidden ingredients that often go into the making of a hit.

Like all successful songwriters, Carm knew when he had a good song and when he had a bad one. About a year after we arrived in New York, he wrote a two-note tune he liked very much. He called it "Cherie" and we made an arrangement and played it on the bandstand. But he wasn't happy with the lyric; halfway through the song I heard him whispering, "No good, no good, not it." All of us forgot about the song but Carmen.

When Prohibition was repealed, Carm thought the nation was ready for a drinking song, and he remembered the melody that had been haunting him for more than a year. He wrote new lyrics, retitled the song "Let's Drink," and again we made an arrangement for the vocal trio. When they were finished, my brother shook his head sadly. "Still no good," he said. "Throw it away."

He and Johnny Loeb were trading ideas for tunes one day and Carm began humming those two notes. Johnny was as intrigued as my brother. They tried for half a day to come up with a new lyric and title and couldn't. Then Johnny suggested they go up to the apartment of a friend of his, Eddie Heyman, who had written "Body and Soul" in collaboration with Johnny Green. Johnny had been Carm's first collaborator on "Little Coquette."

Heyman liked the tune, too. He had an idea for it the moment Carm began humming.

"I got it," he said. "Boo Hoo."

They stared at him blankly.

"Boo Hoo," he repeated. "You got me cryin' for you."

Now the three of them went to work, scribbling furiously, asking each other for words that rhymed. At the height of the collaboration, Eddie suddenly remembered he had a boat to catch to Bermuda. He waved good-by and Carm and Johnny didn't leave the apartment until "Boo Hoo" was a finished product. The lead sheet would read: "Boo Hoo. Melody by Carmen Lombardo. Lyrics by Carmen Lombardo, Johnny Loeb and Eddie Heyman." The song went on to become a best-seller played around the world. It topped the Hit Parade for seventeen straight weeks. It was banned in Nazi Germany because the three authors had names that were obviously non-Aryan.

That started the Lombardo-Loeb partnership, which lasted for more than thirty years. They would write "A Sailboat in the Moonlight," "It Seems Like Old Times," and many other hits, and they would write the lyrics and music for two musicals, *Arabian Nights* and *Paradise Island*, when we began producing summer shows at the Jones Beach Marine Theater.

Carm had an instinct for potential hits, no matter who wrote them. In the fall of 1933, we were playing the Chicago World's Fair and doubling at the Dells, a well-known roadhouse. Rehearsing in the roadhouse one afternoon, we received a batch of songs from the Irving Berlin Music Company. Berlin's firm had for a long time now been publishing the works of other composers, besides his own.

Most of the songs we received were what the firm considered their top numbers, the ones they exploited and hoped to get in the repertoires of the best-known bands. Carm and I never were interested in that type of song. We were always looking for something distinctive, almost discarded, that we could promote ourselves and have identified with our band. We'd established that policy with Phil Julius, the Berlin Company song plugger, in our early days in Chicago. We still operated that way.

And so we went through the latest Berlin Company offerings and rejected all of them but one. Carm was fascinated by something called "Annie Doesn't Live Here Anymore," written by Joe Young, Johnny Burke, and Harold Spina. Freddie Kreitzer played it on the piano and Carm sang it. He said, "This one's a hit, Guy." I wasn't convinced and asked him why. "Because it's unusual," Carm said. "And it tells a story."

He liked the song's beat, its lyric, and especially the sequence about the guy in the top hat who took Annie away and . . . now "Annie Doesn't Live Here Anymore." I went along with him, called Dave Dreyer, general manager of the firm in New York, and asked for an exclusive on it. I wanted it alone for six weeks. Surprised because the song wasn't going anywhere, Dave said, "You can have it for six months."

So we made an arrangement out of "Annie," began playing it at the Dells, and got an immediate reaction from the dancers who stopped at the bandstand and asked the meaning of the lyrics.

They liked the bouncy tune but they were looking for a meaning in the lyrics. The college kids interpreted the man in the top hat as a sharp city character, a lover who cast a hypnotic spell over Annie and took her away. Others saw it as a Depression song that told a story of a poor girl who may have died of hard times. They cast the man in the top hat as an undertaker who had come to take Annie away. But no matter how they interpreted "Annie," all it proved was that Carmen Lombardo often knew a hit even before the experts on Tin Pan Alley. We still get requests to play "Annie Doesn't Live Here Anymore" today.

Picking out hit songs became almost a game with us. We didn't consider ourselves the greatest music brains in the world, nor were we infallible. We just knew what we liked and more often than not were successful in taking a lightly regarded song and putting it on the best-seller lists. We did the same thing with a song from England that was on the wrong side of a record. The publisher thought he had a hit in something called "Tweedle-Dee-Dee."

We were more interested in the flip-side "When the Organ Played at Twilight." We were playing it at the Roosevelt the night the publisher came in and told us he hadn't even considered the organ song as a possible hit. He had big plans for "Tweedle-Dee-Dee." The publisher shook his head; he couldn't understand what we liked about the other one. What we liked was the opportunity to record it with an organ effect, and it became another of our biggest records in the thirties.

As I have mentioned, the two writers to whose judgment we bowed, whose songs we were always eager to introduce, were Walter Donaldson and Irving Berlin. They rarely wrote a song that failed to become a hit. Donaldson, in our first few years in New York, was riding the crest of one success after another. Berlin, strangely, had gone dry between 1929 and 1932 and was not writing as much as he used to.

Walter Donaldson epitomized Tin Pan Alley. He was your Hollywood version of the songwriter who lived for wine, women, song and the racetracks. He could spend the advance he received from a new composition almost as fast as it had taken him to write it. He must have earned several million dollars in royalties through the twenties, and yet when we met him at the Pavillon Royal in the summer of 1930, he was broke.

He had been writing for the Irving Berlin Music Company since shortly after the end of the war. Irving's firm had made almost as much out of Donaldson's songs as those written by the master himself. Donaldson had composed such classics as "Mammy," "My Buddy," "My Blue Heaven," "Yes Sir, That's My Baby." The year before we arrived in New York, he had collaborated with Gus Kahn on the score for *Whoopee* and after that success had left Berlin to form a publishing partnership with two of Tin Pan Alley's most knowledgeable businessmen—Mose Gumble and Walter Douglas. The firm's chief commodity, of course, was "songs by Walter Donaldson." Its chief expense was Walter Donaldson, who would demand and get advances even before he had an idea for a song.

When the Depression hit, the Donaldson, Gumble and Douglas Company was even in more trouble than the other companies in the Brill Building, which were not quite as free in advancing large sums of money to writers. The sale of sheet music had been sharply curtailed by hard times, and radio's impact on the music business was just beginning.

Regardless of the economy, Walter Donaldson continued to live in the Great Gatsby style. He maintained a suite in the Park Central Hotel, and when he wasn't composing on a spur-of-the-moment basis he spent his time golfing at the Long Island courses and speculating at the Long Island racetracks. When caddies were receiving a dollar at the Lido and Rockville country clubs, two of Donaldson's favorite haunts, their earning potential skyrocketed the moment the songwriter appeared on the first tee. He never paid a caddy less than twenty dollars a round.

He arrived at the racetracks in rented limousines, often bringing with him a party of song pluggers. And he usually borrowed cab fare when they returned to New York.

It was on one of his stopovers after a day of golf that I first met Donaldson. He had come into the Pavillon for dinner and sat at a table and listened to the band, and during an intermission he introduced himself. He just happened to have a song with him, something called "Little White Lies," and he was offering the band the opportunity to play it first. I jumped at it, we played it, then introduced it on the air for the first time, and "Little White Lies" became an all-time best-seller. I was more convinced than ever that a Walter Donaldson offering was a virtual guarantee of success.

I began to romance him that fall, going out of my way to be friendly, inviting him to our Sunday night parties at the Riverside Drive apartment, making the rounds of the night clubs with him after we finished the Roosevelt Hotel stint. A few times I lent him rent money. I enjoyed his company and I knew there were more songs inside this man, songs we would get first. One night, Lilliebell, Walter, and I closed Leon and Eddies on West Fifty-second Street about four o'clock, and I dropped him off at the Park Central.

Three hours later he awakened me. During that time, instead of going to sleep, he had composed a song. He wanted me to introduce it that night at the Roosevelt. If I liked it, I had permission to play it on radio that night. It was a Friday and we had recently started another commercial program in addition to the Robert Burns Monday show. I sent over Larry Owen with instructions to make an arrangement by two o'clock, which would give us time to rehearse the new number. The song was called "What Did You Do to Me?" and we had an arrangement of a pretty melody without a lyric. We decided to make an instrumental out of it and introduce it that night.

As we were preparing to ascend the bandstand that night at 7:15, Donaldson called. He wanted me to change the title to "You're Driving Me Crazy." My reaction was: "That's rather crazy, Walter. You sure?" He was sure and Carmen, with his usual instinct, liked it better than the old title. So we played it at the Grill, and later in the WABC studio Norman Brokenshire was intoning, "For the first time on the air, 'You're Driving Me Crazy.' "

Meanwhile Donaldson had invited his partners, Gumble and Douglas, to dinner at an Italian restaurant. He was always discovering Italian restaurants and the partners were wondering where he had dug up a stake that enabled him to pick up the dinner tab. At ten o'clock, Walter asked the proprietor to bring over a radio. He wanted to hear the Lombardo program. When Brokenshire introduced the new Donaldson song, Gumble and Douglas began congratulating him. "You're Driving Me Crazy" certainly sounded like a hit. They needed one because Walter had drained the till. And as they were congratulating him on this wonderful song, he excused himself to the men's room. They didn't see him again that night and Gumble grumbled when he got the check.

We played that song for the next three days and now it had a lyric and it was being sung and hummed and whistled all around town. Meanwhile Gumble and Douglas were looking for Donaldson, who had vanished. The firm had a hit song, but it didn't have it on paper.

They didn't see Walter until he finally showed up at the office a week later, asking for a $5,000 advance on "You're Driving Me Crazy." Gumble said he didn't have it; the firm was broke. Walter suggested he borrow the money. After all, he argued, the firm was taking no chances; the song was a hit before it was even officially published. The partners took out a bank loan and never regretted the decision. "You're Driving Me Crazy" was one of the major hits of the thirties.

Donaldson, of course, was a past master in the art of obtaining advances. Most writers depended on advances as the major source of their annual incomes. They also knew that, if a publisher was willing to come up with cash in advance, the chances were greater that the song would sell. An advance virtually guaranteed that the publisher would exploit and plug the tune. But for Donaldson advances were spending money.

He told me about the time in 1927 that he had decided to spread his songs around, no longer offering them exclusively to the Berlin Company. He had found a profitable market, for instance, in the Leo Feist Music Company, which was generous in giving him advances.

The money hadn't lasted through a long day at the Hialeah Racetrack in Miami, and Walter had a hot tip on the last race. He couldn't find a bookmaker willing to give him credit, but help came in the form of a chance meeting with Saul Borenstein, a top executive with the Berlin firm.

He noticed that Donaldson appeared uncharacteristically forlorn and said to him, "How about giving us a song, Walter."

The reaction was instantaneous. Donaldson perked up. "I have one right here in my pocket." Borenstein asked how much he wanted and Donaldson said he'd settle for $10,000.

"All I've got is about $500 in my pocket. But I'm willing to add a check for a couple of grand. You can get a bookie to cash it." Donaldson agreed but the cash and check weren't forthcoming until he fulfilled his part of the bargain—the name of the song. At the moment Donaldson's mind was occupied with the names of horses in the next race, not song titles. But he never had to look far for an inspiration. His glance took in the sky, the red ball of sun setting over Miami. "The name of the song," he said, "is 'At Sundown.'"

He got his money and it covered expenses for the last race at Hialeah. Then he went home, broke as usual. Two days later the Berlin Company had the song, "At Sundown," another Donaldson hit.

We weren't the only musical celebrities to come out of London, Ontario. One of the objects of our early hero worship was Cliff Friend, who was writing songs even before we left for Cleveland. We renewed acquaintance with him when we got to New York and found him an established writer with a large number of ASCAP credits to his name.

Cliff had a story about advances, too, quite at variance with the Walter Donaldson *modus operandi*. He had written a song and it was ready for delivery when he walked into the prestigious Remick Music Company and sought out Joe Keith, the general manager. "I've got a big one in my pocket, Joe," he said. "And I want a big advance—$10,000." He began humming, "Just Give Me a June Night, a June Night and You." Keith was impressed, wrote out a check for the amount requested, and the song vanished in the company's huge stack of files.

Cliff never heard a word about that song. With that kind of advance, he had expected a big exploitation campaign. He had his money but he didn't have the hit he had anticipated. It rankled. A year to the day after selling the song, he walked into Keith's office and gave him the same routine. He had a great tune; he wanted a ten-grand advance. He hummed "Just Give Me a June Night, a June Night and You." Keith was as impressed as he had been the year before. He wrote out the check. But this time, the song didn't get lost. And the Remick Company more than made up its double advance.

Paradoxically, the advent of radio was no boon to the music industry in the first years after the stock market crash. Radio had decimated the sale of sheet music. People were throwing away their pianos to make room for the new cabinet furniture out of which emanated live entertainment.

They were also getting rid of the old phonographs. Why bother with buying records when all that free music was available through the new medium? More and more dance bands began appearing on radio, and although we all helped popularize tunes and make hits out of them, there wasn't an awful lot of money to be made out of a song. Carmen had that experience with "Boo Hoo," certainly one of the most widely played of the era. It was No. 1 on the Hit Parade for seventeen straight weeks, yet sold only about 50,000 records and perhaps 100,000 copies of sheet music.

But this depression in their industry hardly slowed down the frenetic pace of the song pluggers. They competed with each other more fiercely than before. We continued to be besieged, a veritable honeycomb attracting a swarm of bees. The big firms had ten to fifteen pluggers working out of their New York offices, each trying to make friends with the bandleader at the Roosevelt or the Commdore or the St. Regis. There might be fifty pluggers at the Roosevelt every night, sitting at tables, praying you would come around and ask them what they were selling. If you asked, they'd start singing.

And each had his unique style of salesmanship. It was a matter of life and death to catch a bandleader's ear and they tried every conceivable method. We had established our reputation as being a tough band to get to, the first rehearsal we had at the Roosevelt. That didn't stop the sales pitches, and I must admit sometimes they worked.

One of the most ingenious was Charlie Warren, a tiny man who plugged for the Shapiro-Bernstein firm. His brother Harry

was one of the best-known songwriters in the business. We called
Charlie "Mousie," and it was difficult to ignore his friendliness
and his hard-working approach to his job. He always seemed to
know where to find me. I would be walking along the street and
there would come Mousie, sidling up, singing his newest wares. It
wasn't in my nature to tell him to get lost.

Even when were spending our summers on Long Island and I
had become wrapped up in boating as a hobby, I couldn't escape
Mousie. I had a thirty-five-foot runabout and was getting ready to
start up the motor one day, when I noticed something foreign on
the dashboard. It was the copy of a song entitled "I Just Couldn't
Say Goodbye." And a little note from Mousie. Ordinarily, I would
have thrown the song overboard, but I had to admire Charlie's ingenuity. I brought the song back with me and we played it during
rehearsal. It became a hit.

They were all gregarious, those song pluggers, and so were many
of the music publishing executives, most of whom had started in
the business as songwriters. Three of my closest friends were Harry
Link, music manager at Feist; Sammy Stept, a former bandleader
whom we had first met in Cleveland, and Rocco Vocco, a publisher. But when we got together socially with our wives or for a
ride on the boat, they all understood that we weren't there to
discuss songs.

Harry Link was in the Walter Donaldson mold, a dedicated
horse player and golfer, a teller of tall tales who could keep an audience captivated. He had this habit of talking with a handkerchief; no story would be launched until he had taken one out of
his pocket and begun twisting it. The stories were legion and most
of them concerned what could have happened had fate not
stepped in to prevent him from making a fortune at the racetrack.

A tall spare man, Harry, with his lovely blond wife Dottie, had
written a big hit in the early thirties, "These Foolish Things
Remind Me of You." But he was to earn a handsome living
selling songs, not writing them. At the Leo Feist Company,
Harry's job was to promote the hundreds of numbers that came
out of the big Metro-Goldwyn-Mayer musical pictures, which the
firm published. He was always talking about buying "a little house
in the country," but he never achieved it until years later when he

purchased a two-acre place on the North Shore of Long Island. The money, of course, never came from his winnings at the track.

In those early Depression years when sheet music wasn't selling, the occupants of Tin Pan Alley gravitated toward horse playing, seeking the buck they couldn't make in their own businesses. They would descend on Lindy's for lunch, all carrying scratch sheets and comparing notes. Usually they would stop at Harry's table; the story was "if you knew what Link was playing, you could eliminate a sure loser."

But with all his preoccupation with the horses, Harry always found time to keep my brothers and me amused when we were touring on the road. Every day he would call, telling us the latest story making the Broadway rounds. Or he would send telegrams containing doggerel, riddles, and gags.

One Friday during that period, the band was in Cincinnati and we had already been deluged by wires from Link. We were due home in about a week, and I was invited by friends to spend an afternoon at the racetrack in Covington, Kentucky, just across the river. I was strictly a two-dollar bettor and occasionally enjoyed an outing at the races.

Entering the track, I noticed a Western Union office and it occurred to me that I ought to recognize the Link telegrams and send him one in return. The man in the office said I would have to receive permission from a Pinkerton security guard. I told him I had this gag in mind; I wanted to tout a horse that had already won so that a friend in New York would curse his luck at not having received the tip in time. The Pinkerton man thought it was funny.

The first race had just finished with a seventeen-dollar winner and my wire read: "Bet So and So, first race Litonia." I figured Harry would get a charge out of it, a tip from Guy Lombardo, the bandleader who couldn't even speak the language of the racetracks. He would look at the time on the telegram and appreciate the joke.

The next race produced another long shot and I got caught up with my gag. I sent him another wire, giving him the winner of the second, Litonia, which had paid twenty-two dollars. The third race went to a favorite and this time the wire simply asked, "How we doing? Guy." But the fourth-race winner paid an astronomical forty-six dollars and I sent him another past-post tip. By this time, I figured, Harry would really have something to laugh about.

Back at the hotel, a Western Union boy was waiting. The telegram was from Link's secretary. It said, "Mr. Link in Atlantic City. Will give him info when he arrives Tuesday." Monday was the Fourth of July.

I began to realize the implications of my little joke. When Harry returned to town and saw the accumulated telegrams, it would not dawn on him that they had been sent after the races were run. All that would matter is that he had not been around to receive information that could have earned him a fortune.

Tuesday morning, the phone started ringing in my room. Mr. Link was calling. I couldn't get myself to speak to him. I told the operator to tell him I wasn't in the room. And that afternoon, I called Lilliebell. The first thing she said was, "Oh my God, what have you done to Harry? He's beside himself. He might commit suicide. He was in Atlantic City when you sent him the wires, he was trying to sell a song to Isham Jones. Why didn't you call him, instead of sending those wires? Incidentally, how much did you win?"

I told her the story and Lilliebell didn't think it was funny. "Everybody in New York feels sorry for him. He's been going around town, showing those wires, saying it could only happen to Harry Link. He went to his favorite bookie, Brooks, and waved those wires in front of his face. He called him a lucky s.o.b. He had it figured he would have bet $100 on the first tip which would have brought him back $850. Then knowing that if the tip came from Lombardo, who never touted anybody before, he would have bet all of that on the next one. By that time he figured he would have almost $10,000. He told the bookie he would have insured the next tip and parlayed all of that and when the third one came in, he'd have had more than a quarter of a million. He left the bookie, almost crying, saying how he wouldn't have bought just a little cottage on the island. He'd have bought a mansion."

Lilliebell concluded the sad tale by saying that Harry had told his woes to everybody he knew on Broadway. The saddest part of the story, she said, was Harry's punch-line ending, which went:

"The worst part of it is I wasted my weekend in Atlantic City. That goddamned Isham Jones never even listened to my song."

I finally answered Harry's call and sympathized with the story and clucked at Harry's quarter-million-dollar lost weekend. He brightened up when I told him I was going to the racetrack again with the same gold mine of information.

But the gag didn't last that long. The next night, Harry and Dottie took Lilliebell to a Paul Whiteman opening at the Ambassador Roof. It was a big premiere: Paul was introducing a new singer, Mildred Bailey, and all of Harry's colleagues and competitors had turned out. He spent the night hopping from table to table, showing his wires, which by now were as twisted as his handkerchiefs.

When Whiteman sat down at their table, Harry brought out the wires once again, repeating the story for the thousandth time. The maestro had tears in his eyes. Lilliebell couldn't stand it any longer. She said to Harry, "Did you ever look at the time of those wires? They were sent after the races were over."

Harry paled. He didn't know whether to be happy that he had not after all lost a fortune; on the other hand, he was being deprived of the best racetrack story he had ever told. I got a wire from him that night, masterful for its brevity. It said, "You rat."

Most of the bandleaders had racetrack stories. That was mine. Ben Bernie, a devoted horse player, had another. One of his best friends was Banjo Santly—his Harry Link—an ex-vaudevillian who had become a songwriter and scored with "There's Yes, Yes in Your Eyes." Banjo had gone into business with his brothers and the firm had done well. All of the brothers, except Banjo, had made money and kept it. Banjo's went to the racetracks.

A small, lovable character, Banjo could usually be found in Bernie's company. Ben loved the Damon Runyon type of character and Banjo certainly fitted the category. Like Donaldson, too, his royalties went to the bookmakers. Down on his luck, unable to even place a bet on credit, he brightened up considerably one day when Bernie invited him to come along for a few days to Saratoga. "The only trouble," he told his host, "is I wouldn't even have a deuce to make a bet." Bernie told him not to worry.

They checked into adjoining rooms at the Grand Union Hotel

and Ben asked his guest to be patient for one night. "I've been invited over to the Whitneys' for a party on the lake," he said. "I expect when I get there, they're going to give me the name of a two-
year-old they've entered tomorrow. They have the best two-year-
olds in the world, but this one has never raced. If they think it
will win, we got ourselves a sure winner. Now don't leave the
room all night and tomorrow we'll get ourselves healthy."

Banjo didn't exactly live up to his end of the bargain. He
walked around town, ran into an old friend, now touting for a living, and received gratis the name of a winner in one of the next
day's two-year-old maiden races. The next morning, Bernie took
him to the track in a chauffeur-driven limousine, paid his way in,
and kept silent until the race in which Banjo had a tip.

"I didn't want to give you the name of the winner until it was
almost post time," Ben said, "because I was afraid you'd spread it
all over the track and cut down the odds. Now here's the horse,
the Whitney entry. They think he's going to be a champ. He's
listed at seven to one. What I'm gonna do is loan you a hundred
bucks to bet on it. But you already owe me two hundred, so after
it wins, I expect you to pay me back. Okay?"

It was agreeable to Banjo, all but the part about betting the
Whitney horse. After all he had it straight from a tout's mouth
that another horse would win. And this one was listed at fifteen to
one. His money would not be entrusted to the Whitney colors.

They watched the race together, Ben and Banjo, after the latter
had assured him that he had placed his hundred on the information emanating from the party at the lake. Ben, who suffered from
a back ailment, leaned on his familiar cane and became more and
more confident as the horses broke out of the gate.

The Whitney horse broke fast and left distance between the
rest of the pack. "You got the bet down?" he asked. Banjo answered in the affirmative, quavering, and by the time they hit the
stretch, the Whitney horse was leading by twenty lengths. "You
get the bet down?" Ben asked again. And Banjo, hoping for a miracle, croaked out another yes.

The miracle never came to pass. The Whitney horse paid sixteen dollars and Bernie clapped his pal on the back and said,
"Now you go over and get paid and don't forget you owe me three

hundred." They say this about Banjo; he did not head for the
nearest exit, he looked Bernie in the eye and told him, "I bet
another horse. I didn't like the odds on the Whitney entry."

And racegoers who were at Saratoga that day still talk about the
usually unflappable Ben Bernie using his cane for other than sup-
portive purposes. He unleashed it on Banjo's shoulders, punctuat-
ing each stroke with a question: "You got the bet down, Banjo?"

But to label all writers and salesmen of songs picaresque is to do
an injustice to the most successful composer of them all, Irving
Berlin. I have never met a man with such humility, with so many
self-doubts at the height of his career, with so little of the out-
ward trappings of success. He was simply a modest, humble man,
born out of poverty, and nothing had ever changed his approach
to life. Not all the best-selling songs through the first three decades of the twentieth century, not even his marriage to Ellin
Mackay, whose father, Clarence, was one of the wealthiest and
most socially prominent men in the nation.

He had been born in Southern Russia in 1888, the son of Moses
Baline, a cantor who migrated to this country with his family of
eight children, five years later. Israel grew up in the teeming streets
of New York's Lower East Side, and by the time his father died
in 1896 he was answering to the name of Izzy. The older children
went to work in the sweatshops and Izzy helped his mother at
home.

Slight and dark, Izzy Baline was earning his own living before
he was fourteen. He sold newspapers, sang in saloons, and passed
the hat for a blind pianist. His first hero was Harry Von Tilzer,
the top songwriter of the day, and when he was eighteen, he got a
job with the great man, plugging his songs at Tony Pastor's Music
Hall. A year later, he had his first song published ("Marie from
Sunny Italy") and signed it "I. Berlin."

His rise in the music business was meteoric. Never loath to admit
his lack of education, musical or otherwise, he composed both
words and music. Soon he attracted the attention of publisher-
composer Ted Snyder, a partner in the firm of Waterson and
Snyder. Irving went to work for the company, writing songs in collaboration with Snyder, receiving a drawing account of twenty-five
dollars a week. In a few years, he was flooding the market with

one hit after another, and Snyder made him a third partner. The
firm was now known as Waterson, Snyder and Berlin and attained
a solid financial position, largely on the strength of Berlin's earliest works. In time it would be succeeded by the Irving Berlin
Music Company.

The song that earned him an international reputation was "Alexander's Ragtime Band." He wrote it in 1911 at a time when virtually all his works were in the comedy or ragtime idiom of the day.
The following year he married Dorothy Goetz, who was to die
five months later from the typhoid fever she contacted on their
honeymoon in Cuba. The tragedy inspired Berlin to write his first
important ballad, "When I Lost You." With the advent of World
War I, he enlisted in the Army, wrote an all-soldier show, *Yip
Yip Yaphank*, and out of it emerged the best-known service song
of all time, "Oh, How I Hate to Get Up in the Morning."

Sigmund Spaeth, the noted musical historian, wrote a book
some years ago, A *History of Popular Music in America*, which I
think best describes Berlin's talents. I quote a passage from his
tribute to the composer:

Berlin is by no means unaware of his abilities, but has remained a
surprisingly simple and modest person. He gives as much credit to
hard work and a certain amount of luck as to his unquestionable
talent. He is quite frank also as to his lack of any real education.
Years ago he was inclined to make a virtue of the fact that he could
neither read nor write notes and played the piano only on the black
keys, using an ingenious mechanism for shifting the entire keyboard
into the desired tonality after he had thus picked out the substance
of his tunes.

. . . Irving Berlin has a rare instinct for the perfect combination of
text and tune, as exemplified even by the short, slogan-like phrases
that he often uses for titles (What'll I Do?, All Alone, Remember,
and Always). But he succeeds invariably in giving a new angle to
what may have been essentially old material, musically as well as
verbally. It is those surprising touches of originality that make so
many of the songs memorable.

White Christmas might have turned into another Goodnight
Sweetheart, after a rather conventional start, but the second line
immediately lifted it into something quite individual . . . A Pretty

Girl Is Like a Melody opened with a suggestion of Poor Butterfly, but quickly asserted itself in a single change of melody and harmony and went on logically to complete a most interesting structure. Even Cheek to Cheek, with its clear and perhaps unconscious echo of the start of Chopin's Polanaise in A-Flat, became distinctively Berlin after fewer than a dozen notes.

For such a gift of using basic patterns to produce new and exciting effects, there can be no other word than "genius." All the great composers of the world had it by nature, even though they added to it all the possible resources of scholarship and deliberate technique . . . Berlin has been criticized by his competitors, maligned by his inferiors and snubbed by those who consider themselves musically superior. All of them would pay a fortune for his unerring grasp of popular taste and his unique ability to satisfy it. He remains, as previously recorded, "the most successful songwriter of all time."

My brothers and I had admired Irving Berlin since the formation of our first four-man group before the start of World War I. We had played his songs from the very beginning, and they were a major part of our repertoire as we graduated into a full-scale band and began to achieve a national reputation in Chicago. Unconsciously, I guess, the band's philosophy matched Berlin's. We wanted to play songs with identifiable, pretty melodies, simple to listen to, simple to understand. We wanted to musically entertain, not musically educate. Composer Berlin felt the same way.

Yet something happened to Irving after his brilliant successes in the year 1927. He had reached what seemed to be his pinnacle with such songs as "Blue Skies" and "Russian Lullaby." A year later, his one tune of distinction was "Marie." And then virtually nothing for the next four years. Certainly nothing compared to the prolific parade of Berlin hits stretching back two decades.

I was to learn of his humility and insecurity one spring night in 1931 when he walked into the Roosevelt Grill. We had in the past year introduced and made best-sellers of three Walter Donaldson songs: "Little White Lies," "Sweet Jennie Lee," and "You're Driving Me Crazy." Irving sat down with Carmen and myself, looking glum. He said:

"Boys, I think I've lost it. Mickey (Donaldson's nickname) has just had three big hits in a row and I haven't been able to come up with a real good one in the last two or three years." I hadn't realized it; you just naturally assumed that Irving Berlin was writing his three or four smashes a year, as always. I tried to console him. "Irving, there's no better writer in the world. I know it from the number of requests I get for your numbers every night. You just probably haven't been trying to write songs."

"I don't know what it is," he said. "I just can't seem to get the feeling of today. Donaldson has it and Gershwin and Cole Porter and Jerome Kern. They've been doing wonderful things in the past couple of years. Me, nothing. Would you do me a favor? Play me some of those Donaldson hits. He's got that little bounce to his songs I can't seem to get."

And so we played them as Berlin sat in a chair in back of the brass section and listened. Then he asked if we'd mind if he came back for the next couple of nights. We were only too happy to oblige.

He came back and extended his stay to two weeks, sitting at a ringside table, listening intently to our entire portfolio. He particularly liked Cole Porter's "Love for Sale" and Jerome Kern's "The Song Is You." I can remember him saying, "I wish I could write like that." Talk about humility from the acknowledged master of his trade! On his final visit, he said he'd come back in a week or so and maybe he'd have something we might want to play.

He brought in three songs and Carm and I took him to the little room in the Roosevelt we reserved just for listening to new offerings. He picked on those black keys and sang the lyrics in his inimitable squeak. Then with great timidity he asked what we thought of them. Naturally, we were prejudiced. Irving Berlin could not write a song that sounded bad to the Lombardos. "Well," he said in departing, "if you want to introduce one of them on the air, next Monday night, you have my permission. Maybe if it gets to be a hit, it will encourage me to start writing popular songs again."

And that Monday on the Robert Burns Panatella show, we introduced Irving Berlin's "new big hit, his first in three years." We rushed back to the Roosevelt for our late stint, and the headwaiter had a message to call Irving Berlin. He was unhappy. "Guy, I want to thank you and the boys for putting that thing on the air. You've had a lot of patience with me, listening to my songs and making an arrangement for the one you just played and putting it on the air. You are nice people and I appreciate your friendship. But that was a terrible song. Tear it up and forget about it."

It was the first time we had ever heard a writer tell us to forget one of his songs. It proved what we had come to learn. The great ones knew when they had a bad song, wanted no part of it, no matter if it survived commercially. When other writers had an arrangement in our book, they would encourage us to play it, hoping somehow it would break through, mediocre or not. I think my brother Carmen was like Berlin in that respect. His aforementioned adventures with "Boo Hoo" were an example.

My next encounter with a Berlin song had a happier ending. We were on our way to play our first Hollywood engagement in the celebrated Cocoanut Grove. It was the winter of 1933 and we had stopped off to have dinner with my mother and father at the Benjamin Franklin Hotel in Philadelphia. A four-piece string quartet was playing a number in the dining room that I had never heard before.

The melody was enchanting and I kept trying to hum it after the quartet launched into another number. I couldn't get it out of my mind; finally at the end of the set, I went up the leader and asked him the name of the song.

He said, "Oh, that's a new one called 'Easter Parade.' It's from Irving Berlin's new show *As Thousands Cheer*. They're trying it out here in Philly before they take it to Broadway."

I didn't have time to try to locate Irving in Philadelphia to tell him that if this was a sample of the work he was doing these days, he need never worry again about his ability to produce winners. Instead we had a train to catch to Los Angeles. I borrowed the sheet music from the leader and took it with me on the trip. By the time we opened at the Cocoanut Grove, we had an arrangement of "Easter Parade" ready. The people on the West Coast were ecstatic about the beautiful song; it became one of our biggest hits. And, of course, it became one of Irving Berlin's—in the same league with "White Christmas" and "God Bless America."

You might say it started a second career for Berlin. He would begin writing now for the Hollywood musicals and every so often come back to Broadway with such smash musicals as *Louisiana Purchase* and *Annie Get Your Gun*. The Easter song was included in the 1948 film *Easter Parade*, starring Fred Astaire and Judy Garland, and it enjoyed a renaissance that has lasted until today.

"White Christmas," which Berlin wrote for *Holiday Inn*, starring Bing Crosby and Astaire, was the classic example of how the master craftsman could interpret the feeling of his nation. It was written after the start of World War II, and Berlin, a veteran of the earlier great war, put himself into the minds of soldiers everywhere. He pictured them on Pacific islands and in malarial jungles as the joyous holiday approached. The first line told the story of their longing for home: "I'm dreaming of a White Christmas."

The song would also help the career of Bing Crosby; although he was the most popular singer in the country at that time, it added a dimension to his reputation as a crooner. Now he would be identified forever with "White Christmas," rather than his signature song, "When the Blue of the Night Meets the Gold of the Day . . ." His record of the simple and beautiful Irving Berlin message continues to be the best-selling of all time.

But I would always remember Irving Berlin, not so much for his contribution to American music and for all his songs in our repertoire, as for his humility and ability to discard a number he did not feel was up to his personal standards.

If the Depression did much to boost the fortunes of songwriters with talent, it also created somewhat of a problem for Guy Lombardo and the Royal Canadians. The songs that were popularized on radio by the big bands of the day somehow gave a lot of people delusions of grandeur. The hit tunes sounded so simple, so easy to create. Suddenly amateur songwriters began crawling out of the woodwork. They believed that all it took was rhyming June with Moon to attain fame and fortune. The bad times cried out for get-rich-quick ideas, and song-writing seemed an easy and quick route to prosperity.

It became a frightening experience just entering the lobby of the Roosevelt. Every day, there would be dozens of people, almost as many as the song pluggers, trying desperately to get your ear, to

try their tunes. Many came from various parts of the country on
borrowed money in the hope that, if a Guy Lombardo or Bing
Crosby would listen to their creations, the path to glory would
have been hurdled.

And, of course, 99 per cent of them wrote without a knowledge
of fundamentals, without melody or construction, and with lyrics
that may have rhymed but never said anything. I would receive
thousands of songs in the office and send them back unopened. If
you opened the envelope you were exposing yourself to a suit from
a professional songwriter; if for instance, the amateur effort had a
"moon" idea and you fooled around with it, you could always
expect to hear from somebody who would accuse you of plagiarism.

It happened to Carmen once. No matter where he went, people
would come up to him with ideas, send him their songs in the
mail. Carm, always warm and sympathetic, was less sales-resistant
than I. Once we were playing an engagement in Washington and
he was taking an afternoon nap in his hotel room when the phone
wakened him. The operator said the caller was a war veteran, a
paraplegic in a wheel chair. Carm accepted the call.

The man introduced himself as Stanley Rochinsky and said he
had an idea for a song. "Oh no," Carm groaned. But the caller
pressed on with the title of his song, "Powder Your Face with
Sunshine." Carm came fully awake. The title gave him immediate
ideas and he invited Rochinsky to bring up the lyrics. Carm went
to work at once. He changed the lyrics and wrote a sprightly tune
for it. The song became an instantaneous hit.

It also cost him some time away from the band. A few weeks
later he was served with legal papers. He was being sued by a man
who said he had written a tune for that song. Carm had never
seen or heard it. He was able to prove in court that he had
changed the lyrics extensively and had written a completely
different melody. He made money out of the song, but he would
never accept an idea from a stranger again.

Many of the aspiring songwriters were taken for a ride. The
Depression gave birth to a number of unscrupulous promoters
who called themselves publishers. Working out of cubicles, they
would advertise in the pulp magazines for yet unpublished writers,
asking them to send tunes for appraisal. The critique would

always be favorable and the sucker would be told to send along $100 for the cost of printing the song. Then would come another request, this time for $500; the promoter was so keen on the song that he would guarantee it would be heard by the big bandleaders, the vocal artists.

Those who fell for the scheme would never hear from the promoter again, other than the assurance that the song had made the rounds and, tough luck, try again. So they would come to New York and plead, telling of mortgaging their houses, asking me what I had thought of their song and what could they do to improve it. I could only tell them the song had never been submitted and that unfortunately we did not deal with amateur writers. I eventually had to use a side entrance to the Roosevelt to save myself the spectacle of pleading supplicants who never had a chance in the first place.

But through the thirties and forties, Tin Pan Alley kept turning out the nation's popular music, mainly from Broadway's Brill Building. The first few years of the Depression decade were difficult for the industry; as mentioned before, sheet music sales had been drastically curtailed by the advent of radio. Talking pictures, many of them musical now, helped decimate that part of the business. For a quarter, one could hear (and see) Jeanette MacDonald and Nelson Eddy, Al Jolson and Eddie Cantor. It beat the homemade music of the player piano.

The sale of recordings also suffered during that period when radio was still a novelty and old phonographs were being retired to make room for the new pieces of furniture with names like RCA, Philco, Zenith, and Atwater Kent. It was not until the Big Band era began to mature in the middle of the decade and jukeboxes found their way into taverns and lunch wagons that the recording industry would once again reap profits from the tunesmiths of Tin Pan Alley.

My own band's association with the record business dates back to 1924 before we had conquered Cleveland. Our first record on the old Gennett label, put out by a company in Indiana, was produced on a weird contraption with immense horns and the stylus recorded on hot wax. The recording studio's temperature must have been over a hundred degrees. It was kept that way so the wax wouldn't cool.

The songs we recorded never made an impact because we had not yet fully developed our sound and style. They were "So This Is Venice" and "Cy." Today, the record is a collector's item, worth perhaps ten dollars.

But in 1927, when we were Cleveland's No. 1 band, we accepted a contract from Columbia Records, which was signing up every popular regional orchestra it could bring into the fold. That summer we made two records, almost under protest when the company representative insisted on a stereotyped arrangement that made us sound like any other band. The recording of "Charmaine" did receive some notice, probably because the song was a good one.

All of the big recording companies were after us following our radio success in Chicago, but we still had several years left on the Columbia contract. The company set up an impressive recording session this time, sending out Eddie King, the leading artist's and repertory director in the country. He listened to the band at the Granada for a few nights and was obviously much disturbed.

"I don't know how I'm going to make a decent recording of this music," he told me. "I know it has something, I can see all the people dancing to it. But I don't know how it's going to come out on wax."

The problem, as he saw it, was that there just wasn't enough sound coming from our drummer, George Gowans. We could hear him setting the tempo, but the dancers couldn't. And neither could Eddie King, who tried to get George to make more racket.

I disabused him of the idea, telling him, "We just don't play that way. The last records we made for Columbia weren't in our style. Please let us play our music the way we know best."

Our style was simply quieter and slower than the other bands of the day. Where they took thirty seconds to play a song, our tempo stretched it out to almost a minute.

King decided to go along; the Lombardos were becoming known throughout the Midwest by a radio audience. He gave us permission to do it our way.

We cut about twenty sides for him, and those sessions were to begin an intricate process that I have followed ever since in making records. The important thing was to balance the band perfectly and know exactly where each instrument should be stationed in relation to the microphone. To retain the soft and sweet sound, for instance, it would be necessary to move Carm and Lebe farther back from the mikes than their normal position on the bandstand. Both can push the needle of a volume indicator almost to a breaking point on certain notes.

So at the first session, I carefully balanced the band to my satisfaction with each man's chair in exact position. When we came in for the second session, the cleaning men had moved the chairs and I had to repeat the process. That gave birth to a routine that I have followed to this day in making records. It never fails to intrigue recording technicians. If there is going to be more than one session, I will walk around the floor and put tacks in, indicating where each chair is to be placed. They remain there for the duration, saving all members of the band a memory search for the position they occupied at the previous session.

I got a fill-in from Ted Collins, then an executive at Columbia and later Kate Smith's manager, as to exactly what happened when Eddie King brought back the masters to New York. The records had come back from the processing department late in the afternoon and the company president, vice-president, board of directors, and assorted executives had flocked into the auditioning studio to hear the new band from Chicago.

The first record King put on was "Coquette" and, according to Collins, the reaction was completely negative. How was anybody going to dance to that? the executives were complaining. You could hardly hear the rhythm. How were they expected to sell it?

They tried increasing the revolutions per minute and ended up with a product that sounded more like a screech. King took the floor and stood up for the band from Canada. It wasn't what the executives thought in the studio, he said; what mattered was the reception it would get from the public. He had seen the reception at firsthand; the completely filled dance floor at the Granada, the crowds on line outside, waiting to get in. This was the only way the Lombardos knew how to play and their leader had made it plain they weren't going to play any other way.

Eddie King, the protagonist, won out. The records were released. The first one had "Coquette" on one side and "Beloved" on the other. It started slowly and then the college students latched onto it. They always have been the ones in the forefront of the newest musical trends. Then the best advertising of all—word of mouth—took over and the "Coquette" record was to sell over a million copies, as would a half-dozen other releases that followed. This was in the recording boom of the late twenties, when million-copy sales were not as unusual as they would become in the early Depression days.

One of the best friends I made in Chicago and who was to play a big part in our recording history was Jack Kapp, the Brunswick representative in that city. He had been a fan of ours since he heard our first broadcasts from Cleveland and he had tried everything in his power to get us to sign with his company.

We couldn't because of our contract with Columbia, but I did give Carm, Lebe, and several other members of the band permission to make a record for him under the name of "The Louisiana Rhythm Kings." It was played in Dixieland style with "Mississippi Mud" on one side and "Nobody's Sweetheart Now" on the other. The Columbia executives screamed when they heard it; they weren't fooled by the name of the band and enjoined us from ever attempting a similar stunt. The record, today, is a much more valuable collector's item than the 1924 effort.

The Columbia contract ran out after we arrived in New York, and now we were really deluged with offers to sign up with every company in the field. Victor Records had offered us a $25,000 down payment and a contract calling for $100,000 a year, and on Jules Stein's advice we had tentatively agreed to sign. The Brunswick Company, for whom Kapp worked, had failed, and he had formed his own outfit, Decca Records.

Kapp appealed to me not to sign with Victor, but to come in with his new company. "The two hottest properties in the country today," he told me, "are the Lombardo band and this new singer, Bing Crosby. I would love to start off my new company by announcing I have both under contract."

The idea intrigued me. I felt that Crosby was the best popular singer I had heard since coming to New York, and had in fact recommended him to Bill Paley, who gave him his first regular radio program. And I valued my friendship with Jack Kapp and felt a certain loyalty to him for seeking out the Royal Canadians long before we became known. I told Jules Stein of my decision to cancel the Victor contract and go with Decca. He threw up his hands. "If friendship and loyalty mean more to you than money," he said, "how can I argue?"

The Victor company was not to give up without a fight. The night we closed our 1931 spring engagement at the Roosevelt, a young man came up to the bandstand with a huge floral arrangement. The first thing I noticed was that it came from Victor; I was touched that the company had apparently decided to be gracious about losing out on the contract. The young man pointed to an envelope hidden in the arrangement. "You better look inside."

It developed that the messenger boy was a process server. The envelope contained a subpoena announcing a Victor suit against the Royal Canadians for breach of contract. The company claimed they had set up a staff just to handle Lombardo recordings and were suing for damages. But our agreement had been verbal and I had never signed anything.

Decca's first record in 1934, a Jack Kapp dream come true, featured our band on one side ("Moonglow") and Bing Crosby on the other ("Love in Bloom"). The record is still in print.

But Kapp could not survive the times and his company went into bankruptcy. We signed on with Victor and stayed only for the duration of the contract, by which time Jack had restored his company and we were back again on the Decca label. The association was to last for years and produce four gold records commemorating million-plus sales. They included "Winter Wonderland," "Easter Parade," "Third Man Theme," and "Humoresque." The last featured a new addition to the band—twin pianos. We had by the forties come up with this novelty, setting up a fine pianist, Frank Vignuea, alongside Fred Kreitzer.

The "Third Man" record was a departure from the way the

song was played when it was introduced as the theme song for the movie by the same name. In the movie a zither carried the harmony. I wanted it played on a more familiar instrument and selected our guitarist at the time, Don Rodney, to carry the melody.

Decca put out "Third Man Theme" as a cover record, never expecting a gold record. Covers were usually produced by rival companies as competition to the original recording of a song, and even Jack Kapp was surprised at its sales.

We would later switch to Capitol Records, which had shown an appreciation and feeling for our music. With the tremendous output still owned by Decca and the new albums that Capitol produced, the Royal Canadians would maintain a batting average of from a quarter to half a million copies sold for every record we made. Some years we would sell as many as 11 million records, and the total to this day would reach 300 million records, more than has ever been sold by either a musical aggregation or vocalist.

The sales would be helped by the coin-operated jukeboxes that began appearing in the mid thirties. Hits that would first be heard on jukeboxes created a demand for records to be played in the more sophisticated sound systems being installed in homes in the prosperous fifties. But the Tin Pan Alley that we had known almost from childhood would change with the coming of rock-and-roll and with the ability of amateur groups to record in garages and cellars on new tape machines.

The songwriters we knew, too, moved to Hollywood to make music for the films. The capital of the music business would no longer be the Brill Building; it would now be located in Nashville with strange new companies glutting the market with rock and country and western and soul. The hits as we knew them would diminish to perhaps a few a year; the Nashville products would enjoy meteoric and very brief successes.

Only a Burt Bacharach, among the younger writers, would compose songs during the last decade to compare with the creations of Berlin, Porter, Kern, Donaldson, Richard Rodgers, and the great writers who inhabited Tin Pan Alley.

Guy Lombardo and the Royal Canadians would continue to

play those old songs, the standards, for the audiences that remembered them and for the people who still danced cheek to cheek. We would endure when so many of the other big bands would break up because we could never forget that Tin Pan Alley gave us the music that was our trademark.

6. The Era of the Big Bands

We could hardly be counted a major force in the band business until our success in Chicago. The big names belonged to the pioneer leaders who emerged during and shortly after World War I and proved that popular music as played by ten or more men was equally enjoyable for dancing and listening.

Paul Whiteman wasn't the first of the pioneers but he certainly was the most successful in establishing the pattern that most bands followed in the twenties. He brought the symphonic sound to the business, leaned on talented arrangers, and featured vocal soloists and even a trio.

But there were others who helped set the foundation for the booming Big Band era that reached such unparalleled proportions in the thirties and forties. A number of them, like Whiteman, originated on the West Coast, made names for themselves, and came to New York after the war to attain national recognition. In that number were Art Hickman, who may have been the first to invade the East, Abe Lyman, and George Olson.

All of them featured a bouncy, foot-tapping style that through the twenties would be called jazz. Even our band, later to be scoffed at by so-called jazz purists who had a different interpretation of the word, would play that kind of cadence in our early, formative years.

They came from all corners of the nation, the early bandleaders, seeking to fill the ever-increasing demand for postwar dance music. We started like most of the others, a virtual pickup crew of four men, playing engagements in the ballrooms around the London area that were replacing the community halls with new dance facilities.

The pioneers were a step ahead of us in enlarging their bands to ten or more men. Ballrooms were springing up all over, and leading hotels found it profitable to provide rooms that were set aside exclusively for dancing. Like us, but a few years earlier, the musicians began moving out of their home towns for the big cities.

We had already received guidance from some of those pioneers:

Jean Goldkette, a talented pianist who had come to this country from France, made a reputation in Detroit and later graduated the most talented sidemen in the business, including Russ Morgan, Tommy and Jimmy Dorsey, Bix Beiderbecke, and Joe Venuti. It was Goldkette, you may remember, who first allowed eighteen-year-old Carmen to sit in with his band and learn what was demanded of a saxophonist.

There was Isham Jones, who we regarded as second only to Whiteman, when we were listening to phonograph records and deciding to expand into a big band. Jones gave us further impetus when he accepted that invitation to my twenty-first birthday party, out of which Lebert emerged a professional trumpet player.

And there was the Coon-Saunders orchestra, which had gained a national reputation by getting exposure in Kansas City's Muehlbach Hotel and Radio Station WDAF. The Kansas City Nighthawks had given us the inspiration to get to Cleveland with the hopes of receiving exposure on radio. Later they would be competing with us on Chicago radio.

But the one man who probably more than any other solidified the business and hastened the era of the Big Bands was Jules Stein. He had started his Music Corporation of America in Chicago and to that city gravitated bands from all over the country, seeking the buildup and engagements they would get if MCA took them in the fold. Before the second half of the twenties, most bands had booked themselves; now they had heard that Jules Stein could do it better and more profitably.

I had not gone looking for MCA when we were reaching the

height of our popularity in Cleveland. Perhaps I had an innate suspicion of booking agents; more probably I felt that we had made it big on our own, had no end of engagements lined up, and saw no reason to pay an agent's commission. But Jules Stein sold me with his plans for getting us to New York, with his flattering opinion that he wanted the Royal Canadians to break the New York market for him, a move in which he had failed with other bands.

I have never regretted signing up with Jules Stein nor been able to state in certainty that Guy Lombardo and His Royal Canadians would have made it to the top without MCA. In retrospect it was the wisest business decision I ever made.

And it began paying off immediately. Jules's brother, Billy, got us to Chicago via Al Quodbach and his Granada Cafe. The brothers were helpful, too, in persuading Al to install a radio wire in the cafe; they shared the weekly hookup costs with the band and the reluctant proprietor. The impact of radio and its role in earning a national reputation for the band was not lost on Jules Stein. He would not bring us to New York until he had arranged a similar setup in the best possible hotel he could find for us.

That job was made a little easier for Stein in the winter of 1928, when Bill Paley's foremost sports announcer, Ted Husing, came into the Granada after he had broadcast a Northwestern-Illinois football game. He liked the band so much he phoned his boss and arranged for a one-night broadcast on the CBS network out of Chicago. Paley listened and he was not buying a pig in a poke when Stein got him to approve a commercial radio program even before we arrived in New York.

The Big Band era was really a series of events and it coincided with our early years in New York, in a depression during which blue-chip businesses would struggle to keep alive. Certainly the chancy industry of show business seemed destined for a worse fate. Yet the bands would flourish and prosper for the next twenty years, one event after another occurring to keep them healthy.

If Paul Whiteman and our predecessors set the tone for the big bands that would follow, the Royal Canadians proved a formula. We proved that a hotel room like the Roosevelt Grill could double and triple its take by employing a band that had become na-

Guy, with Lilliebell, accepting the trophy for that race.

Guy and *Tempo* VII. Trying it out in Bay City, Michigan.

Guy with Gar Wood, the racing champion he most admired. 1946.

Two Long Islanders, Perry Como of Sands Point and Carm Lombardo of Woodmere, celebrate all-star opening of new arena in Hempstead, 1948.

Lilliebell Lombardo.

Guy and Lilliebell's twentieth wedding anniversary, celebrated in Los Angeles. Standing: the Lombardo brothers and Rose Marie, Fay Emerson and husband Elliott Roosevelt. Second and third from left: Alan Ladd and his wife Sue Carroll. Second from right, sitting: Mrs. Jules Stein.

At President Dwight D. Eisenhower's inaugural in 1953, where Guy was suddenly displaced by Fred Waring. Left to right, front row: Guy, Fred Waring, Mrs. Elvira Doud, Jeannette MacDonald, Mrs. Eisenhower, President Eisenhower, Lily Pons, George Murphy. Behind Guy is Lauritz Melchoir; behind Mrs. Eisenhower are Esther Williams and James Melton. *(Photo by Maurice Johnson, United Press International Photo.)*

tionally celebrated on network radio. When we arrived in New York, only a few hotels featured name bands. After a year or two, there were perhaps a dozen all following the same formula, filling the air on radio and the hotel rooms they played in. Jules Stein began bringing in more and more of his bands from Chicago and points west.

The customers didn't have much money but they had to part with very little to hear Rudy Vallee and Guy Lombardo and Paul Whiteman and Vincent Lopez and Fred Waring on radio. All of us became national names and visitors who came to New York for business or special occasions would flock into the Roosevelt, the Commodore, the Biltmore, the Astor, the St. Regis, the New Yorker, the new Waldorf Astoria, to all the hotels that featured their favorite bands introduced to them over radio.

And bands and their personalities became conversation pieces. Was Rudy Vallee a musician or basically an entertainer with that tremulous voice he sent through his bell-shaped megaphone? What kind of reeds did those Lombardos use to get their special sound? Who was imitating whom: Bing Crosby or Russ Columbo? Later there would be arguments about and between Tommy and Jimmy Dorsey, about Benny Goodman and Glenn Miller, and about a skinny kid named Sinatra. Was his rendition of "Marie" better than the original by Jack Leonard?

And as the names of the bandleaders and vocalists became household words with the radio listeners, a new boom began. People around the country who couldn't get to the big cities where the bands were playing in an ever-increasing number of hotel rooms began demanding to see, hear, and dance to what had come to be known as the "Big Bands." Ballrooms began a renaissance in the small towns.

I remember one in Pottstown, Pennsylvania, owned by a man named Ray Harkenstein. A building tycoon, he had fallen on hard times and was practically broke in 1932. He got the bright idea of using surplus supplies to build a palatial ballroom, but he wouldn't open it until MCA booked our band for the premiere.

The demand for the bands spilled over to the Broadway movie houses that featured a stage-show policy. Suddenly the top names in vaudeville—Al Jolson, Sophie Tucker, Will Rogers, Eddie Cantor, Jack Benny—were being replaced by the bandleaders and their men who had become known on radio and records. Between engagements in the hotels, MCA and its new competitor, the General Artists Corporation, would book their bands on theater circuits that might take them to half a dozen cities. They would still meet radio network commitments from wherever they were playing.

It turned out to be an expensive proposition for the theaters because of demands by union stagehands to be paid for moving the bandstand, the chairs, the instruments before and after the other acts on the show; and by the Musicians' Union, which insisted that a standby band play for the acts. The Big Band theater policy might have enjoyed a short life had not Bob Weitman, the young managing director of the Paramount Theater on Broadway, come up with a novel idea.

We had been playing the Paramount theaters in New York and in circuit cities since the fall of 1930. When we returned for the 1935 engagement, Weitman had put into effect his idea to eliminate the killing demands by unions. He had perfected a band pit that came up from the basement by elevator and set into place in front of the stage.

We would ascend from the cellar ready to play, arriving dramatically under the glare of a spotlight, and those early audiences considered it a marvel of technology. More important, we were now in the pit and could play for the line of girls, occasional adagio dancers, and comedians who were part of the show. And the Paramount Theater no longer had to hire almost as many stagehands as musicians in the band for our part of the show.

The idea caught on. Soon there were elevator-riding bands in the Roxy, Capitol, Strand, Rivoli, and other theaters on Broadway. The big houses in the major cities borrowed the idea, too, and the complaints about band shows being too expensive vanished. The Weitman idea would make stars of the new bands that were coming along to fill the demand of the theater circuits.

It was in these theaters that reputations would be made for Benny Goodman, Tommy Dorsey, Harry James, Glenn Miller, and others. And it was at the Paramount that Goodman would usher in the new sound he called "swing" and would win even more converts for the Big Bands, many of which latched onto his style. By 1938, the Big Band era was bursting at the seams and there were lucrative jobs to be had for the good ones in hotels, on radio, in ballrooms and theaters. The movie industry got in on the act, too, signing up as many name bands as they could get.

Another event that kept the business healthy in the late thirties was the arrival of the jukebox. Suddenly they appeared in taverns and diners across the country. You could play a record for a nickel while quaffing a beer or nursing a cup of coffee, and most of them featured bands and their vocalists. All of a sudden, the public was demanding more and more records. The jukeboxes were making the hits, and the recording industry was busy filling orders for discs that would be played in the home on more modern turntable equipment.

Jack Kapp of Decca would begin selling single records for thirty-five cents, and the volume of sales reached proportions far beyond the halcyon days before radio and the Depression. Now more and more bands were called on to make recordings, and the Big Band era moved into the war years of the forties, solidly entrenched as a thriving aspect of show business.

Later I will deal with the decline of the era. In between are memories of the bandleaders I came to know, of the role I was fortunate enough to play in their careers, of the incidents that made up the life of the Royal Canadians during what was an epochal period in our history.

An incident stands out illustrative of radio's search to find an identity in the first years of the thirties. The bands had proved they could attract an audience and the executives of the networks and advertising agencies were falling over themselves looking for new ones. It is ever thus in the entertainment industry; a trend is milked to bursting point.

Our band had been among the pioneers of commercial radio along with Paul Whiteman, Rudy Vallee, Vincent Lopez, Ben Bernie, Fred Waring, George Olson, Abe Lyman, and Phil Harris. Now the rush was on for new names and other segments of show business were being ignored, notably the star comedians who were losing their bread and butter as vaudeville was being mortally wounded by talking pictures and radio.

The situation was brought home to me on a Sunday night in 1932, shortly after we had moved upstairs from our Riverside Drive apartment to the penthouse suite that had been occupied by George Gershwin. The composer had sublet his premises to us when he moved to Hollywood to write for the movies, and Lilliebell, again with brother Joe's help, had decorated the duplex with the primary purpose of making it comfortable for entertaining. Every Sunday night was open house at the Lombardos' and our guests included most of Broadway's show business personalities.

On this particular evening, I wandered into the small room we had set up as a bar, and found Jack Benny sitting alone, gazing dolefully at his drink. The reason for the melancholy? Jack, who had reached star billing as a vaudeville entertainer, had just finished thirteen weeks on a fifteen-minute radio program sponsored by Canada Dry and had been informed that his option was not being picked up.

"There just doesn't seem to be any room on radio for comedians," he said. The only consolation I could afford him was that nobody had found the right formula yet. The comedians who had been put on the air, like Eddie Cantor and Ed Wynn, operated out of a vacuum in a studio without an audience. Radio was presenting them in the same manner that had worked for the bands, behind a glass screen to eliminate foreign sounds. That was the way it worked in a recording studio.

But a comedian needed laughs. He needed an audience. It was difficult to gauge whether his lines were going over. There was little inspiration looking at a glass screen behind which technicians were working, usually too busy to even smile at a punch line.

Our band was fortunate enough to be in a position to help change that situation. That winter we took on an added radio program in which we featured a low-budget variety show, including dancers and a comedian. With what I had learned from Jack Benny, I insisted on a live audience. The applause that followed each act enlivened the show considerably, and shortly after, Eddie Cantor followed suit and stepped out of his soundproofed glass booth. In came the audience and thus began new careers for Jack

Benny, Bob Hope, Fred Allen, Burns and Allen, and so many others who were to become national institutions.

George Burns and Gracie Allen were my all-time favorites. They were contemporaries of Jack Benny and faced the same dilemma. After struggling to become headliners in the twenties, they found themselves with dismal prospects as vaudeville began declining. They had appeared on several early Eddie Cantor shows and received good notices, but few avenues seemed to be open to them.

Meanwhile a strange thing was happening on our Robert Burns show, the one that reached across the country, that had proved the attraction of orchestras. We had the top rating of any band show, but somehow the program wasn't selling cigars. The ad agency was quick to come up with what was to become an integral part of broadcasting. They made a survey. They learned that most of our listeners were college students. And college students didn't buy cigars.

The advertising agency responsible for the program suggested we add two minutes of comedy to the show. They wanted to know if we had a preference. My choice was the team of Burns and Allen, with whom we had toured on a Paramount theater circuit the year before. They were a delightful act, the straight man with his ever-present cigar and uncanny sense of timing and his refreshingly whimsical wife and partner who may have reinvented the malaprop. I felt that if anybody could sell cigars George and Gracie could.

The first show received a negative reaction. CBS was inundated by letters and telegrams from the college audience. "What are you doing to Lombardo?" they asked. They wanted music, not comedy. We had to work out a compromise.

For the next program it was announced at the beginning that our band would play throughout the entire half hour. When Burns and Allen came on for their two one-minute spots, the Lombardo fans could still hear the Royal Canadians, although we diminished our volume. The comedy team came on during the middle of a number and talked as we played. That satisfied the college kids and brought to the audience an additional coterie of fans who enjoyed Burns and Allen. The program was the first big break they received on radio and it was all they needed.

I couldn't have been happier that George's and Gracie's career took off on a Guy Lombardo program. I owed them much for making bearable the difficult working conditions on that circuit tour the year before. Unflappable George and down-to-earth Gracie were not only always good for a laugh but were fascinating companions.

The early-day theater tours before Bob Weitman came up with his elevated band pits were sheer drudgery. You worked seven days a week. You did seven shows a day. You arrived the first day of the engagement for a 6 A.M. rehearsal at the theater to get ready for the opening show at 10:30. The musicians had to leave their instruments in the basement, several floors below the stage, and that meant carrying them upstairs seven times a day. It was a testimonial to our youth that we could survive six weeks of these conditions in six different cities. Only the Brooklyn Paramount, which we played the week after its Broadway namesake's run, had an elevator to take us to our dressing rooms.

I had been exposed to vaudevillians for a long time, ever since Lebe had worked at the little theater in London and on through our first tour with Corinne Arbuckle. I knew them as a breed entirely apart from the rest of us. George Burns was first and foremost a vaudevillian, as I was to learn when we traveled the Paramount circuit together. Gracie Allen, on the other hand, might have been a favorite next-door neighbor, sweet, compliant, practical, and never onstage when she was off it.

George knew all the tricks of the vaudevillian's trade and some never invented. They provided me with a steady source of amusement. His routine wouldn't vary as we came into a city. He would send ahead Gracie and baggage to the hotel and proceed forthwith to the theater to check the billing.

I believe it was in Indianapolis that I checked into my own room and had hardly hung up my clothes when there was a phone call from the manager of the theater. He wanted to know who the hell was George Burns.

The team of Burns and Allen had a lucrative contract on the circuit and I so informed the irate manager, who fumed, "Well, he's not going to tell me how to run my theater. He wants his name featured as prominently as the band's. You're my attraction and if he keeps pestering me, I'm going to leave him off the bill, contract or no contract."

I managed to placate him, suggesting he print up an extra sign, in which Burns and Allen would be featured alone as "Added Attraction." It apparently satisfied George Burns; he had made his point about not being overlooked in the billing, a mortal wound for a vaudevillian.

George and Gracie were to become my lifelong friends as well as superstars of the industry on radio, television, and the movies. Neither of them ever changed and it was never more apparent than the first time George worked alone some thirty years later. I was vacationing in Lake Tahoe, Nevada, at the lovely cottage Bill Harrah maintained for the star acts at his mammoth club, and George was about to debut as a single. Gracie had decided to give up show business and its rigors, preferring to become a homebody, to play bridge, and enjoy all the pleasures she had missed on the road. Now Lilliebell and I were sitting with her at a table in Harrah's awaiting George's debut.

"I've never been so nervous in my life," she confessed as George came onstage, flicking ashes from his cigar. "I don't even know if I can stand it. I almost wish I were up there with him again."

And as George cracked jokes and sang old-time vaudeville refrains with equal aplomb, Gracie Allen, America's favorite scatterbrain, peered at adjoining tables to ascertain how the material was being received. Satisfied finally at the ovation and encore calls, she sighed and said, "I feel better. He'll do all right without me."

It was a sad prophecy. Gracie died a few months later.

If we were to play a small role in the evolution of comedians on the air, the Royal Canadians fell into a bigger one in the development of a sizable number of bands. It was one of the by-products of success. We had helped create the demand for more and more dance orchestras, and now in the early thirties combinations were being organized with the sole purpose of duplicating the Lombardo sound. At first flattering, the trend began to get annoying.

One would have thought we employed magical tricks to attain

our sound. It was as if we owned the secret to a new weapon. Ridiculous as it sounds, the band suddenly became the target for a network of spies.

We almost reached the point of having to hire a guard in our band room. One night, a spy sneaked in and picked up a reed thrown away by a saxophone player because it was cracked. For weeks, he tried to sell the cracked reed around town, claiming it was the secret behind our success.

Then there was the agent who invested in a nightly table at the Grill, paying strict attention to every detail on the bandstand: how the musicians held their instruments, how they fingered the keys, how they breathed. He thought he had unraveled the secret one night when he noticed a peculiar action on the part of Derf Higman. Derf had completed a long passage on his sax and decided his reed was a little too wet. So he slipped a piece of music paper between the reed and the mouthpiece and laid it aside to dry. The intelligence agent rushed out convinced he had the secret. For about a month after that some saxophone players around New York were trying to make music with a piece of paper stuck in the reed.

But there were more intelligent musicians around who realized that there was no secret to the Lombardo sound. We had developed our style through evolution and the part of it that was most identifiable was the slow fox trot beat, which made dancing easy and enjoyable. Art Kessel, a bandleader who preceded us in Chicago, once told MCA executive Karl Kramer, "Everyone in the business learned a little bit from the Lombardo success.

"At first all of us used to make fun of Guy's music," he said. "But there was envy in our joshing and I must admit that while I never set out to capture the Lombardo style, I did seek to put in my band certain things I didn't have before and which came to me after hearing Lombardo. The first and most important was the slow beat . . . I believe if there had been no Lombardo success in the twenties, there would have been no Tommy Dorsey ten years later. While these bands may seem worlds apart, Dorsey did adopt the slow Lombardo beat and remained with it throughout his career.

"I say we all learned from Lombardo and I wasn't kidding when

I said to Guy after I returned from a big one-night tour, 'How much do I owe you?' There were a lot of other leaders who could ask the same question."

The three best-known bands that deliberately copied our style were led by Jan Garber, Sammy Kaye, and Blue Baron. Garber had started a band that played fast music and enjoyed a moderate reputation. Then he happened to hear a small orchestra led by saxophone player Freddie Large, who came from the same area we did and who was a friend of ours. Freddie had moved to the States shortly after we did, and came about as close to sounding like Carmen as was possible. In fact, his band sounded like ours even before Louis Bleet had helped to fully develop our style in Cleveland.

Freddie, however, was having a tough time getting started, and it wasn't until Garber heard him that his prospects improved. Garber, who had made his name in Atlanta, dissolved his former band and took on Freddie Large's crew. His was the only band that sounded remotely like us when he became a rival bandleader in Chicago. I never resented his success because he was quick to admit that his style was pretty much like ours.

I could not feel as charitable toward Sammy Kaye. It got under my skin to see Sammy and his musicians who were playing in a hotel a short distance from the Roosevelt come into the Grill and station themselves behind the bandstand. They were there for no other purpose than to listen closely and try to imitate our sound. I never treated Sammy discourteously, but I have to admit now that I regarded the band watch as an intrusion.

Still, we were in an admirable position to help bands we considered deserving. We had influence with MCA and with CBS and both the talent agency and the radio network were often willing to listen to our recommendations. Thus it was that Eddie Duchin, the young pianist who had built such a solid reputation playing between orchestra breaks at the Central Park Casino, came to see Carmen one day to ask his advice. He had dreams about starting his own orchestra. The hitch was that he had signed a contract with Sid Solomon, who owned the club, a hangout for society folk and politicians.

Carm knew that Jules Stein was constantly seeking out new

band personalities, and he told him about the talented Eddie and his desire to form his own band. MCA purchased his contract from Solomon for $25,000 and the band Duchin put together would become a permanent fixture at the beautiful new Waldorf Astoria.

A few years earlier, we had a similar experience with a bespectacled young man with a soft Southern accent. He was going through a period almost identical to that of the Royal Canadians when we were desperately trying to stay in Cleveland and avoid the ignominy of returning home as failures.

Kay Kyser had come off the campus of the University of North Carolina with a small band, ready and eager to conquer the North. They had landed in Cleveland and the only job they had found was in a Chinese restaurant, which had almost been the fate of the crew from London, Ontario. Now we had returned to Cleveland during a theater tour, and the young man visited us backstage, inviting us to the Golden Pheasant, his place of employment. The invitation reminded me so much of a younger Guy Lombardo seeking advice from established bandleaders that I hastened to accept.

Carm, Lebe, and I were royally entertained by Kay Kyser. His musicians were sound, they had their own identity, and each one of them had a certain comedic bent that we had never quite achieved when we were straining for funny effects in vaudeville. The most amusing member of the crew, in an understated way that wasn't at all corny, was Kyser himself.

After the show, Kay sat down with us and told us his problem, so reminiscent of our first days in Cleveland. He was having trouble getting booked. When they closed at the Golden Pheasant in a couple of weeks, it looked like they'd have to go back to North Carolina. I got hold of Billy Stein and asked him to take a look at the band; I thought it was talented enough to earn a shot with MCA.

Billy called back in a few days, saying, "That guy you recommended, that Kyser. He's a nut. I walk into this restaurant to hear a band and the first thing I see is the leader on the floor. He is pushing a knife with his nose. How do you expect us to sell that? If that's what he's peddling how can we ever get him on the air?"

But we kept after Billy and almost in self-defense he finally signed the Kay Kyser band. Kay would become a big name in the Big Band era, one of the best-known attractions on radio and television with his Kyser College of Musical Knowledge. And then at the height of his success, he would pack it in and return to North Carolina in the early fifties.

The last year we played at the Roosevelt Grill, 1963, Kay Kyser returned to New York for just one night. He brought with him a heart-warming gesture that meant much to the Lombardo brothers.

I noticed a familiar-looking face that I couldn't quite place, even though he was sitting at ringside. I kept peering and he finally stood up and yelled at me, "It's your old pal. Kay Kyser. Don't you recognize me?"

I hadn't because Kay wasn't wearing glasses and I had never seen him without them. After the show, my brothers and I joined him at his table. Where had he been? How come we hadn't heard from him? What was he doing here?

"To tell you the truth, boys," he said, "I heard this was your last season at the Roosevelt and I couldn't take the chance that I might not catch up with you again. So I came up for this one night. I simply wanted to thank you for what you did for me. I don't know how many songwriters and song pluggers and bandleaders ever thanked you for your help. I just want to be one of them."

There is a deep satisfaction in discovering new talent, and as the band began tracing and retracing its way across the country, opportunity to help aspiring young musicians constantly presented itself. So it was the first time we played New Orleans in 1934. We arrived at Mardi Gras time and the city fathers were generous in their reception, providing each member of the band with a car to ride in the ticker tape parade. The cars also came equipped with carnival queens to accompany the Royal Canadians.

We were scheduled to begin an engagement at the Club Forest on the night after the parade, and all of us dropped in for the closing show of the Anson Weeks orchestra, which featured singer Bob Crosby. I had known both of them in New York and wanted to greet them. I noticed, however, that neither Weeks nor Crosby was on the bandstand during the performance. I asked the maître d' where they were and he informed me they were in the gambling casino in one of the club's side rooms.

He invited me to visit the casino, saying, "I'm sure they'd like to see you." I told him I'd rather wait till they came out. But they didn't, the leader and the name singer, and the band finished a final number without them. Meanwhile emissaries from management were coming to the table, insisting I come to the casino. I resisted; Al Quodbach had given me an early lesson about the dangers of casino gambling, especially for an employee of a club who wanted to take home his weekly paycheck.

Weeks and Crosby finally came into the room as the musicians were putting away their instruments. Both looked perturbed as they stopped at the table. I suspected the reason and they confirmed it. They didn't have any money to pay the band. Their fee—I think it was $3,500—had been left with the stickmen. They rode back to the hotel with me somewhat cheered; the manager had advanced the bandsmen's salaries on the condition that the money would be taken out of Weeks's and Crosby's salaries the next time they played the club.

I almost had to laugh at the unceasing efforts to get Carm, Lebe, and me into the casino during our engagement. We never succumbed, and on the final night the manager came up again, saying, "The boys in the casino want to say good-by to you."

"I never said hello," I told him. "Why should I say good-by."

We had better things to do with our time. Everywhere, especially on Bourbon Street, there were small clubs and in them were fine musicians. It was springtime and warm enough so that the doors of the clubs were open. Up and down the street, sounds poured out, sweet, penetrating, Dixieland and improvised jazz. One night, walking alone, I heard the sound of a trumpet, different and more piercing than any I had experienced. I walked into the tiny club, which was almost empty. On the bandstand was an olive-skinned trumpet player, hardly more than a boy. He was leading a four-man group and a girl vocalist sat beside them.

They were putting as much into the show as if the place overflowed with patrons. And the trumpet player so impressed me I ran back to the hotel and got Carm and Lebe out of bed. They came back with me, Carm grumbling that I was probably thinking about reviving the Dixieland and jazz numbers we used to play in our early days. I wasn't thinking about that at all; I wanted to find out if my brothers were as impressed with this different personality as I.

They were. We talked to him after the show, found out his name was Louis Prima, that he was nineteen years old and had just started his first engagement. One night he asked us to come to his house for dinner, and we met his mother and father, ate Italian dishes with a touch of Creole, and left feeling like members of the family.

We came to hear Louis every night we could and I finally asked him if he would like to come to New York. I was sure I could find a job for him; I hadn't heard his type of music in the big town. Louis' folks were rather reluctant but they gave him their consent. I had one place in mind for him, a well-known night spot on Fifty-second Street, Leon and Eddie's. I knew Eddie Davis, one of the partners. He was an ex-vaudevillian who emceed the show at his club and I felt I could talk him into hiring Prima's combo and use Louis as an emcee the night Eddie took off. I told Prima I would let him know if the job was open.

Back in New York to make our first appearance in the Waldorf Astoria, I sought out Eddie Davis the first chance I had, told him about my discovery, described his personality, and suggested he could prove a boon to business. Eddie wanted to know the size of the combo; he liked the idea of a five-man group and said, "Tell him to come. If he's as good as you say he is, I can use him."

Up from New Orleans came Louis Prima and band and I took him over immediately to see Eddie Davis. We sat down and talked and Eddie excused himself, motioning for me to follow. "I don't know how to tell you this, Guy. But I can't use him. I just found out the union won't let me get rid of the band I was going to replace him with."

I did not take the news kindly. How could Eddie, my friend, do this after I had uprooted five kids from New Orleans and brought them to New York for a guaranteed job that was now nonexistent? Eddie apologized, saying his hands were tied.

I booked rooms at the Waldorf for Louis and his crew and contacted Irving Mills, who handled our record dates, to see if he could find work for the combo. Irving said he'd try and, to keep them in eating money, he'd have Louis make jazz records. Satisfied that Louis was in good hands, I left for an engagement at the Cocoanut Grove in Los Angeles.

Some weeks later on the Coast, I picked up a copy of *Variety*. There was a Page One story about New York's new sensation, Louis Prima and band, which was doing capacity business in a new Fifty-second Street club, the Famous Door. It was a few doors down the street from Leon and Eddie's. The review was ecstatic, mentioning new jazz sounds never before heard in New York, and it mentioned that among the prominent ringsiders at opening night was Eddie Davis. Louis Prima's success at the Famous Door brought a gold rush to Fifty-second Street as other jazz and swing combos followed in newly opened clubs. It came to be known as Swing Street and Louis Prima would later say that it was really founded by Guy Lombardo.

When we got back to New York, I could not resist the urge to needle Eddie Davis. He admitted he'd made the biggest mistake of his life and then he had a confession. "I didn't tell you the real reason I didn't hire the kid. To tell you the truth, I thought he was colored and I just couldn't take a chance on losing customers."

That reason was the tragedy of our day. The management of hotels and the night-club owners simply refused to break the color line, fearing financial consequences. Many of the best bands in the country were black—Duke Ellington, Louis Armstrong, Cab Calloway, Fletcher Henderson—but job opportunities were difficult to find outside of Harlem.

Eddie Davis on first seeing olive-skinned and swarthy Louis Prima and knowing that he came from New Orleans, had simply assumed he was a black man. The shame is not so much that he lost a gold mine but that he capitulated to the prejudice of the times. The color line would be broken only a few years later when Benny Goodman came to the Paramount Theater and had the audience dancing in the aisles. Two black men—Teddy Wilson at the piano and Lionel Hampton on the vibes—were among his talented performers.

And when Goodman, riding success, was asked to play at the Waldorf Astoria, he brought an integrated band to the Park Avenue hotel for the first time. He would have had it no other way. It was an act of courage as historic and important as the Branch Rickey move that brought Jackie Robinson to major-league baseball.

Our first of many trips to the West Coast was made in 1933 after much soul-searching and an assist from Phil Harris. He had come to New York from San Francisco, taken advantage of the radio time available to bands with distinctive styles, and become one of our best friends among the bandleaders. His vocalist was a lovely girl named Leah Raye, who would later become Mrs. Sonny Werblin.

Phil was one of the regulars on the boat I had purchased when we were playing summer engagements at the Pavillon Royal. He had just signed on for an engagement at the Hotel Pennsylvania Roof, started working on his first radio program, and had several best-selling records on the market. Witty and entertaining, he also spoke a kind of musician's language. He frequently used the word, "man" as a form of address and was the first to acquaint me with the hip jargon that would become popular in the sixties.

We cruised off Point Lookout, catching fish, inhaling salt spray, and I remember Harris saying, "Man, this is the life. It's almost as good as the Coast."

That reminded me that the Coast had been beckoning the Lombardo band. Inquiries had been coming in almost weekly from the Ambassador Hotel's Cocoanut Grove in Los Angeles. They wanted us to play there for most of the winter season. I hadn't paid much attention to the offer because we were booked at the Roosevelt.

I mentioned it to Phil and he said, "Man, you got to get out there. You'll never play in a room more beautiful; they got real coconuts in the trees and fake monkeys with lights in their eyes. You look around that room and all you see is movie stars. Man, get out there tomorrow if you can swing it."

Suddenly the way opened up and I wasn't sure I was happy about the chain of circumstances. The Roosevelt Hotel and several others in the area of Grand Central Terminal had been fighting to stay alive since the stock market crash. Bands helped; they brought tourists and nationwide publicity. The Royal Canadians had made the Roosevelt Grill one of the best-known attractions in the city. But the hotel management was still hard put to meet mortgage payments.

In 1933, the New York Central Railroad, holders of mortgages on a number of hotels in the area, decided to foreclose and take over their operations. Into the management moved efficiency experts, studying the books and seeking ways to cut expenses.

The expert assigned to the Roosevelt came immediately upon one budget expense that seemed out of line. He noted that the Royal Canadians were being paid $2,000 a week, plus a percentage of the Grill's receipts. Pursuing the matter, he checked around with the Musicians' Union and asked, "How much should it cost the hotel for a ten-piece band?" Told that the going rate was about $1,000 a week for union musicians, he quickly moved to set the matter right. We were informed we would have to take a cut in salary. Jules Stein could argue and point to the figures that proved our band had almost quadrupled the take in the Grill since we came to work in 1929. The New York Central man remained adamant.

We terminated our association with the Roosevelt, unhappy at losing what we had come to consider a permanent home in New York for the fall and winter months. The unhappiness was tempered by the offer to play the Cocoanut Grove in the winter and spring and the Waldorf Astoria in the summer. Phil Harris's glowing exposition of what life would be like on the Coast also helped soften the blow.

He had certainly not given us a wrong steer about the glamorous setting in which we would be playing. For a bunch of young Canadians, it was heady stuff to mingle every night with the Hollywood stars, to be accepted as part of the movie colony's royalty.

Opening night at the Cocoanut Grove remains among the fondest memories of my life. I looked out at a panorama of the most recognizable faces in the world, the so-called stars of the silver screen. Immediately in front of the bandstand sat the powerful men who directed the fortunes of the Metro-Goldwyn-Mayer empire, Louis B. Mayer and Irving Thalberg among them.

The table to the right was occupied by Jean Harlow and a large party. To the left sat Marlene Dietrich and company. Both would take time out from dancing with escorts to reach up and shake the hand of a bandleader who had to wonder how he had arrived in such exalted company.

I doubt if I have ever seen so many photographers in one room, before or since. They gave me no time to relax during intermission. They ascended the bandstand bringing a parade of subjects to pose with me. I knew their faces from seeing them in movies: Joan Crawford, Carole Lombard, Jeanette MacDonald, Franchot Tone.

Home in Hollywood was a poolside bungalow on the sumptuous grounds of the Ambassador Hotel. I was thirty-one and still pinching myself on occasion to make sure all this was not happening in a dream. Emissaries from Louis B. Mayer and other studio magnates were constantly approaching the bandstand with messages that the Royal Canadians were wanted for the movies. Sorry, fellas, I could tell them, the band is booked solid for the next twelve months. Maybe next year.

And Clark Gable would dance by and wave. And Jeanette MacDonald, Nelson Eddy, Gene Raymond, Errol Flynn, Ronald Colman, Ginger Rogers, Loretta Young. Their smiles said they loved the band and here, in a make-believe setting during a time when the world was facing the reality of poverty, I was the richest of men.

Once again the feeling of well-being stood in the way of resolution to maintain the formula that had made us successful. Our major radio show was still the Robert Burns program, changed only in format by the location of our studio, three thousand miles from where we had started. Our ratings were still at the very top, and one of our few rivals in popularity was Fred Waring and his Pennsylvanians. Fred's band featured chorus and vocal groups.

Advertising men pay attention to trends. If Fred Waring could catch on with his chorus, why not increase Guy Lombardo's popularity by adding another dimension to his band. So reasoned John Reiber, president of the agency responsible for our program. He came out from New York to see me, positively rhapsodic about the idea. I was less escatic, we were number one, why change?

He was insistent and I vacillated; how could a few more singers hurt us? Maybe he was right about adding a dimension. So we added eight voices to the band, four male, four female. We must have auditioned half the singers in California. I found out what a mistake it was as soon as we returned from our first radio program with the new format. Waiting at the Cocoanut Grove was a stack of telegrams from radio editors around the country. They were hardly complimentary; they accused the Lombardos of going Hollywood.

Reiber prevailed upon me to try it for another week; people have to get accustomed to a new idea, he told me. For the second program, the new chorus replaced Carmen's solos and the trio's best numbers. There were even more telegrams waiting for us. The radio editors weren't objecting so much to the quality of the chorus; what bothered them was that our band was no longer Lombardo, it was synthetic Waring. The people who made up the Lombardo audience didn't tune in to hear Waring. They could get him another night in the week.

I called Reiber and asked him to come to the Grove. He arrived and couldn't find a place to sit; every table was occupied. I gathered my telegrams and motioned him to follow me to the control room.

I showed him the wires, saying, "John, every one of these important radio editors around the country is raising hell. This is Wednesday night and you look out there in the room and nobody's been able to get in for an hour; that's why we had to come in here for a place to sit. They love us here, John, and they loved us on radio before the damned choir. We're a dance band, John, and that's all we are. You want a dance band, you got us, the best. You want a choir, you get Waring. He's the best."

Reiber sighed. He had to make a gesture of surrender and he did it gracefully. He snatched at a telegram and wrote on the back of it: "To whom it may concern: Guy Lombardo is to continue playing his music as he has been all these years. We're perfectly happy with him and want him to stay with us." He signed it and took the next train to New York.

Fred Waring and I were to continue a public enemy routine for many years, much in the manner of Jack Benny and Fred Allen, Ben Bernie and Walter Winchell. We had been friends for years, but we got a kick out of insulting each other on the air.

I think it all started during the height of radio's domination of the entertainment industry, in the middle of the thirties, when hour-long variety shows like Eddie Cantor's and Rudy Vallee's were high points of the week in virtually every household, and when almost every name band in the country had its own program. Fred fired the first shot by referring to me on one of his shows as "old man Lombardo." I must have been thirty-five at the time.

I answered him on my own show by reminding him that I had heard him on radio in Detroit, "way back when his brother, Tom, was playing the musical saw." I remembered I had fallen off my mother's lap laughing.

Another time, Fred sounded believably angry when he accused me of pirating members of his band. He was referring to Bill Flannagan, a young blond guitar player whom we had hired to double as a vocalist.

I asked him on the air what he was complaining about. "He's got fifty musicians. Can't he spare one?"

The fact of the matter was that Bill had consulted Fred before leaving and received his blessing. We played the fake feud to the hilt. In the middle of a Waring show, Carm, Lebe, Victor, and I burst into his studio and carried him out, screaming in protest. It may all sound corny, now, but I think the fans of both our shows enjoyed the comedy.

I will have to admit that Waring had the last laugh many years later. He had actively campaigned for the election of Dwight Eisenhower in 1952 and been named chairman of the entertainment committee for the Inaugural Ball in Washington. Our band had been invited to play as we had before for all of Franklin Roosevelt's Inaugurals as well as for Harry Truman's. We were to appear in the National Armory, the largest of the five or six ballrooms at which guests would dance.

I received a call to get to the armory at six o'clock, three hours before we started working. It was explained that all the performers were to gather for a photo with the new President and his First Lady. It was the kind of picture most prized by everybody in show business; it would appear in Sunday rotogravure magazines, in *Life* and *Look*, a two-page color spread picking out America's favorite entertainers posing with Ike and Mamie.

I have always been a bug about punctuality and I arrived perhaps ten minutes early. I was recognized by a Secret Service man who had met me at previous Inaugurals and he said, "Good you came early, Mr. Lombardo, we've been marking out where the President and Mrs. Eisenhower are going to stand. See that chalk mark, well, you walk over there and stand about a foot away from it. That way you'll be standing near the President when the picture is taken."

It sounded nice. I walked over to the indicated spot in my white tie and tails, and soon the performers began trooping in, people like Walter Pidgeon, Greer Garson, Bob Hope, every one a household word. There must have been forty of them in a line and the President and Mamie walked through an aisle of Secret Service men and placed themselves beside me. The photographers lifted their cameras, and just before the flashbulbs began popping somebody wedged himself between the President and me, pushing me back.

It was Fred Waring, and when that big spread appeared in the media it showed him rubbing elbows with the President. If you looked hard, you might have caught part of my face behind Waring's shoulder.

Another Lombardo adversary was Rudy Vallee. He had preceded us to New York by about a year and had appeared on network radio before we did. He was a personality and a showman and so regarded himself, more so than as a bandleader. His megaphone helped build his reputation as a singer, and in 1928 he was being heard over WABC by wire from the Heigh-Ho Club on East Fifty-third Street. He had adopted a slow tempo for his band, which some music critics said he had copied from the Lombardos, who had been the only orchestra using that beat. Vallee always indignantly denied that, commenting that he'd been playing that way before the Royal Canadians had ever been heard of.

Be that as it may, Rudy's success did hasten our desire to get to

New York before other bands began adopting the same style. I first ran into him at the Pavillon Royal, where he also had been appearing. He showed up, very much the celebrity of the day, with a big entourage including publicity men and song pluggers. In the party was a beautiful girl, the daughter of an NBC executive. She sat next to Rudy, but he obviously wasn't paying much attention to her. He was busy reading next week's radio script.

I came over to the table and shook hands all around, and the girl asked if I would dance with her; she said she'd always wanted to dance to our band. We danced a number and came back to the table. Vallee was standing up. He was leaving. He turned and walked out, without saying good-by. The poor girl followed him out the door.

The next day I received a call from Rocco Vocco, a music publisher who was a mutual friend of Vallee's and mine. He was perturbed. "What did you do to Rudy?" he asked. "I called him to see if he'd be my guest at your opening night at the Roosevelt next fall and he turned me down. He said you weren't a friend of his. What happened? What did you do?"

I laughed. "I didn't do anything. He wasn't paying any attention to his girl and when she asked me to dance with her, I did. Tell him to come to the opening."

Vallee showed up for the opening and I smiled to myself when he introduced me to his beautiful dark-haired companion, Fay Webb, who would later become his wife. The first thing he said was, "She is not going to dance with you. I've already warned her about that." Rudy apparently considered himself the vagabond lover of one of the songs he made popular, but he certainly did not brook competition.

Neither did he mind approaching the competition when it came to finding him a bargain. Vallee had always been known for his parsimony and he never minded the reputation. A few years later when his variety program was among the most sucessful on radio, Lebe said to me one night he had run into Vallee, who had asked whether I would mind finding him a boat. By that time I had become known as somewhat of an authority on boats, having progressed from the twenty-four-foot runabout I had purchased my first summer in Long Beach to the fifty-five-foot houseboat I now owned.

I contacted Rudy at Manny Wolfe's restaurant and asked what he had in mind. He said he had seen a nineteen-foot Chris-Craft at the boat show, but thought it was a little expensive. He wondered if I knew anybody who might get him a better price. I called a friend of mine who sold boats and he said that what Rudy wanted cost about $1,150, that there wasn't much markup, but maybe he could save him $75.

I called Rudy with the information and he seemed shocked. "I didn't want a new boat. I was thinking about a used one." Could I look around and see if anything was available?

The captain of my houseboat was getting it ready for the season at City Island, which had a variety of boatyards and I asked him if he could fill Vallee's order. He spent almost a week at the task, finally locating in Larchmont just what Rudy seemed to want. It had red leather seats, was only a couple of years old, and the captain made an offer of $650, which was accepted. Rudy said he was delighted; he'd let me know shortly. That was the last time I heard from him on the matter.

An Eddie Cantor bout with the flu changed Rudy's mind. The comedian couldn't make it to his radio show and he asked Rudy to take over the hour as a last-minute replacement. The custom was that substitutes didn't get paid; they could either expect an exchange appearance on their own show or a handsome gift. When Eddie asked Rudy what he wanted, he said a boat. But with slightly different specifications. He wanted a twenty-four-foot Chris-Craft. Brand new, naturally.

If I never could quite deliver for Rudy Vallee, I had better luck with a bandleader named Jack Denny. Unfortunately his lack of appreciation boomeranged on his aspirations.

Jules Stein had added him to the MCA stable, and my brothers and I thought Denny's was one of best new bands we had heard since coming to New York. When we were asked by CBS executives to recommend the bands that would precede and follow our Saturday night remotes from the Roosevelt, I had no hesitancy in suggesting Denny, who was playing an engagement in Montreal.

Our Saturday night show was aired from 11 to 11:30. We arranged for Denny to follow us from 11:30 to midnight. Given that exposure and backing it up with fine musicianship, the Denny band soon began receiving impressive offers from all over. He selected the choicest plum of all to play at the opening of the Waldorf Roof in the summer of 1932. The hotel had been built the year before.

I was very happy for the young man until I heard from Walter Donaldson's music firm. You may remember that in the spring of '32, we had introduced Donaldson's "You're Driving Me Crazy," and it had become a big hit. Now, I was told, Jack Denny was complaining that he hadn't been offered the song first.

Shortly before his opening, Denny came to the Roosevelt with Jules Stein. I sat down with them and said to Jules, "See all those song pluggers sitting there in back of the room. They're a pain in the neck. If they didn't cut me in on their songs, I'd throw them the hell out of here."

Denny's ears perked up. So that's how Lombardo got all those songs! He announced he was going to try the same technique. He opened at the Waldorf with great fanfare and unlimited prospects. But the Waldorf patrons were no longer hearing the beautiful arrangements of tried and true songs that Denny had brought them from the Mont Royal in Montreal. Now they were getting the junk Jack Denny was accepting from every song plugger who promised him a percentage of the profits. He didn't finish out the summer.

It may have been a cruel thing I did; I never really expected that Denny would buy that ridiculous proposition whole, nor that it would almost end a promising career. I simply allowed myself the luxury of bowing to what I considered justifiable resentment. I wasn't big enough to forget that a man I had helped could complain that I was able to introduce a song before he did.

There were happier experiences. We were fortunate enough, for example, to help Lawrence Welk get his start in New York. This would occur after our two-year absence from the Roosevelt, when the New York Central finally went back to running a railroad and gave up trying to operate hotels. A new management took over the Roosevelt, and in 1935 we would return and play there continuously for almost thirty years more.

We had met Welk in Chicago a few years before. He had a successful band that toured the Midwest and was popular in cities like Pittsburgh and Cincinnati. He had just finished a Pittsburgh job, was off for a few days, and had come to Chicago expressly to meet us. He had an introduction from Phil Julius, the Irving Berlin song plugger.

He watched our band every night, and we were impressed by his technical knowledge and curiosity. The night he left, he asked Carmen if he could borrow a hundred dollars. Carm obliged and the money came back the next afternoon, special delivery. It puzzled Carm and he wondered about it to Phil Julius. "He must not have needed it very bad if he could get it back so quickly."

Julius laughed. "He's a funny guy. He wanted very much to know if you boys liked him. And that was his way of finding out."

We were able to open many doors for Welk, continuing to be impressed by how hard he worked to improve his band. And when we returned to the Roosevelt, the management had a favor to ask. They wanted us to recommend the bands that would replace us in the summer. The first summer we recommended Benny Goodman. The customers thought he played too loud. The next year we suggested Welk, and he did a creditable job, playing familiar, danceable tunes. Even then, Lawrence was beginning to perfect that style of introducing songs that was so different from ours.

He would introduce each song title with a brief story, each soloist the same way, and that style later would work for him on television, a medium he would conquer with a permanency attained by no other band. When he was playing the Roosevelt, however, he had to contend with the fact that this was the home of the Lombardo brothers and in the minds of the loyal patrons all other bands suffered by comparison.

We were instrumental, too, in launching Freddy Martin as a bandleader. Freddy was a saxophone salesman when we first met him in Cleveland, and after Carm heard him playing demonstration tunes he characteristically delivered an instinctive opinion. "You ought to be playing the sax with a band, not selling them."

It happened that Carm's opinion coincided with a decision we

A television show being taped live at the Lombardos' restaurant East Point House on Long Island. 1955. (*Photo by Jerry Saltsberg & Associates.*)

Standing: Kenny Gardner. Seated: Carmen, Victor, Guy, and Lebert. About 1947.

Guy's favorite photo of his wife, 1953. *(Photo by the Glickman Studios, Freeport, L.I.)*

Guy takes his last remaining boat, his mahogany cruiser *Tempo*, for a spin. He makes his Jones Beach entrance on this boat for the opening of the show. (*Photo by Barry Kramer.*)

Lauritz Melchior, Robert Moses, and Guy on the Jones Beach set of *Arabian Nights*, watching Mary Martin ride an elephant. *(Photo by Barry Kramer.)*

Guy, Robert Moses, and Mike Todd, Jr., discussing the forthcoming *Around the World in 80 Days*. Jones Beach. *(Photo by Barry Kramer.)*

Song of Norway at Jones Beach. *(Photo by Barry Kramer.)*

Guy and Richard Rodgers discuss the Rodgers and Hammerstein musical *South Pacific* before its production at the Jones Beach Marine Theater. *(Photo by Barry Kramer.)*

Guy is reunited with old friend Louis Armstrong, whom he hired to play in Jones Beach representation of *Mardi Gras*. He introduces him on stage. *(Photo by Barry Kramer.)*

Sonny Werblin, Guy's first band boy and first president of the New York Jets, with Guy and Milton R. Rackmil, then president of Decca. *(Photo by Barry Kramer.)*

Guy and Arthur Treacher, who provided comedy for *Paradise Island* at Jones Beach in 1962. *(Photo by Barry Kramer.)*

Fred Waring, an old rival, visits Guy and his musical director, the late Mitchell Ayres, at Jones Beach in 1965. *(Photo by Barry Kramer.)*

Xavier Cugat, and Abbe Lane visiting Guy at a Jones Beach show, choreographed by June Taylor, right. 1962. (*Photo by Barry Kramer.*)

The Schaefer Dance Tent at Jones Beach. (*Photo by Barry Kramer.*)

had just made to add a third sax to the band. So Martin became an immediate candidate for the job. Unfortunately, or fortunately as it worked out for the young man, we selected another candidate, Larry Owen. Freddy had no trouble getting a job with the Arnold Johnson orchestra, and we would meet him every once in a while. I suggested to him that he ought to form a band of his own, and one of his first appearances as a bandleader was at the Hotel Bossert in Brooklyn. From that start in 1931, he soon became a name around New York with a big band that included a talented, all-purpose musician named Russ Morgan.

Russ was equally adept at playing the trombone, the piano, and helping out with arrangements. He left Freddy to form a band of his own and by 1935 had developed a singing-trombone style that was uniquely his and immediately recognizable. We became fast friends. I don't think there was a bandleader around who liked the Royal Canadians more than he did, yet he never attempted to abandon his own style by borrowing from ours. He understood what we were doing as much as he recognized that he had his own identity.

Russ had a favorite number he would request us to play whenever he dropped in to hear us either at the Roosevelt or the Paramount Theater. He would stay for one chorus of "When the Organ Plays at Twilight," admiring the mighty Wurlitzer effect we accomplished with the baritone sax and flute. Then he would wave good-by and rush out.

All that made it easy for me when an advertising man, Milton Bioux, who had worked with us on the Robert Burns show, came into the Roosevelt one night with a big package in his pocket. He had just signed up the Philip Morris cigarette people for a prime-time radio show. It would be a band show and he had a list of names, including Russ Morgan's. Which would I choose? I didn't hesitate a second. Russ got the program.

The program made the Morgan name and style known from coast to coast. Equally well known became the midget wearing a bellhop uniform with his line that opened and closed the program: "Call for Phillip Maah-riss."

Among the fruits of the program was a $1,200 weekly salary for Morgan, a long engagement at Broadway's Latin Quarter, and the opportunity to further parlay his burgeoning career with a succession of hit records. He had joined the big names of the Big Band era.

A year later I was startled by a visit from Bioux, who came with the disconcerting news that Russ Morgan wanted to quit the radio show. He hadn't given any reason. Could I talk to him? If it was a matter of money, Bioux thought he could get the sponsor to come up with more.

I asked Russ to come to the Roosevelt and I could see he knew why. He seemed rather sheepish. "You want to know why I'm leaving, right? Well, to tell you the truth, I've gotten to hate the show."

Hate a show that had made him? I asked for an explanation.

"I know you'll think I'm nuts, but I can't stand the midget. I can't stand the look of him and I can't stand the sound of his voice. And I'll never know whether people tune in the show to hear him or us."

Russ Morgan had courage. He left the show to prove himself. He would never again have as large a radio audience as Philip Morris had provided for him, but he was too talented a musician and arranger to sink into oblivion. He took his band on one-night tours and played to capacity audiences. He continued to stay near the top of best-selling record producers among the Big Bands.

And "Music in the Morgan Manner" would outlive the era of the Big Bands.

It hardly seemed possible as the decade of the Depression neared an end that Big Bands would not go on forever. To the names of the bands that had started the trend in the twenties and early thirties now were added the new stars of the business—Benny Goodman, Tommy Dorsey, Glenn Miller. All three and Tommy's older brother, Jimmy, had been among the most sought-after sidemen in the twenties, playing for some of the best-known bands of the day.

Dorsey and Goodman had formed their own orchestras in 1934, when the demand for new bands was at a fever pitch. Prohibition had been repealed and speakeasies had been replaced by night clubs and beautiful dance pavilions such as the Glen Island Casino in Westchester and Frank Daley's Meadowbrook in New Jersey. Now that they could sell liquor, hotels which had been finding it difficult to support and in many cases underwrite top talent suddenly had an additional revenue that enabled them to do so.

The Dorsey brothers first big band would break up in 1935, Tommy and Jimmy going their own ways with new orchestras and finding the going tough until Tommy hit the big time in 1937 with a hit record, "I'm Getting Sentimental over You."

Goodman, meanwhile, also went through three difficult years before his talent was finally recognized. He had been our summer replacement at the Roosevelt, and the patrons had complained he played too loud, especially when the brass section cut loose. Similar complaints were heard from other hotels he played around the country. In Denver, he appeared at one of the city's two amusement parks and could not match the appeal of Kay Kyser, who was playing at the other one.

But Goodman was bringing a new style and beat into the business that appealed to many professional musicians. He was the innovator of the period and suddenly the country was talking about this new music called "swing" and Goodman was recognized as its king. Bands hurried to adopt the style as they had borrowed ours six years earlier. Some, like Tommy Dorsey, played a combination of swing and sweet. By 1937 both Goodman and Dorsey were joining us as the biggest names in the business and the Big Band era was enjoying a boom that compared to the stock market before the crash.

New bands began making names for themselves, many led by graduates of the Goodman and Dorsey organizations. Swing had brought in new dance steps and young people were flocking to hear the bands that played them. Among those who rose to the top in this boom of the final years of the thirties were Glenn Miller, who had played with the Dorsey brothers; Gene Krupa, Goodman's drummer; and Harry James, his trumpeter.

Through all the innovations of the period, through all the new dance crazes—the Lindy Hop, the Big Apple, Truckin',' and Peckin'—the Royal Canadians adapted to the tunes of the day but played them in our own style, which never varied. And we kept on our music list the standards that continued to keep us at the very top of the ratings in record sales, radio time, personal appearances, and theater engagements.

There were now estimated to be eight hundred bands in an industry doing a reported billion-dollar-a-year business. The Lombardo brothers built homes on Long Island and looked forward to remaining on top of an industry they had helped build.

7. The Family Moves Closer

Those early Papa precepts we learned in London may not have been as important as the last one he laid down when we were struggling for a permanent job in the States. "Families should be together at Christmas," he had roared into the phone, half tearful and half furious. In a small town in Ohio, away from the family for the first time, we had agreed with him and pledged we would never be apart again.

But it finally took a tragedy to persuade Papa to move closer to his sons in the band. In 1934, the four of us and our wives were permanently ensconced in New York apartments. But we were on the road much of the time and there were few occasions that we could see the rest of the family other than Christmas.

Lebe's wife, Carol, had been ill for several months when we were getting ready to leave for California for our second engagement at the Cocoanut Grove. She hated the idea of being alone and decided to make the trip with us. A few weeks later she died. The news hit Mama and Papa hard. Perhaps if they had lived closer to New York they might have stayed with Carol and been able to comfort her. This way, they couldn't even get to California in time for the funeral.

They came to New York after our return, expressing this feeling, and opened the way to what I had been considering for a long time. The only reason I hadn't brought it up before was that I was sure Papa wouldn't buy it. He was in semiretirement now and spending much of his time on that farm we had purchased for him outside London. Where as a younger man he had engrossed himself in racing trotting horses and speedboats with his friends, now he had become a gentleman farmer. He loved to garden and to tend his cows. I could never see him leaving all those friends he had made in London or the bucolic pleasures he enjoyed on the farm.

I wondered if he and Mama wouldn't consider moving to a green area somewhere within driving distance of New York. He could still indulge his gardening hobby and it would mean that his sons could visit every Sunday that we were in town. Mama voted for the move; Papa went along with some trepidation, bowing only to the proposition that the family would all be together again.

We were able to find a twenty-acre estate in Stamford, Connecticut. On it was a fine house with twenty-two rooms, more than enough to accommodate Papa, Mama, Elaine, Joseph, and Rose Marie with room left over for visiting sons and their wives. One of the advantages of earning big money in the Depression was the wherewithal to purchase property at a fraction of its value, and my brothers and I were not hard pressed to make the deal.

The move from London to Stamford might be compared to the great journeys of history and probably most specifically to that of Noah's Ark. The caravan consisted of three vehicles, a large new car into which Papa had piled Mama, Elaine, Joseph, Rose Marie, a great Dane named Florrie, and a cat named Tabby. The car pulled a trailer with a solitary occupant, Papa's favorite cow, Elsie. Bringing up the rear was the biggest moving van they could find in Canada, commodious enough to house thirty-five years of accumulated furniture and twenty tons of Canadian hay for Elsie. We could not convince Papa that Elsie would find Connecticut hay equally digestible.

The first problem arose at the border. All passengers, including the animal emigrants, were acceptable, except that Elsie needed papers. Papa remembered they had come with the bill of sale; what he could not remember was what he had done with them. The decision was to go back to London to scour the vacant old house. So car and trailer turned around and went back to the Canadian side. Here the border functionaries came up with a more serious obstacle. Elsie could not be readmitted into Canada under a law excluding bovines from bringing in possible disease from south of the border.

So Papa went back and explained his problem, which fell on the deaf ears of bureaucracy. Back and forth he crossed the toll bridge separating the borders, so many times that the toll collectors finally allowed him to pass through without paying. Elaine ended up the heroine of the saga. She remembered suddenly where Elsie's papers were—in an antique desk in the moving van.

The driver of the van had been waiting at the side of the road until the resolution of this moving Ping-Pong game, and he and his men began removing furniture on the highway until they found the desk. Elsie's papers lay inside and thus did the Family Lombardo and menagerie finally migrate to the United States.

The rest of us were to locate on Long Island, and that involved a series of events, too. We had first become acquainted with the area, of course, when we played the summer engagement at the Pavillon Royal in Valley Stream. We had rented apartments near the ocean and I had purchased a runabout, which gave way the next year to a thirty-four-foot cabin cruiser and finally in 1933 to a veritable yacht, fifty-five feet long, with enough sleeping accommodations to convert it into a houseboat.

Again, the Depression enabled me to acquire a treasure I would otherwise have been unable to afford. We had enjoyed those boating summers on Long Island so much that Lilliebell came up with the idea of a houseboat. Why not just spend our summer vacations on the boat?

While the band was on tour in that bank-holiday spring of 1933, Lilliebell went boat shopping. I wanted one big enough to accommodate overnight guests and fitted with enough accouterments so that city-oriented friends would enjoy both day and moonlight cruises. I told Lilliebell to look for something in the $10,000 price range.

She found what we both wanted in a City Island boatyard. A fifty-five-foot cruiser, it had been custom built by one of the world's best-known shipbuilders for a wealthy family in 1929. Fashioned out of the finest mahogany and with decks of teak, the boat was powered by customized twin engines. The bow contained quarters for a captain and steward, and aft was a fully equipped galley, followed by a stateroom and a large dining salon. In the stern, under a raised deck, was the master stateroom. The boat had sleeping accommodations for six, besides the crew. Two could live on it in luxury.

The shipbuilder's price had been $55,000, perhaps a fifth of what it could be reproduced for today. And the family that had purchased it, shortly before the crash, no longer had the means to maintain it. Now it had lain in the shipyard, almost new for three years, and the price had come down to $13,000. Lilliebell told me about her find over the phone one night. Now that she had seen it, she said, she couldn't live without it. I told her to buy the boat.

She offered $11,000 and it was accepted immediately. When I got home for the summer, I had a yacht. I hired a captain and a steward for $200 a month and set about choosing a name for our summer home on the water. *Tempo* seemed a natural, and every boat I would own in the future would be similarly named, including those I would later drive in speedboating competition.

Lilliebell and brother Joe went to work on décor, and on a Sunday in July the boat had been fitted out in such sumptuous style that I did not hesitate to invite a large party of songwriters and bandleaders to accompany us on our maiden voyage. I decided to head for Point Lookout, on Long Island, where we had spent previous summers. The captain responded yes sir and we were off.

We set sail from the Columbia Yacht Club, close by our Riverside Drive apartment, and enjoyed the majestic view of the Hudson River and New York Harbor. The river was serene, but as we turned east into the open sea of the Atlantic the climate changed from serene to chaotic. We were engulfed suddenly by whitecapped waves accompanied by a strong wind. Our beautiful boat began bobbing up and down like a piece of stray wood. My landlubbing friends began turning green.

Dishes and glasses were breaking in the galley and a large bowl of fruit fell off the dining-salon table. Broken glass was underfoot and one of the passengers fell headlong into the galley and onto the debris. He emerged shaken and bleeding.

I made my way up to the bridge, where the captain was fighting the wheel for dear life. I hadn't realized when I gave him the sailing orders that it was the captain's duty to proceed, even if he had advance knowledge that the conditions in the ocean were not exactly comfortable for a cabin cruiser. From that time on, I would always consult the captain before setting a destination.

Eventually, I would learn that it made more sense to simply dock the boat in Freeport and cruise around the calmer inlets, canals, and bays, venturing out for ocean-fishing only when the captain had optimistic weather information.

The following year we were booked for the months of July and August at the Waldorf, and Lilliebell and I drove out most Sundays to spend the night on the boat. Often we left after our last Waldorf number and enjoyed our new acquisition until late Monday afternoon, in time for me to get back to the job. Many times we went out almost every day in the week.

Our favorite stopping point was a small restaurant called Otto's on the Woodcleft Canal. Otto served steamed clams and seafood dishes to my taste and I would often bring out friends like Phil Harris and Freddy Martin, Harry Link and Sammy Stept. The difficulty was in maintaining one's sense of privacy, a commodity few of us who were big names in the business were able to enjoy.

I have always attempted to be gracious, to fill requests for autographs during band breaks. I never learned to turn down a request, even after we would come out of the restaurant and find a number of uninvited guests on the *Tempo*. Many had rowed over to greet us and the luxury of simply sitting down with friends on the boat for a drink was almost unattainable. We would have to be out in the open water before we were alone.

One day, I noticed that across the canal from Otto's was a good-size piece of vacant property. I asked him who owned it and he said a Mr. Randall, who was a descendant of a pioneer Freeport family and who had done much to develop its waterfront.

Otto called Randall, who came to the restaurant. He asked how much of the property I was interested in and I ventured about a hundred feet. How much did he want for it. He said, "Oh, about $1,800. Is that too much?" I gave him a check and in a few weeks had the deed to the property.

I had purchased the piece of land simply to have a place to tie the boat. People don't venture onto private property as they do a public dock like the one at Otto's. Now I learned the property was useless unless I bulkheaded it. Between the land and the water was a strip of muddy marsh. How would you get off the boat? Otto put me next to a bulkhead builder down the street and I asked how much it would cost for one hundred feet. That would be $1,800, which was what I paid for the property.

The bulkheading did not mean I had solved the mud problem. That strip of mud and water still separated the boat and bulkheading from firm land. What do I do now? I asked the bulkhead man. He said, "You have to fill it in. Dump fill on the little piece of marsh." I was not at all surprised that this new job had a familiar price tag—$1,800.

The next year, I got another brilliant idea. Now that I had a place to tie my boat and a piece of solid ground on which to descend, I could begin cutting down expenses on the operation of the boat. We had a new radio program sponsored by Standard Oil of New Jersey, and I had been told by a company executive that if I wanted gas wholesale all I had to do was install a gas pump on whatever property I owned. He was probably thinking about saving me money on running a car. But boats consume a lot more gas than cars do and the only property I owned was meant for nautical pleasure. I was rather proud of myself when I installed the gas pump in Freeport and saved about five cents a gallon, which seemed to justify the $5,400 I had already laid out for the privilege of a private dock.

I don't know how much money I really saved on that gas pump. We were never sparing of fuel. In the ensuing summers we continued to play the Waldorf but took off the month of August. Now we really made a houseboat out of that yacht. If we felt like taking a trip to Montauk or to the Jersey coast, we just took off with guests.

But every year, there was another improvement to be made on our Freeport property. First we landscaped, installing hedges, trees, flowering bushes. Then we fenced in the front and built a driveway to park the car. Finally we decided that we would no longer take a chance on bad weather, when we had to lay tied at the dock, the boat bobbing on the usually calm canal, making sleep uncomfortable. In 1939, we began to build a house.

It was only going to be a cottage of two rooms or so and a garage with a cot for the captain. We brought in Joe Lombardo, our family designer-architect. When Joe was finished with his pencil, the thirty-by-thirty living room was bigger than the entire house I had anticipated. The dining room, separated by steps from the sunken living room, was almost as big. The kitchen was as large as some I had seen in hotels. The master bedroom was the size of a suite. The house was built on cement columns with an open veranda running around it and a boat slip underneath. I had to go out and purchase another sixty feet of Mr. Randall's property, which cost more than the original hundred.

Small houses were appearing on both sides of South Grove Street, and Lilliebell decided we had better protect our property. So I purchased one hundred feet more, next door, all of which had to be bulkheaded and filled in. For further protection, we purchased two corners across the street.

The home in which we still live thirty-five years later was finished in 1940, about twelve months before Pearl Harbor. With the outbreak of war, gas was sharply curtailed for boat use and the standing joke around the band for a long time would be: "Does anybody want to buy a used gas pump?"

My brothers made Long Island their home, too. Carmen and Florence built a beautiful place with a swimming pool in Woodmere, a few miles away. Lebe had remarried after the tragic loss of his first wife. He had courted a beautiful Pennsylvania oil heiress, Helen Healy, and they were wed in an impressive ceremony in St. Patrick's Cathedral. Now he was the proudest father you could ever meet, carrying entire albums of his four children, a daughter and three sons. He moved the family to Manhasset, on the island's North Shore.

The first of my brothers to present Mama and Papa with grandchildren, however, was Victor. When he came to the band at nineteen in that spring of 1930, a pretty blond girl, Virginia Dabe, who came frequently to the Roosevelt, asked me. "Hey, Guy, who's that new sax player." They were to meet and marry not long after and have two husky sons, Guy Victor and David Carmen. Vic, Ginny, and sons settled in a beachside home on Oak Beach, not far from Jones Beach. Now, by 1941, all of us were in our own homes near each other and Papa and Mama were in Connecticut, little more than an hour away.

8. Carmen—The Reluctant Vocalist

With all the relocation that was going on, I had hardly noticed that Carm was beginning to show visible signs of unhappiness. I guess I just couldn't get myself to believe it. After all we were floating around on top of our profession and Carm's career as a songwriter was providing him with an income almost equal to his share of the band's earnings.

They were considerable during that period when the new bands that had come along were giving rise to what was being called the Big Band era. Goodman, the Dorseys, Glenn Miller, and Harry James were star attractions now, and prices for the big names of the industry were skyrocketing. Our band continued to be among the most wanted and we commanded among the highest fees for appearing on radio or in theaters, for playing dance music in hotel rooms, and for concert engagements.

By now all the bands had become almost as celebrated for their vocalists as for the uniqueness of their style and their high quality of musicianship. Frank Sinatra and the Pied Pipers sang for Tommy Dorsey; Perry Como was with Ted Weems; Tex Beneke with Glenn Miller; the Lane Sisters (Priscilla, Rosemary, and Lola) with Fred Waring; Ray Eberle and Helen O'Connell with Jimmy Dorsey; Helen Forrest with Benny Goodman; Doris Day with Les Brown; Dinah Shore with Xavier Cugat; and Betty Hutton with Vincent Lopez.

And with the Royal Canadians, it was Carmen Lombardo,

soloist and member of the Lombardo trio, along with Derf Higman and Larry Owen. He was our first and only soloist, as
identifiable for the band with his singing as with his sax, clarinet,
and flute. He had never relished that one duty among all the
others he assumed for the band—its musical director, leader of the
sax section, orchestra leader when I had to step off the bandstand.
He played the clarinet solos and the flute obbligatos and he shared
the responsibility with me of choosing the songs we played.

With all that Carm had to know the lyrics to hundreds of songs
in our library and constantly learn the new ones. And with a
limited vocal range, he would have to attempt a Cole Porter tune
like "Night and Day" with a range of an octave and a half to
country-type songs and novelties. He didn't like the job but he
rarely complained about it because he knew as well as I that his
singing was among the band's most valuable trademarks. If he
didn't consider that his vocal efforts were as distinguished as some
of the rising new singers, our loyal patrons appeared to be less discriminating. Singer Carmen Lombardo meant as much to his
band as Frank Sinatra did to Tommy Dorsey.

But it was becoming more than just an odious chore that had to
be borne for the sake of the band. Carm was beginning to hate
the very thought of singing. One reason, perhaps, was his constant
striving for perfection in every aspect of the business. Carm felt he
was simply not as good a singer as most of the names that were
coming into prominence in the late thirties. And suddenly there
began appearing comedians who could get a laugh by doing a Carmen Lombardo impersonation.

Some of them mocked the style, the tremolo that made his
notes quiver, and the precise diction our mother had taught him.
A blind pianist, Alec Templeton, whose music Carm admired, did
a devastating imitation, probably the one that hurt him the most
because it came from somebody he respected. The name Carmen
Lombardo was mentioned on every Fred Allen program as a kind
of running gag.

What I didn't realize was how much all of this was getting to
Carm, who had always appreciated comedy and jokes. I kept
telling him this was wonderful, bringing out the weary cliché about
imitation being the sincerest form of flattery. All the other guys in

the band pressed the same well-meant advice. Carm simmered and burned and continued to hurt silently.

Derf Higman and Larry Owen knew better than I did how much of an effort it was getting to be for Carm to simply stand up to the mike and sing. When they appeared with him as the trio, they could feel him shaking violently and Derf would press close to him on one side and Larry on the other, literally holding him up with physical and moral support.

Carm would later remember, although he never told me at the time, how excruciating the singing chores had become. "What got me worse than anything else," he would say, "was the lights. The worst time of all was when we played a theater. I'd have to step up to the mike to take a solo and those damn lights would hit me square in the eyes, like a guy getting the third degree. You're blind under those lights. You can't see a thing. I felt self-conscious. I began doing little nervous things like fixing my tie. It got worse and worse. One night during a Lady Esther broadcast from a theater, I stepped up to the mike, those lights hit me, and oh my God I still tremble at the memory. I opened my mouth and not a sound came out. Then I was really scared. I did force myself to get through the number somehow but that was my Waterloo. I knew I couldn't keep singing for long."

Carm wouldn't come right out and say he'd like to abandon the solos altogether. He started suggesting we ought to try a new vocalist. It finally dawned on me that my brother would be happy if we could find somebody our audience would accept as his replacement. We made one such attempt in 1938, when I approached Buddy Clark, one of the better-known singers of the day, who had made it on his own without a big band behind him. He eagerly accepted the offer to sing on our Sunday afternoon radio program, sponsored by Bond Bread.

We broadcast the show in the Broadway theater Ed Sullivan later used for his long-running variety program on television. Every week CBS got so many requests for seats from people who wanted to see the program live that we had to play two shows, the rehearsal and one that would be broadcast.

We put Buddy Clark on without fanfare or prior announcement. He simply walked up to the mike and sang, beau-

tifully and professionally, and I could see my brother Carm listening almost in rapture. His expression seemed to say, "Thank God
we've found our man. They don't need me to sing anymore."

He was wrong. When I got back to the Riverside Drive apartment, the sponsor was on the phone. "Who was that singer?" he
asked. I told him and he said, "Look, Guy, we didn't buy Buddy
Clark, we bought Carmen Lombardo."

In one respect I was relieved that the sponsor didn't go for
Buddy Clark. As good as he was, he somehow didn't match the
band. Without Carmen, the vocal solos simply did not sound like
Lombardo. For the next two years, Carm forced himself to sing,
torturing himself as the impersonators grew in number and often
in maliciousness. I simply could not convince him that other well-
known singers like Rudy Vallee and Bing Crosby also had their
share of imitators and that it was one of the penalties of massive
exposure.

But I was also becoming aware that the longer the situation
lasted, the longer my brother would endure very real pain. I made
up my mind that we would get a new singer as soon as we could
find one who blended into our style, who, like Carmen, not only
rendered a song but understood the lyrics to it and how to deliver
its meaning. Carm just didn't mouth words; he sang an entire
story and many vocalists followed that style and learned from it.

Slowly we began to cut down on his solos. He still sang with the
trio but we were in the process of phasing him out. There were
repercussions. The mail from radio listeners came by the sackful,
demanding more Carmen Lombardo numbers, not less. Once at a
theater, when he failed to do a single solo, irate customers asked
for their money back.

My sister Elaine finally came up with the prescription for the
anguish of Carmen Lombardo and his millions of fans. Living
with the folks in Stamford, now, she worked in our office at the
Brill Building, handling the business affairs of our new music
publishing firm. One day in 1940, she had just arrived home and
was about to turn off her car ignition when she heard on the radio
a voice singing "Am I Blue?"

Elaine, of course, had grown up with the band from the beginning, knew every aspect of the business, and had been in contact

with countless musicians and vocalists. No voice had stirred her like the one she was now hearing. She sat in the driveway until she found out to whom it belonged, a young man named Kenny Gardner, who had recently arrived from California and had been given his own fifteen-minute sustaining program.

The following Sunday, all of us were spending the day with Mama and Papa and Elaine turned on the table radio in the kitchen. There was that voice again. She came running out to the living room and got me to the kitchen to hear her find, just as he was signing off. I heard enough to want more. The next day, without telling Elaine, I called the radio station and asked them to send over a sample recording of a Kenny Gardner number. Carm and Lebe listened with me and I said to them, "He's for me. What do you think?" They both nodded.

Several days later, I made Elaine Lombardo a very happy girl. I called her and asked if she'd ever heard of a singer named Kenny Gardner. "For crying out loud, Guy," she said, "what happened to your memory? That's the singer I was trying to tell you about."

I had the last laugh. "I just hired him," I told her.

Kenny was sandy-haired, had a puckish expression, and a sweet baritone voice to match his way with a song. His tonal quality fitted the band's sound, and although it took a year or so before our fans could get used to hearing the Royal Canadians without Carmen Lombardo singing, they finally accepted Kenny and he has remained a Lombardo fixture since.

We did lose him to the war for a while. He and Elaine fell in love and they were married after his induction into the Army as a lieutenant in the U. S. Rangers. Shortly after, he went overseas with the 71st Division, fought his way across Europe, and was in Austria when his division met the Russians just west of Vienna. He returned home a major and rejoined the band.

So our problem in finding a singer for the duration of the war was not yet solved and again we turned to the family for a solution. The youngest Lombardo, Rose Marie, was sixteen in 1941, and we were all thrilled by the lovely contralto she displayed for us at the Sunday family gatherings. On a Saturday night in November, just two weeks before Pearl Harbor, she made her radio debut on our Colgate Toothpaste Hour.

The week before the debut was an exciting time for my young sister. I suppose it was a little wearing, too, because there were so many members of the family around to prepare her for the momentous occasion. Elaine took her around the New York department stores, looking for a debut gown, settling at last for one with a sweet-sixteen look that four Lombardo brothers had to examine before giving final approval. We were less than unanimous in deciding a hair style, almost coming to blows. I think I opted for long hair, Carm for short, Lebe for up, and Vic for down.

Rose Marie did not permit the fuss and bother to affect her premiere. The critics loved her performance and it was no end of enjoyment for me to be able to announce, "And now introducing the newest Lombardo, here is Rose Marie singing . . ."

The fifth Lombardo in the band served her apprenticeship through a period that was almost as physically difficult as our first itinerary through the Midwest with Corinne Arbuckle. These were war years and we no longer could take our private bus across the country or expect to find first-class accommodations waiting for us in overcrowded hotels.

Even getting across country by train was a new adventure each time. Every railroad car was packed beyond capacity with servicemen, and we could hardly complain about having to carry the band's instruments onto the train, find room to put them someplace, and make sure they were there when we disembarked.

Once we were on a car hooked onto the back of a seemingly endless troop train. When we pulled into the station, the car was several hundred yards from the platform. Rose Marie showed us she had become as accustomed to the rigors of a trouper's life as the rest of the band. Uncomplainingly, she leaped off the last step, suitcase in one hand, a plastic bag heaped with evening gowns thrown over her back, and hiked in her high heels over the rough terrain of the roadbed.

Rose Marie began singing with the band at a time when female vocalists were becoming as well known as their male counterparts. We had resisted putting a pretty girl up front as most of the bands were doing, because such a move did not seem to match our identity. But with Carmen's singing days over and with Kenny

Gardner trading his mike for a bayonet, there was a spot open for another member of the family who happened to be feminine.

Rose Marie would never reach the heights attained by such former band singers as Dinah Shore, Ella Fitzgerald, or Peggy Lee, but she would fill a big void in the band throughout the war years and she would enhance our reputation as a family. Meanwhile, she would also cause my brothers and me some concern as to whether we were really equipped to chaperone a sixteen-year-old girl on the road.

She would remember later: "When I joined the band, I really expected I was entering a life of glamour. It was exciting, of course, singing with the number-one band in the country, having people come up to the bandstand with compliments, and seeing your picture in the paper. We would stay in New York for perhaps half a year and then take off on the road, which wasn't glamorous at all. All my brothers made sure they knew where I was every moment and I guess a teen-ager would finally learn that there was nothing glamorous about traveling in crowded trains, living in hotel rooms, and then going to work."

We were on a one-night date in New Bedford, Massachusetts, the night Rose Marie met a handsome young lieutenant, assigned to the amphibian forces of the Army. His name was Hank Becker and Rose Marie was smitten at first sight. For the next two years they corresponded, meeting once or twice when we played the Roosevelt, and I could see that my pretty little sister was becoming more interested in marriage than in her career.

I thought she was much too young and told her several times she ought to wait until at least after the war was over. I was old enough to be my sister's father and I hoped she would take the advice as if it were coming from Papa himself. But Rose Marie, perhaps because of all the mothering and fathering of four brothers, wanted to assert her independence. She and Hank Becker eloped to New Orleans in 1943.

She returned to the band after the honeymoon and we welcomed back the newlyweds happily. Rose Marie would remain with us for another five years until she decided that her career as a band singer was simply not conducive to a happy marriage. Ironically, she would divorce Becker a few years later and marry Sidney

Rogers, an affable hotel man, with whom she would operate an inn in Westhampton Beach, Long Island, and raise three children. The Rogers family now lives in Toledo, where Sid manages an exclusive club.

The personnel of the band was undergoing other changes as we entered the forties. The man I most hated to see leave was my friend Larry Owen, the young bandleader who had encouraged us and helped find a permanent job for us in Cleveland. Two years later he had joined the band as third sax and arranger and proved to be our most valuable acquisition to the original crew from London. Larry had helped form the original Lombardo trio, which consisted of Carm, Derf Higman, and himself.

It had taken another of life's ironies to remove Larry from the organization. He had taken his first drink the night it was offered to him by Eddie Mashurette, our original tuba player and one of the best customers of the Cleveland bootlegger who supplied spirits for most of the bands in the city. Larry's first drink gave him the courage to stand up and lead his own orchestra that night, but he never really liked the taste of alcohol.

It may be recalled that Eddie Mashurette had been an early casualty in Cleveland, forced to leave the band because he had developed a drinking problem. And now in 1939, Larry Owen, one of the most sober and industrious members of the organization, also found himself confronted by alcoholism. He was having trouble with his first wife and he began looking for an escape in the contents of a bottle. It soon became apparent, not only to us but to himself, that he would have to leave unless he conquered the habit. I was to fight back tears the night he said good-by.

Through the war, I never could find a third sax to make us as happy as we had been with Larry. Shortly after the end of hostilities we finally found what we had been looking for. He was Cliff Grass, tall, taciturn, and talented and possessing a way with novelty numbers. He became the new member of the singing trio, which now included Derf Higman and Kenny Gardner. Carmen still made occasional appearances with the trio for old favorites like "Boo Hoo," and Cliff became known for his rendition of "The Chicken Song," in which the hen tells the rooster, "I ain't gonna take it setting down . . ."

And the Larry Owen story would have a happy ending, too. He had divorced his wife, joined Alcoholics Anonymous, and traveled to the Coast, where he played and arranged for a number of bands, including Jan Garber, an old rival.

I called him one day in 1947 and told him how happy the news had made me that he was on the wagon and working again. I also mentioned there was a job with the band anytime he wanted it. Larry did not have to agonize about rejoining his old friends. He accepted the offer. He would later tell me that the chance to rejoin the band was the most important thing that ever happened to him, even more so than being picked over Freddy Martin the first time.

"What they teach you in AA," he said, "is never turn down an opportunity to return to old friends you gave up because of the drinking problem. When you can prove to them that they can depend on you again, you have won the battle."

He proved it, of course. He has never taken a drink in the remaining years and he is still our band manager and chief arranger. And he is happily married now.

We survived the war without Larry's arrangements because we had added another arranger shortly before he left us. It was during a period that there were so many demands for new material that one man could hardly supply all the numbers the Lombardo band would have to play on an ever-increasing number of broadcasts, recording sessions, and theater appearances.

Listening to a late-night radio program, I was struck by the beautifully melodic arrangement of a popular song. I called the station the next day to learn that the arrangement had been handled by a man named Dewey Bergman, and I lost no time asking him to join our organization. Dewey wasn't sure he wanted to. He considered himself a modernist in music, was interested in composing, and most of his work had been with large orchestras that featured big string sections. He felt the last thing he wanted to do was work with a dance band.

We had a long talk and I guess Dewey was impressed by the sincerity of what the Lombardo brothers were trying to do in music. He would remain with the band, even after Larry Owen came back, and he still free-lances for us today.

In *The Sweetest Music This Side of Heaven,* a book written by Booton Herndon in 1964, Dewey Bergman, the modernist, would explain to the author that he never had to compromise his own ideas about music when he came to work for the Royal Canadians.

". . . Their music isn't really as old hat as some of the critics say. Progressive jazz, today, for example, uses a lot of vibrato, just like the Lombardos. And one of the most popular swing bandleaders of all time was Glenn Miller. I used to see him in the Roosevelt every Monday night, sitting quietly at a table, studying Lombardo. He made use of the Lombardo tempos in his own orchestra."

We were making other changes, constantly on the lookout for techniques to meet the new trends in musical tastes. The Lombardo sound would remain the band's keystone, but we were always prepared to give the public the popular dance music of the day. We had played ragtime as kids, the Charleston in the twenties, the jazz that Paul Whiteman popularized, the fox trots and waltzes of the ballrooms. Now we were adding jitterbug numbers as we would later the various phases of the Latin dance craze.

It meant experimentation. For instance, we were the first dance band to popularize twin pianos. Freddie Kreitzer had been our original pianist and he became part of a duo when by coincidence we added a fellow townsman from London. His name was Hugo D'Ippolito, and his father had taught Carmen how to play the flute. Hugo had yearned to be a member of the Lombardo band, but we had never been able to accommodate him until I got the idea of adding a more intricate piano sound. Hugo provided the intricate chords to supplement steady Freddie's standard band piano. The twin piano sound would become as identifying with the Lombardo band as our brass section.

Before that, there had been an addition to the already distinctive sound of the saxophones handled by Carm, Vic, Derf, and Larry. I had become enamored of the even sweeter tone of the soprano sax and purchased three of the little instruments, which resemble the straight configurations of a clarinet. Carm, Derf, and Larry each grabbed one and set out to play an impromptu concert.

They sounded awful, giving up finally in disgust, unanimous in an opinion that you can't teach an old dog new tricks.

Vic had watched the experiment and noticed something that had escaped the older men. The tiny sax was obviously a soft and sensitive instrument that had to be babied. You couldn't approach it as Carm did his regular sax with the hard reed, utilizing the tremendous wind power from his barrel chest. Vic picked up one of the soprano saxes and began testing it. It wasn't long before he found the key to its mystery. Soon he had become one of the most accomplished soprano saxophonists in the country, our soloist on the instrument and featured on many records.

Most bands had added depth to their brass sections, some using as many as four trumpets and four trombones. Ours numbered only two, Lebe on trumpet, and Jim Dillon on trombone. I knew we needed a little more volume, but I wasn't willing to quadruple the section for fear the band's sound would become strident and lose the softness associated with the Lombardo music.

I had heard of a well-known musician named Dudley Fosdick, who had designed an oversized trumpet that sounded like a mellophone. I wondered if that wouldn't be the answer to our problem, and I think it was Lebe who suggested there might be another one like it around somewhere. Instead of instituting a search, I decided to make an effort to get Dudley Fosdick himself.

We were playing a Chicago date, and Dudley was with a band in New York when I called to ask if he'd be interested in joining us. I asked if he could come out to discuss the possibility on his night off and he agreed. He arrived without his mellophone, concerned that his leader might become suspicious if he took it along with him. But he brought a picture of the instrument and we passed it around, inspecting it carefully. With or without his instrument, I wanted Dudley Fosdick and he became the newest member of the band, the best mellophone (or as he called it Fossophone) player in the world. We had another dimension to add to our identity.

The war brought no diminution to the demand for the big bands. We traveled, as did the others, the length of the country, appearing on bond shows, in defense plants, at military camps. Although Kenny Gardner had been taken from us to serve in the fighting forces, most of the band's personnel were exempted because of age or marital status.

I think the period shortly after Kenny came home, with the war over and the band in such demand that our dates were scheduled more than a year in advance, would prove to be the happiest in my life. I had somehow even found time to push a speedboating hobby into a position as a national champion, but even that was not the major reason for being so content with my good fortune.

I now not only had a home, my mother and father close by, my brothers living within a few miles of each other in their own houses, but an entire Lombardo entourage to take into the theaters and radio studios and hotel ballrooms. It was almost as if I were back in London, traveling the dusty lanes of Ontario with Papa and Elaine filling out the Lombardo troupe. Now I could stand on the bandstand and introduce Carmen playing one of his own songs or singing it with the trio; my brother Lebert doing a trumpet solo; my brother Victor on the sweet soprano sax; my sister Rose Marie, the beautiful coloratura singing a love song; and the newest member of our family, our own answer to Frank Sinatra and Perry Como and Ray Eberle, my sister Elaine's husband, Kenny Gardner.

Papa had taught well the lesson of family and nobody had benefited from it more than Guy Lombardo.

This euphoric state lasted only one year. It ended with a decision by Vic, the youngest Lombardo brother in the band, the only one who was not a partner in its management and in the sharing of its profits. Vic had come along too late to achieve that position. He was a small boy when Carm, Lebe, and I had formed our three-way partnership just prior to embarking for the States. He had shared neither the hardships nor tribulations that accompanied us on our way to success.

When he arrived in New York at nineteen, he had to first prove that he was good enough to play with the band, brother or not. That he did and naturally we were delighted. But my brothers and I felt that making him a partner in a going organization he hadn't helped build was not quite fair. Perhaps we resisted the move, also, because Vic had still to prove to us that he could handle the added responsibilities of becoming part of the band's management team. And he had come to us with a background of spending, of borrowing, of hocking instruments and clothing.

From the standpoint of his musicianship, we had never regretted the decision to add Vic to the crew. He made many valuable contributions, his soprano sax becoming as well known in its own way as Carm's sax and clarinet and Lebe's trumpet.

By the end of the war, Vic had a growing family. One day in 1946, he asked me for a raise and I turned him down; he said he'd quit and I didn't discourage him.

Vic stormed out and returned the next day, saying he would stay on only until we could find a man to replace him. He continued playing with us while we were auditioning for the replacement, and in the meantime began looking around for the nucleus of a band he announced he was starting on his own. He had consulted with his wife, Ginny, and they had decided to take the plunge. He would make it on his own.

We wished him well and Carm and Lebe would bring back reports about the preparations he was making for his new career as a bandleader. He had rented an office and was listening to about forty men a day, carefully selecting his personnel. He was offering top salaries and paying an arranger to work around the clock putting together orchestral arrangements at $125 apiece. Vic had sold his house to finance the new orchestra and now he was facing two important decisions. The first was the kind of music he would play, in what style and sound. He had learned one important element from his brothers about the formula for success in the band business, and that was to play music in a manner that would make it immediately identifiable with the band.

Vic's forte was the soprano sax and he had mastered the technique of playing it with such virtuosity that he could get haunting, sweet strains out of the instrument to a degree unmatched by others. His arranger wrote in a part for the soprano sax in many of the new band's numbers, making for unique instrumentation.

The other decision was what to name the band. Vic talked to a lot of people and many advised him not to use the name Lombardo. My brother saw no reason to be ashamed of his own name and the Victor Lombardo orchestra began accepting bookings. But he became incensed when he learned how the bookers were advertising the band. One ad read: "Here comes that Guy, Victor Lombardo." The word "Guy" had been printed in larger letters than "Victor," giving the misleading impression it was some kind of offshoot of his older brother's band. He corrected that soon enough.

The new band received excellent reviews. Vic's personality was warm, he performed well as a master of ceremonies and bandleader, and the critics were quick to praise the identifying soprano sax. He was booked into a number of the bigger hotel rooms around the country, including the Hotel New Yorker in New York, the Edgewater Beach in Chicago, and the celebrated Aragon Ballroom in Los Angeles. But Vic couldn't have picked a worse time to start an orchestra. The Big Band era was beginning to wind down.

More unsettling to Vic's peace of mind was the constant travel, the giving up of a home life. Ginny was on the road with him, his two boys were installed in the New York Military Academy, and home was a hotel room, with few opportunities to see their sons and the rest of the family.

Dozens of new bands were beginning to form after World War II. Leaders who had been pressed into service returned to form new organizations. Many of their best musicians had formed bands of their own while they were away. Locations demanding the services of big bands had mushroomed around the country, some financed by defense plants in the vicinity. But a new band had to travel, as Victor was to learn. He no longer could count on six months in New York with the Royal Canadians.

The bubble of the big band popularity began to burst in the summer of 1946. Attendance figures started to decline in ballrooms, night clubs, and on one-night tour dates. The 20-percent amusement tax, installed as a wartime measure, was not taken off. People who had spent their incomes in a sort of there's-no-tomorrow abandon, during the war, stopped seeking every-night entertainment and began buying the cars, homes, and appliances that had not been available during the hostilities.

Salaries had doubled and trebled during the war and they continued high and rising after it. A new bandleader like Vic had taken on a tremendous payroll and he found himself accepting every date the road had to offer. He also began to find toward the end of the forties that ballrooms that had been operating on a full six-night week were beginning to cut down to three and four.

Hotels and night clubs were also beginning to cut down in the face of the spiraling costs of keeping bands, especially the top names like Benny Goodman, Tommy Dorsey, Harry James, and Artie Shaw, who were demanding as much as $7,500 for a week's work. Before the war, they could command a guarantee of $1,800 a night on tour. Now they wanted $3,000 to $4,000 for one-nighters.

Vic had neither the following built up over the years that could guarantee him the kind of money being paid the big names nor the radio time to give him the exposure he needed. And so he traveled with Ginny, each becoming more exhausted with the succession of train and bus rides and hotel rooms and widening separation from family.

Carm knew what was happening and he asked me if it would be all right with me if he called Vic and offered him his old job at a raise in salary. I had lost Vic and then Rose Marie to marriage and I missed them both. I told him to make the call: no strings, no recriminations, no I-told-you-so. If Vic wanted to come back, we'd love to have him. One night in 1950, Vic and Ginny, after traveling all day by bus, playing a night date and facing another bus ride the next day, came back to their hotel and the phone was ringing. It was Carm, warm and emotional, the family's patch-up man.

"Come on back, Vic," he said. "You know Guy, he's too stubborn to call you himself, but I talked to him and he wants you. You've proved you could do it on your own, but I know how bad things are getting to be in the business. Now come back to the family. Your old job is waiting and there's a big fat raise. We need you."

Ginny was listening. She had stood by Vic and the strain was showing. Now they could see their sons again. The business of becoming as important a bandleader as his brother now faded before the more important consideration of providing a home for his wife and kids. He came back and there was another Lombardo on our bandstand again.

206 AULD ACQUAINTANCE

We kept adding new personalities as some of the original members of the crew from London left for one reason or another. Jim Dillon, our original trombonist, decided he had had enough of travel and retired to run a piano-tuning business in New York. Bern Davies, a Carmen Lombardo student of the saxophone, had been our first bass horn player and his wife had been traveling with the band since they were married. Now she was becoming a mother and Bern retired, too. Muff Henry, our guitarist, became ill and died.

We had replaced Larry Owen with Cliff Grass, who would remain with us for thirty years. Muff Henry's replacement was a talented guitarist-singer named Don Rodney, whom we featured on our million-selling gold record of "Third Man Theme."

And when Rodney left to become a solo performer in 1951, we were fortunate enough to get Bill Flannagan from the Fred Waring organization. Now of the original crew of ten who had left London and found fame in Cleveland, five were left: the three Lombardos, Freddie Kreitzer and George Gowans.

Bill Flannagan was the type of musician we were constantly seeking out to increase our versatility, our ability to adjust to whatever musical trend was coming along. We would play in the idiom of the day but never abandon our sound. Bill would be the man to feature in the country and western songs that were becoming popular, the hillbilly music he had learned in southern Illinois, where he grew up. He was an all-around musician, having played the euphonium in a Navy band before taking up the trombone. With our band, he sang and played the guitar, doubling on the euphonium, or baritone horn, which produces a beautiful mellow tone.

My brother Joe, the antique dealer who had spent several years in Hollywood as a set designer, made many trips abroad and in Paris found a strange little instrument called a clavietta, resembling a harmonica but with a tiny keyboard like that of a piano. Joe brought it back with him and presented it to me in case somebody in the orchestra would like to try his hand at it. Bill Flannagan was the only one who could get a lovely sound out of it and his rendition of "Moon River" on the clavietta was one of the numbers most in demand by our audiences.

Bill was another of the musicians who joined us rather reluctantly, with a preconceived idea implanted by the so-called progressive musicians of the day, who referred to the Lombardo music as corny. He had never heard us and he almost balked at the idea of having to play a two-beat rhythm rather than the equally accented four beats in vogue among the swing bands.

He had reservations about playing what they were calling the old-fashioned rhythms of the "Mickey Mouse bands." But he changed his mind after his first appearance.

"I looked around me," he would recall, "and saw all the other guys in the band happily playing away, tapping their feet, and I looked out on the dance floor and saw the people dancing and having a wonderful time. I had been kidding myself. These people dancing weren't looking for an education; they were looking for a good time and they were getting it to music they knew and loved. I tapped my feet, too, and I was happy to be part of the band."

And so we continued playing what we knew and what the public accepted and loved as some of the newer bandleaders began playing for their own amusement and began changing their styles for listening rather than dancing. Big brass sections were turning people away rather than on and radio stations were beginning to feature name singers on records, rather than depending almost exclusively on the big bands.

The industry was changing. Vocalists like Frank Sinatra, Perry Como, Rosemary Clooney, Nat "King" Cole, Doris Day, and Dinah Shore, groups like the Andrew Sisters, the Boswell Sisters, the Ink Spots, the Mills Brothers were beginning to compete with the bands for domination of record sales. The latter part of the forties saw a sharp curtailment of band remotes from hotels as disk jockeys began appearing in every city for the all-night listener. The record spinners were now choosing and playing the records that would become hits and they were using singers more often than bands.

The bands began cutting down on personnel and the band bookers were finding fewer locations to place their clients. Theaters were no longer starring bands in stage shows; in fact, many of them abandoned the movie and stage show policy altogether.

Television was coming in and theater owners were concerned that they might lose evening audiences altogether.

Despite the gloomy picture, we were fortunate enough to meet the challenge by simply adhering to our formula of producing our style of dance music. Through the late forties and early fifties we were selling an average of 11,000,000 records a year. Our four gold records—were the most produced by a band.

But the bulk of sales was not so much from the million-selling hits as the tremendous number of records that sold from 250,000 to 500,000 copies at a time. They added up to a volume that would earn us the position as number-one recording artists of all time.

Meanwhile my parents were adjusting to life in the United States and to their home in Stamford. Papa had been lonely the first few months, and one day he decided to pack a bag, get into his car, and visit his old friends in London. It had taken him two hours to try to find his way out of the city and he had returned home in high dudgeon. Now he set about making new friends. He also puttered with his car, created a huge garden that required daily maintenance, and personally tended to the care, feeding, and milking of Elsie, his cow.

Mama looked forward to the Sundays that her sons in the band were in New York. We would come trooping up with our wives and often with friends, crowding that big house and noisily partaking of the bountiful table at the head of which Papa sat proudly. We would discuss matters of moment like what Rose Marie would do after she got out of high school.

Rose Marie remembered the day that discussion came up. "I hadn't even entered high school," she recalled, "and now everybody was hollering at the top of their lungs about where I would go to college. Guy stood up in his chair and outshouted the rest of the family. He said if I didn't want to go to college, I didn't have to. From then on, I didn't worry about college anymore."

In August 1951 we came up for the most momentous Sunday of them all. Papa was seventy-eight and celebrating his fiftieth wedding anniversary. He was in the best of health, and Mama, only a few years younger, bustled around seeing that all the guests were served and entertained. Among the guests was a large contingent from London, including the mayor. Papa even obliged with several of his baritone numbers.

A few years later, he suffered a heart attack and died. Elaine called me with the news. Just two days before, she said, he had been happily puttering away, singing in his full, rich baritone "Somewhere a Voice Is Calling."

I was to learn as I helped make the funeral arrangements how fruitful Papa had made his new life in Stamford. My brother Joe was supervising the bringing in of hundreds of chairs for the service and they counted up to many more than I expected would be needed.

"You'd be surprised," Joe said, "about all the people he came to know and who came to know him in Stamford. You and Carm and Lebe and Vic only come up on Sundays, which the folks always reserved for the family. But you never had a chance to see what went on during the rest of the week. People came here from all over town for advice and guidance and friendship. He made hundreds of good friends in this town."

Mama would survive her husband by only a few years. Both left behind seven children who would never forget how much they owed them.

9. The Tempo Moves to Water

In 1946 an article appeared in *Motor Boating* magazine which began with the following paragraphs:

"Lap, heat and total race records smashed—a new champion crowned—probably the most breath-taking 30-mile duel in motor boat racing history—a spectator crowd of 250,000 (some estimate 300,000)—that's the story of the 39th A.P.B.A. Gold Cup Championships, held on the Detroit River, September 2, 1946.

"Guy Lombardo, of Freeport, N.Y., the nationally famous band leader, who mixes motors and melody with equal facility, is the new champion to enter the charmed circle of Gold Cup winners, and he accomplished his objective during his first campaign with big racing boats."

My father had never meant music to be the all-consuming factor in his oldest son's life. It had been his own passport to America, but, as an adolescent immigrant in London, he had found out soon enough there were other skills and interests to acquire. The most important was the business of learning the English language.

My mother would remember that Gaetano Lombardo was a source of much amusement for the student body of St. Peter's Parochial School, which he attended at the same time he was serving his apprenticeship at Carmelo Paladino's tailoring shop. He was several years older than the rest of his classmates, a tall fifteen-year-old who had difficulty finding a place for his feet under the small desks of the sixth-grade classroom.

He survived that, learned his English, worked on losing his accent and becoming part of the community. One of his pleasures was singing in the church and YMCA choirs. Another was an interest in American sports involving speed. By the time he married Angelina Paladino, he had become firmly assimilated in the community, participating in the racing of trotting horses, an amateur sport of the day, hardly more organized than one horse owner challenging another to a match race.

I was about ten when Papa purchased a fine trotting mare to race with his friends. The mare served another purpose, as noted before. Carm and I were rewarded for distinguished performances at music lessons by getting a ride in the buggy the mare pulled. Another reward, which pleased me even more, was the opportunity to board Papa's newly acquired motor launch.

I doubt it could go faster than six miles per hour. Its main function was not to establish speed records, but to entertain Papa's friends and occasionally Carm or me. It had a little canopy and under it he would seat his guests for after-work excursions on the Thames. The times I got to go, I can remember helping him lug aboard crocks of cheese and cases of Canadian ale. Sometimes I would take over the controls as the older men were eating and drinking.

Two of his most frequent guests were neighbors with a long-standing rivalry as to who owned London's fastest trotter. Now they became interested in boating and set out to prove they could operate the city's speediest water craft. Both purchased fine speedboats with powerful inboard engines and during the course of an entire winter tinkered with the motors, honing them up for a race the following summer.

They had those engines in barns and often Papa would allow me to visit one or the other after I had completed my lessons. I had been impressed with the control of live power that sent Papa's boat flying at six miles per hour. Now I was enthralled at what these rivals were trying to do to energize their motors to more impressive speeds.

The ice was hardly out of the river in May when my father's

friends put on their match race, the first of what would become an annual event. Papa acted as starter and the riverbank was filled with curious spectators. They started at the center of town, sped to Spring Lake, and headed back for Papa's boat, which was the finish line. It was an eight-mile round trip and they raced neck and neck, covering the distance in less than fifteen minutes. I forget who won; I remember only that in the ensuing years first one then the other would reach Papa's outboard first. What was mind-boggling was that both averaged 34 mph the first time, and it seemed incredible to me that a boat could do more than half a mile a minute.

My proximity to those neighborhood match races every summer created an interest in speedboat racing that I would never lose. As I got older, I would often make summer trips to the Gold Cup races at the Detroit Yacht Club, the world's best-known racing course. The Gold Cup was the World Series and Superbowl of speedboating, and the skill of the drivers left me in awe.

In 1920 I had the supreme thrill of seeing Gar Wood break the world's speed record in winning the Gold Cup. His boat averaged seventy miles per hour for an entire mile lap. I think if I had not already set my course on becoming a bandleader, my next choice would have been to follow a career as a race-boat driver. Papa had indeed provided me with other options than music.

But I couldn't give the thought more than passing notice. There were the years of struggle ahead to firmly establish ourselves in the band business, to fight just to remain in Cleveland and then push further.

I never really got a chance to resume my love for the water and for boating until we got our first summer job at the old Cleveland Yacht Club. There I had numerous opportunities for cruising at the invitation of friendly boatowners. The urge to race a boat would have to be curbed until I built my house on the Freeport waterfront.

I had purchased a speedy little boat the first summer we played the Pavillon Royal and rented a house near Point Lookout. It was a twenty-four-foot Sea Lion with a Chrysler engine that propelled it up to speeds of 35 mph. The next year I found a thirty-footer with a Sterlng petrol engine that went 40 mph. I was going up in speed, but Lilliebell was more interested in comfort. That was when we purchased our fifty-five-foot cruiser, our yacht. Even with the big boat, however, I always kept a speedboat after purchasing the property in Freeport.

I became an avid reader of the motorboat magazines, keeping up with developments in the sport, following the exploits of Gar Wood, who had always been an idol more revered than Babe Ruth, Jack Dempsey or Red Grange. The 225-class was the most popular in racing and in 1935 their speeds rose dramatically with the invention of three-point suspension.

Up to that time, most race boats were the v-bottom type; the new design literally drove a boat on a cushion of air, riding on two sponsons and the prop—thus three-point suspension. Where before few but the championship drivers could go more than 60 mph, 80 mph became commonplace.

I saw one close up while we were playing an engagement at the Toronto Exposition in 1939 and made my mind up on the spot to acquire it. I was told to call a boatyard in New Jersey and ordered one to be shipped to Freeport. It arrived at about the time we were moving into the new house, one of the few two-seaters of the model that could go as fast as 80 mph. I couldn't wait to get it into the water.

The new neighbor who owned a band did not find favor with the homeowners along the Woodcleft Canal, who enjoyed leisurely cruises on the creeks and canals leading into the bay. They looked askance every time I took the boat out on the creek and streaked by, trailing a huge wake.

I had named the boat *Tempo* and had to build a crane to lift it out of the water, because it was so fragile you couldn't leave it in the creek overnight. By the spring of 1940 I figured that I had mastered the boat's controls to the point I wanted to engage in competition.

One morning as I was preparing to take it out, I noticed a little outboard flash by with racing numbers on its side. The driver was a boy hardly in his teens and I called out to him, asking if he would pull over. I wondered if he knew where I could race my boat, and after looking over the 225 admiringly he suggested a place in New Jersey. He said that I had the right boat because they were having a 225-class race, but he also reminded me that some of the best drivers in the world would be in it.

I checked it out, learned that the boy knew what he was talking about, packed the boat in a trailer, put in a spare battery and my gardener, who doubled as my mechanic, accompanied me to the race. I had never been in one in my life.

All I knew about starting a race, for instance, was that there was a five-minute warning gun to get the boats out onto the course and a one-minute run to position the contestants to get off to a flying start.

I thought I could remember all that, and when the five-minute gun sounded I headed my boat for all the others that were milling around waiting to get off flying. It didn't seem that I had been out on the course for more than a minute when I suddenly developed a very lonely feeling. Looking around, I found it hard to believe my boat was all alone and the others had already passed the starting line and were distant specks in the water. I headed for the pits.

My mechanic wanted to know what had happened, and all I could tell him was that I hadn't heard the starting gun. He said he hadn't either. The noise of the motors had drowned it out. We waited, embarrassed, as the first heat of the race was completed and Pops Cooper, the winner, came into the pits. He drove a boat he called *Tops* and had beaten out the race favorite, George Schrafft, the candy family heir, who was one of the biggest names in racing.

Pops was a charming little guy and I decided, as the boats got ready for the next heat, that this time I would follow the lead of a winner. Whatever Cooper did at the start I would do. Now all of the boats were turning and maneuvering and I kept my eye on *Tops*, following its every movement. When Pops flew up to the starting line, I was right behind him.

Off we went, my first official race start, and the next thing I knew my boat was back in the pits again, right in back of Pops Cooper. He had suffered a puncture in the hull and had made immediately for the pits. My debut as a racing driver had been about as successful as some of the band's earlier premieres. In two heats I had failed to find the starting line and then I had failed to find the race.

Back in Freeport, I flagged down the young man in the racing outboard again, told him about my sad experience, and asked if he could advise me where to learn the knack of starting. He said he had been to a number of races with his father, and his suggestion was that I enter a race in Red Bank, New Jersey, the following week.

"But get there a day early," he advised. "And practice running up to the starting gun. Pick a spot about a half minute behind the starting line and don't listen for the gun. The motors are too loud. Look for the blue smoke the gun gives off when it's fired."

I took his advice. All that day before the Red Bank race, I practiced. By the end of the day, I had gotten the starting technique down to a science. I picked out a spot on the pier, which figured to be the starting line, and timed myself to hit that spot wide open, without beating the gun. But I was going full speed at the proper time, and if I could do it in the race I figured to get a good start.

Starting, I would learn later, was one of the most important aspects of the race. The slow starters have to plow through the wakes of the boats ahead. They are, in effect, racing in the aerated water created by the lead boats. The Red Bank race would be especially difficult for laggardly starters because it had an enormous field of twenty-two entries, the largest bunch of 225s ever assembled at one time.

The all-day starting practice certainly helped. I watched for the starter's gun smoke, picked out my spot on the pier, and hit the starting line all-out. Suddenly I began to have that lonely feeling all over again. Looking ahead of me, I saw nothing but water. I seemed to be all alone. So I looked back and saw a fleet of monsters bearing down on me. Involuntarily I slowed down. By the time I hit the first turn, at least six of those boats had passed me, throwing water in my face. I was genuinely frightened, feeling I was about to be cut in two.

But I finished and back at the pits the various mechanics and drivers started asking questions. Why had I slowed down? I had the only boat that had gotten off to a good start. Why hadn't I just kept going? They were answering their own questions and telling me that I could have won the race by myself.

So I learned another lesson: disregard the boats behind and never look back; worry only about your own craft and how to maneuver past the ones in front.

I was not entirely disappointed with my efforts at Red Bank. Out of that field of twenty-two I managed to finish fourth the next two heats. Top people in racing, the officials and wealthy owners of the best boats, had suspected that I had entered the competition to publicize the band. I assured them it wasn't so; I just happened to be crazy about the sport and the more I learned about it the crazier I got. I left Red Bank with a warm feeling, somewhat like a rookie in his first professional golf tournament who had finished among the leaders and won acceptance and respect.

The next race was in Washington and again I finished fourth. Another respectable showing, but I knew I had a long way to get to the top, since I neither had the experience nor a finely tuned boat like such stars as Danny Foster, Danny Arena, Zammie Simmons, and Georgie Schrafft.

There was much to learn and I set my mind to it, gaining confidence with each race, even learning how to endure the pain that often is the lot of competitors in all sports. In an early race in Cincinnati, I learned that the Ohio River could act up almost as tumultuously as the Atlantic Ocean near my home.

In that race the water was so rough my boat was bouncing almost six feet in the air at full speed. I was not in a boat as much as in a projectile that hit cement, took off like a rocket, and bounced again. The ordeal was not only violent but bone-shaking, and I found myself fighting the wheel, abosrbing the impacts, and holding on for dear life.

Safety belts aren't used by speedboat racers. In case of an accident, should a driver's boat capsize, he would go down with it and probably drown. It is felt he has a better chance of surviving if he is thrown clear. So my boat had a specially designed footrest on the floor board which I would push against as hard as I could to remain wedged into the seat.

In the Cincinnati race, the boat's hull took such a severe pounding from the waves that the oil line was cut in half at a point just above my legs. They were being drenched by scalding oil pumping out from the severed line.

One never knows what he will do in an emergency until it occurs. I remember my mind racing with ideas as the burning sensation in the legs became more acute. If I pulled my feet off the footrest, I'd probably be thrown out of the boat. I could throttle back and certainly lose a race I had a chance to win. But more important, if I did that I would endanger the boats in back of me.

I really had no other choice than to go ahead and hope to finish the race as speedily as possible. When it was over, I had earned a victory at the expense of burning-oil scars that I still carry on my legs today.

That may have been my second victory and I remember it better than the first, which occurred in the summer of 1942, just as boat racing was winding down for the duration of the war. The Gold Cup class boats, the big jobs with custom-built engines measuring a minimum of 650 cubic inches and so expensive that only millionaires could afford to race them, had fallen out of favor and the only entry in the 1942 race was Zammie Simmons of the mattress-manufacturing family, who had been dominating the class since 1939. He won the 1942 Gold Cup, merely by sending his *My Sin* around the course for the required number of laps.

So with the big names of racing virtually retired during 1942, and with the acquisition of a new *Tempo*, which I purchased from Joe Taggart, a well-known driver who had been winning in the 225 class, I began entering every race scheduled that year. The first one I won was a marathon affair from Atlantic City to Cape May. The band was appearing in Atlantic City and I just happened to have the boat along for a race that wasn't as much a test of speed as a lesson in navigation through the creeks that intertwine between the two seaside resorts.

I received my first winner's trophy on the bandstand that night and had to concede to the presentation committee that the reason I won was because I could find my way through weeds better than the other contestants. And that started me off on a circuit of twenty-two races that season, of which I won twenty-one. I was

named national champion for 1942. Racing would not be resumed
until 1946.

I moved up to the Gold Cup class more by accident than
design. In the early spring of 1946, I read an ad in *Motorboat*
magazine. Zammie Simmons, with whom I had become friendly
in the two years I had been racing, was putting his championship
boat, *My Sin*, on the market to the highest bidder. The boat had
dominated the field since 1939, when he set back the challenge of
Count Theo Rossi of Italy and established a Gold Cup record of
66 mph for the ninety-mile race.

Simmons must have put at least $100,000 into *My Sin*. It came
equipped with a specially built Zumbach-Miller engine and nothing had been built in the prewar days that could match it. Now
Simmons had retired to Nogales, Arizona, and the boat was available to anybody who could afford it.

It was certainly beyond my means, but I sat down and wrote
Simmons a letter, offering to drive the boat in the forthcoming
summer races. I would race it under the Simmons banner and pay
all expenses. I told him I would have loved to buy the boat out-
right but did not feel I could pay nearly what it was worth. I just
wanted to compete with the big-name drivers in a boat that
matched theirs for power.

He called me a week later at the Roosevelt and asked if I'd be
willing to pay $6,001 for *My Sin*. Flabbergasted, I answered in the
affirmative. He explained that he had only received one bid and
that was for $6,000. If I would up the ante one dollar, he'd be
delighted to sell the boat; he had watched my development as a
driver and he thought I could compete against his old rivals.

My Sin, which would become *Tempo VI*, was shipped to
Freeport, a beautiful hull, awaiting its motor. The engine, hand-
crafted by Charles Zumbach, one of the most renowned machinists in the world, was in his New York shop, for its annual winter
checkup. I visited Zumbach, showed him my title to the boat, and
told him I expected to race it but wondered if he could send it to
Freeport so I could try it out before the racing season.

The machinery came out by truck next week, four Indianapolis
race-car engines measuring 151 cubic inches each, and fitted onto
a common crankshaft. *My Sin*'s power plant had taken Zumbach a

year to build with his own hands and had cost $50,000 in Depression money. Now it was lifted lovingly off the truck by four of his German machinists, who put it on the ground and covered it with canvas.

The machinists were to spend three days putting the engines into the boat, meticulously sparing no detail, using wrenches of every size and weight, tightening each nut and bolt. Finally the sixteen-cylinder engines with eight carburetors and a magneto were put into place just a week before the year's first important race, the Red Bank Sweepstakes. The machinists accompanied *Tempo* VI to the races, directing it onto the racecourse, telling me when to step on the starter, when to pull the choke. I had not had the time I wanted to try out my new *Tempo*, but the mechanics had done their work well. I won the sweepstakes easily, against most of the big names who were only just returning to postwar racing. My next stop would be the Gold Cup on Labor Day in Detroit.

The Gold Cup was the Kentucky Derby of boat racing. Unlike the thoroughbred scene, however, it was not the first event of speedboating's Triple Crown. The Red Bank Sweepstakes came first, the Gold Cup followed, and the President's Cup in Washington completed the cycle. As winner of the first leg, I suddenly found myself a big name in the sport.

Gold Cup officials kept calling me to make sure I would race, that the band had not taken on an engagement for Labor Day. I assured them I would be there. They also wanted to know if I had any suggestions about changing the conditions of the race. I had one that would change the course of Gold Cup racing. It had bothered me to see in the years just before the war that only extremely wealthy people could own Gold Cup class boats, with engines that had to measure a minimum of 650 cubic inches and a maximum of 750. Those boats were the property of multimillionaires like Zammie Simmons, Horace Dodge, Harold Wilson of the wealthy Canadian family, and Count Rossi of Italy. They had virtually eliminated competition because they had the means to purchase the most powerful boats.

I suggested that the Gold Cup be an unlimited class, open to all, big and small. Smaller boats might have a chance if those big complicated craft developed trouble. And engines could now be purchased from war surplus that had even more horsepower than the Gold Cup boats.

For instance, the powerful Allison engine with 1,500 horse-power could be purchased for as little as $200. Of course to fit one into a race boat, a gearbox costing about $2,000 was also necessary, but it was still a small price to pay for an engine that stood a good chance in Gold Cup competition. My *Tempo*, for instance, had only 450 horsepower. The officials consulted among themselves and with the judges and came up with an affirmative response to my suggestion. The Gold Cup was thrown open to large and small boats alike. It would be truly an unlimited class.

Labor Day, 1946, dawned cool and cloudy on the Detroit River. By race time, more than 200,000 spectators jammed the riverbank, among them my entire family from Papa and Mama to Lilliebell. I received an undue amount of attention from reporters, most of whom asked if I really wasn't in the race for the publicity.

There were seventeen entries, five of them, including my own, that were still considered Gold Cup boats. But now there were also ten of the 225-class boats; two were 135-cubic-inch hydros. I did not race in the first qualifying heat, which turned out to be a terrific contest between a powerful Allison-engined boat, *Miss Golden Gate III*, driven by Danny Arena, and *Miss Canada*, owned and driven by Harold Wilson. Wilson was leading most of the way until he developed supercharger trouble and Arena coasted in the winner.

There was no drama for the spectators in the second qualifying heat, in which I was entered. By the second lap I was full-out, had passed the entire fleet, and at the finish I was a lap and a half ahead of the second boat. I had never slowed down as it became apparent that all I had to do was keep going to win the heat. When I came into the pits, I was told I had broken Gar Wood's record for a thirty-mile heat, which he negotiated at 70 mph. I had watched him set that world's record twenty-six years before. Now I owned the new record, 70.8 mph.

There were only five boats that had finished the two qualifying heats as I went into the semifinal, well aware that Danny Arena in his *Miss Golden Gate* was a dangerous contender. Although he got off first and I trailed in fourth, I was able to pass him before the first lap was over. He pushed me hard and I later heard that the spectators were jumping up and down in excitement as it seemed *Miss Golden Gate* would finally overtake *Tempo*. But suddenly Danny Arena's boat lost speed and by the time the race was over I had lapped him. I now had virtually won the Gold Cup because I had the most points for the two heats I had won and a 4.9 minute lead over second-place *Miss Golden Gate*. He would have to beat me by more than five minutes in the final heat to take the cup.

And Danny Arena tried. There were only five boats left for the final heat and he came out roaring with *Miss Golden Gate*. In the second lap of the second heat, I had established another world's record of 73.29 mph. Only ninety minutes later in the first lap of the finals, Arena would beat that record and keep beating it each succeeding lap until he had reached 76.79 mph. Some spectators would later say they thought his boat was exceeding 100 mph. But *Tempo VI* was keeping up, not far behind in second place. All I had to worry about was that my boat finished; Arena had hardly cut into my time or point lead.

And then with two laps left, *Miss Golden Gate* lay dead in the water. Its oil line had ruptured earlier in the race, but the boat's magnificent power plant carried on even with faulty lubrication until it finally quit. I crossed the finish line by myself with yet another world's record. I had also beaten Zammie Simmons' 1939 mark for the ninety-mile race, averaging over 68 mph.

The entire Lombardo clan seemed to be caught up in the flush of that victory. I saw Carm and Lebe hugging each other, Lilliebell kissing my other brothers and sisters. And off to the side, holding tightly to Mama, was the proudest Lombardo of all, Papa. He was thinking aloud, wishfully, when I greeted him.

"You know what would be wonderful, Guy? If somehow the people in London could get a look at this championship boat."

It was not that difficult to arrange. My home town is only 110 miles from Detroit, and it would be just as easy to ship the boat home via London rather than Buffalo. The mechanics accompanied Papa and the boat, which was put on display in the main town square for two days. Gaetano Lombardo was on hand personally to explain the boat's fine points and to remind the home folks that his son had learned speedboating on the Thames.

Now I needed only the President's Cup in Washington to win the Triple Crown. I knew it would be a difficult task because *Miss Golden Gate,* equipped with that powerful Allison engine, had proven to be faster than mine and had only lost because it had developed trouble twice in three heats.

My fears were not unwarranted. Dan Foster, who was the boat's co-owner with Dan Arena, would be at the controls in the Washington race. Both men had years of combined experience behind them as drivers, and they pooled all their talents to make sure that this time nothing could go wrong, that the Allison was installed perfectly and in balance. Among the spectators on the banks of the Potomac to watch what had been billed as the race of the century was President Harry Truman.

For my part I hadn't neglected homework either. I knew by now that winning a race often depended on correctly preparing for it. One had to do everything he could to make his boat foolproof, to guard against a gas tank falling off or a prop breaking. The mechanics and I had overlooked nothing that might cause an accident, and I was confident *Tempo VI* was in perfect racing trim.

All of that could not win the President's Cup for me. Danny Foster's 1,500 horsepower proved too much for *Tempo*'s 450 or so. The course seemed shorter than the one in Detroit and he would come out of the turn and be gone, while it took me the length of the course to catch up. That Foster-Arena monster simply outsped *Tempo* in three heats, winning each one by three to four seconds.

Although I was acclaimed the national champion for 1946, I felt I had to make changes if I was to retain the title the next year. The most important would have to be a new engine with more horsepower. Foster and Arena had proved the efficacy of their Allison and others would follow. I called on Charles Zumbach and asked him what he thought about buying a war-surplus engine.

I can still see the shock on the brilliant old machinist's face. I was asking him to discard the creation it had taken him a year to build with his own hands. It had won three Gold Cups—two for

Zammie Simmons and one for me. And now I was asking him to replace the engine. He just looked at me, unable to find words.

A week later I had acquired an Allison from Bell Aircraft surplus and sent it to Zumbach in New York with instructions to begin the conversion. He never got the chance. The next day he was in the hospital suffering from a heart attack. Stricken by the news, fearful that the rejection of his engine had brought about the attack, I went to the hospital as soon as he was allowed visitors. I hoped I could speed his recovery by telling him I had changed my mind, that *Tempo* would race with the Zumbach engine the following year.

A few weeks after he got out of the hospital, Charles Zumbach shot himself. I would never know if this man, who had striven for perfection all his life, committed suicide because he couldn't go back to his physically demanding job or because he simply would not accept the fact that his engine had become outdated for Gold Cup racing. I do know that he destroyed every diagram and every blueprint that mapped out his engine. In overhauling the engine that winter, his mechanics had to work from memory.

As I was winner of last year's Gold Cup, it was my prerogative to pick the site for the 1947 race. The custom was to select one's home waters, preferably a course with viewing facilities for spectators. Where to begin? In the New York area, you could attract a lot of people to the Hudson River on both the Manhattan and New Jersey sides. But that wasn't really home; Long Island was. The island, unfortunately, did not have a river big enough for the race; what it had was the ocean, the Long Island Sound, the Great South Bay, and canals.

I took my problem to Robert Moses, the master builder who had created Jones Beach only a few miles from Freeport. We had never met in person, but the band had played several summers at the Jones Beach Boardwalk Cafe and he was extremely cordial. I told him that I had the opportunity of bringing the Gold Cup race to New York for the first time and that it would have to be on a Sunday late in August. He was not enchanted.

"Sunday is the day that gets the biggest boat traffic on the island," he reminded me. "People are out fishing and cruising. It could be a big problem to seal off a large area, presuming there is one, without a lot of boatmen getting mad."

I told him I understood, I'd simply have to tell Detroit we'd race there again. They'd love to have it.

"Now wait a minute," he interrupted. "I didn't say it wouldn't be a good thing for New York to have the race. The problem is finding the right spot. I'll get back to you."

The way he got back was in typical Robert Moses style. That same night at the Roosevelt Hotel, a delegation from the Coast Guard descended on the Grill armed with maps and charts. "Mr. Moses called this afternoon," the spokesman said. "He wants us to find a spot that can accommodate at least a hundred thousand spectators, that will disrupt the least amount of Sunday boat traffic, and has the least likelihood of acting up rough for your speedboats." I left it up to the Coast Guard, and they spent the next two months studying every available location, finally coming up with Jacob Riis Park in the Rockaways.

The park, on the shores of Jamaica Bay, had a long railing for spectators. The bay, the first day I visited it, seemed as calm as a lake. Bob Moses liked it because that body of water did not attract nearly as many boatmen as Great South Bay over the Nassau County line to the east. The only pessimistic opinion I received was from Frank Ripp, a friend who raced a 225-class boat. He warned that if we should happen to encounter a northeast wind the day of the race it would blow debris all over the bay and that contestants would find the course a hellhole.

I told him we had no other choice and August 7 was selected as the date for the race. The week before, boats began arriving from all over the country, the drivers testing them on what they called the most placid waters they had ever raced on. I awakened that Sunday morning to a northeaster, blowing at 12 mph, and when I arrived at Jamaica Bay it looked like an ocean flecked with white-caps. Frank Ripp's prediction about debris had been on the nose; you could see floating logs from the pits. By the time of the 1:00 P.M. start it was raining.

The weather hadn't dampened the size of the crowd. Newspaper reporters estimated that more than a hundred thousand were on hand. And since the regulations demanded that the race go on no matter the conditions, I found myself roaring off to the fastest start I could remember. I still had Charles Zumbach's engine and I had to pray that the mechanics had known where every nut and bolt were supposed to go without a diagram to help them.

It may have been the most reckless race I ever competed in, not being sure my engine was perfectly installed, disregarding the floating debris that was slowing up every boat behind me. The northeaster was blowing against the incoming tide, creating a short, steep chop that discouraged the boats with wide, flat planing surfaces.

I won the first heat with little trouble, while Danny Foster, in *Miss Pepsi* V, and Al Fallon, who had purchased *Miss Great Lakes* from him, competed for second. Both had Allison engines, but the added horsepower did them little good that day; it would have been foolhardy going full-out in the face of the floating obstacles on the course. I had won that first lap by taking chances to compensate for inferior speed.

And now in the second lap my good luck would not hold up. *Tempo*'s starboard sponson began disintegrating under the frightful pounding of the high speeds under the heavy chop. I didn't even realize what was happening as the boat began to lose speed. Danny Arena, now driving *Miss Notre Dame*, caught me on the second lap. I finished the heat, a poor fifth.

In the pits, the mechanics advised me not to take the boat out again. In overhauling the engine without Zumbach, they had neglected to put in a new oil line and my oil pressure was dangerously low. But with one first-place finish and one fifth, I was still not out of the Gold Cup. I determined to race in the final. The wind had shifted and the course was calmer now. I went against everything I had taught myself: to compete only if I was sure nothing could go wrong with my boat.

Although the ruptured sponson had not been fully repaired, the wound had been patched up and my mechanics begged me to take it easy. I could not heed their advice if I was to catch the leader, *Miss Pepsi*, which had a point total of 700. *Miss Great Lakes* was second with 450, and I was third with 427. I still had a chance if I could get some speed out of my boat and the others would lay back, careful to avoid the floating debris.

But *Tempo* could never make it, although my gallant boat tried for most of the race before I hit a piece of debris. Lubrication trouble finally forced me out of it. Danny Foster in *Miss Pepsi* had beaten me for the second straight time.

Although I mourned Charles Zumbach's passing, I no longer felt an obligation to go on racing with his engine. In a few weeks, *Tempo* had been outfitted with an Allison and I would beat Foster later that month in the National Sweepstakes Regatta at Red Bank, New Jersey.

I would win other races that year, but the President's Cup in Washington continued to elude me. I was ahead going into the final heat when my propeller shaft tore loose from its mooring, flew aft, sheared off the rudder and disappeared in a great cloud over the muddy Potomac.

The frightening explosion, which threw me out of the boat, was the result of the engine running away and suddenly cutting itself off. They retrieved me from the river, a black object covered with oil and miraculously unhurt. It would be my last race of the year and I would carry the memory of it on the bandstand as we toured across the country. Often Carm would catch me at a rehearsal, staring into space, and he would bring me back into the reality of the band business.

"For chrissakes, Mr. Gold Cup," he would say. "Will you start thinking about the next number and forget about your next engine."

But I made sure that *Tempo* would be ready for the next Gold Cup. Now it had an Allison as powerful as Foster's and Arena's and Fallon's and a new crew that would work on overhauling it during the winter and seeing that it was perfectly installed. I tried not to let my brothers notice my preoccupation with a hobby that had become an obsession. I wanted the 1948 Gold Cup almost more than the assurance that we were still the top-grossing band in America.

That next Gold Cup in Detroit would be known as "Boating's Black Sunday." Only one out of twenty-two fabulously expensive craft would finish the race and it would not be mine, despite the knowledge that we had entered the race in perfect trim, with ev-

Guy and old friend Lawrence Welk at the Rainbow Grill. (*Photo by Barry Kramer.*)

Prime Minister Pierre Trudeau of Canada seeks out Guy on the bandstand at the 125th Anniversary Ball for the city of Hamilton, Ontario. 1971. (*Photo by the Hamilton* [*Ont.*] Spectator.)

Carmen Lombardo.

Guy and Lilliebell's current pets, Missy (the poodle) and Daisy. Lilliebell's concern for animals often filled the house with a motley collection
of both the pedigreed and the strayed.

Three moods of Guy Lombardo: reflective as he introduces a song from the bandstand, saying hello to an "auld acquaintance," and posing as Mr. New Year's Eve. (*First two photos by CBS, third by Barry Kramer.*)

Lombardo at rehearsal at the Waldorf-Astoria for the 1974 New Year's Eve broadcast. At right, he gets report from the director. (N.Y. Daily News *Photos.*)

A typical scene at the Waldorf-Astoria on New Year's Eve. (*Photo by Wagner International Photos.*)

Guy Lombardo as he is today. *(Photo by CBS.)*

erything that could possibly go wrong with it checked out and with confidence in my own driving ability.

I had *Tempo* in a favorable starting position for the first heat, nursing it along, planning to get up to 125 mph before we hit the first turn. In front of my boat was Morlan Visel's *Hurricane* from California, untested in major racing, a big humpbacked affair that seemed perpetually airborne. My plan was to hit the starting line at full speed, cut across his wake and go inside at the first turning buoy.

And so it went as the starter's gun went off. I was flying at 125 mph at least, heading for Visel's wake, when his boat's rudder and prop suddenly failed and veered into the path of the oncoming *Tempo.* If I kept going, I would have crashed into him at tremendous speed; if I swerved in the opposite direction, I would have hit a pier that jutted into the river at that point. Hundreds of spectators crowded the pier and my boat would surely have killed some of them. Hardly thinking, I spun my wheel and shut off the engine, sending *Tempo* into a broadsiding stall.

For a moment it seemed my beautiful boat would achieve a miracle of stability and stay right side up. That was the last thought I can remember. *Tempo* dug her port sponsons into the churning wake, whirled on her side, and flipped over in a huge cascade of spray, splotched with debris and the floating form of a forty-six-year-old orchestra leader turned racing driver.

Weeks later, with a cast on a broken arm, I would read an account of the accident in *Yachting* magazine, which described the final scene of the near tragedy. "Lombardo floated unconscious in the water and *Hurricane* lay inert nearby like a large dog feigning innocence after upsetting the dinner table . . ."

But I did not know about that after it happened, nor about much of anything else that followed for the next few days. I regained consciousness and wondered where I was. I was lying head down in a swimming position and my hands were in front of my face. I looked for my wrist watch to find out what time it was. The watch was missing. I felt along my arm and met stabbing pain. What was I doing in the water? What had happened? Where was my boat?

The patrol boat came along and I told them to watch out for

my arm. They pulled me aboard and I felt blood on my face. I kept asking for my boat and they pointed to pieces of it in the water. "It's at the bottom of the river," somebody said.

All through the ambulance ride to the hospital, all through the ministrations of the doctors and the nurses, setting the arm, putting a cast on it, I felt apart from what was going on. I kept asking for my boat and the doctor kept insisting that I get into a hospital bed.

"Oh no," I told him. "I've got to get back to the race. My friends are waiting for me. My wife will be worried."

He told me I was in a state of shock, he could not permit me to leave, but I walked out anyhow, somehow got back to the Detroit Yacht Club. It was a scene, I suppose, out of a scenario. Injured hero returns, arm in cast, face covered with adhesive bandages, crowd on feet cheering the brave matador. I was not conscious enough to appreciate that all the excitement was on my behalf.

I was too busy looking for Lilliebell, who had arrived at the hospital while they were working on me, who had been going up to the operating room while I was walking out. She arrived finally and with the rest of my family and yacht club officials tried to get me inside the building to rest.

Still I would have none of it. Later they told me how I gave orders to dredge up the boat from the bottom of the river. I stood on the riverbank alone watching the crane pull up the shattered remains of my boat, saw that they put it on a trailer. Onlookers reported that I looked happy, told everybody I felt wonderful, kept repeating a promise that the boat would soon be fixed up good as new and racing.

Out on the river, the race was over. Only Danny Foster, driving Al Fallon's *Miss Great Lakes*, had been left for the final heat, and the officials made him go around the thirty miles, around battered and sinking boats as he waved his fist at them, asking to be flagged down and end "Boating's Black Sunday."

Strangely none of the dire events of the day seemed to dampen my spirits as Lilliebell and I went back to the hotel room, packed, and took a plane home. It wasn't until late at night that she finally got me to take a dish of soup in Freeport. I went to sleep peacefully and it wasn't until the middle of the next day that I awakened and relived the experience of the 1948 Gold Cup race in Detroit.

The consequences of the debacle were more provoking to Guy Lombardo, bandleader, than they would be to Guy Lombardo, race driver. I would get a new boat and win more races and the Gold Cup committee would change its rules prohibiting inexperienced drivers with unsafe boats to simply enter the big race without a short qualifying heat. Danny Foster and I had both suggested that before; we didn't care that a boat could not get up to 100 mph speeds. If it could just prove it was able to get around a three-mile course at, say, 70 mph, at least a measure of safety would have been provided for the championship boats.

The band embarked on its fall engagements with a one-armed leader. The cast itched and I would reach into it with the baton and scratch furiously. I tried to hide it from the audience and would scratch facing the band, which often sent Lebe into convulsions as he was about to launch a trumpet solo. Even more bothersome, I had never learned how to knot a bow tie one-handed. So I used clip-ons, constantly worried they would fall off at an energetic baton wave.

That exercise in discomfort lasted about a month. The only thing that assuaged my wounds during that period was a story Carm brought back from Italy, where he had been vacationing while I was racing.

He and Florence had been touring the country in a car with a chauffeur who doubled as a guide and who rarely made conversation except to describe points of interest. Once when they got back to the car, the driver was reading a local newspaper.

The front-page headline concerned the famous American raceboat driver, Guy Lombardo, who had lost the Gold Cup race because he had been thrown out of his boat. Guy Lombardo, it turned out, was the Italian hero who had replaced Count Rossi as the greatest name in racing. They had been rooting for Lombardo since Rossi quit the sport. Now the driver was wondering if Carmen had ever heard of this other Lombardo—Guy.

"He's my brother," my excitable brother shouted. "What happened to him? I've got to get to a phone." It took him a day to reach Lilliebell before he learned the extent of my injuries, and when he finally got me on the phone, I could hear his voice crackling with excitement. "All of a sudden, my guide is talking to me," he said. "He's treating me like some kind of nobility. They never heard of Guy Lombardo, bandleader, over here. But they sure know Lombardo the race driver."

Carm had not been enthralled with my racing career. It wasn't that it interfered with the band, since I did all my racing either during the summer vacation or on days when I could get back to New York for the night's performance. What I didn't know at the time and was to learn only later was that my brother resented the fact that I now had an interest that he didn't share.

It had never been that way for the forty years we had been doing things together. All our efforts had been combined to make the band a success. Even Carm's song-writing career was a matter of sharing. He would bow to my judgment despite protracted arguments, would accept the proposition that the songs he wrote did not automatically go into the band's repertoire. We shared all business ventures; we were never apart; the butlers we hired for our homes were twin brothers.

But through the years I was racing, I felt a certain antagonism in my brother. Often he displayed an irascibility toward me that was completely foreign to the generous, friendly, warmhearted Carmen I knew and loved. He never mentioned the racing except for that one time he got back from Italy, and that was more in wonderment that I could be better known for my boats than my band. I suppose we had a communications gap on the subject and I was not astute enough to realize it.

Lilliebell and Lebert began to worry about the racing also. They were more concerned with my physical safety. Lebe got to the point that he simply would not attend races. He admitted he was terrified of seeing a repetition of the '47 and '48 Gold Cup incidents, both of which might have turned out tragically. Lilliebell knew how much the sport meant to me; she would never come out and admit her fears, but she tried several times to dissuade me from continuing my quest for new trophies and new speed records. She said the sport was for younger men.

I fought that. I had been blessed with good health, and when I started the racing career at forty I had never felt better in my life.

I was forty-four when I won the Gold Cup and felt like twenty. I was being lumped in now with the sports heroes of the day. It was a heady feeling.

The only time I ever felt fear was during a race in Detroit when I drove a boat other than my own. This was shortly after *Tempo* had been damaged in the Jamaica Bay Gold Cup and I had promised sponsors of the Harmsworth Trophy race in Detroit that my boat would be repaired by Labor Day, the day of the event. We had worked on *Tempo* in Freeport, but the piston blew up again and I had to call the committee to say I would not be able to race.

They begged me not to tell anybody; they'd get me a boat. They had billed me as the star attraction and my absence in the race would sharply curtail attendance. I agreed finally, wondering what I was getting myself into.

What I got into was *Miss Great Lakes*, owned by Al Fallon. This monstrous boat with an Allison engine had been driven by Danny Foster, Danny Arena, and Fallon, had beaten me in the President's Cup, and finished ahead of me in the '47 Gold Cup. Danny Foster had been thrown out of it only a few days before and the boat had been damaged. Now it was repaired, and just a few minutes before the race Al Fallon was giving me instructions on how to drive it. I had never driven an Allison-powered boat before.

The boat was a two-seater and Fallon would accompany me during the race. We took a quick spin before the start, with Al giving me the comforting news that *Great Lakes* had not been tested since its accident. Now we had been towed out to the starting point and Al was showing me how to start the engine.

I looked at the by-now familiar riverbank, with perhaps forty thousand spectators crowding it. And for the first time, I began having qualms. I remember thinking, What the hell am I doing here, in front of all these people, driving a boat that has always been my enemy, a boat I know nothing about? How did I ever get into this business?

And suddenly there was no time for thinking. Al Fallon had reached over and turned the starter and we were off and into the turn with all the other boats and I was racing blind. I hadn't even had time to learn the instruments. "Head for the arrow," Al told me, and I could make it out barely, four and a half miles from the starting line on the Belle Island Bridge, which was the point you turned around and went back.

Besides all my problems, I had another one, which began giving me acute physical discomfort almost from the moment the boat started pounding the water. There was no footrest, no place for the foot that was not on the accelerator. And I had forgotten to bring along an athletic supporter.

I couldn't brace myself in the seat as I was accustomed to do in *Tempo*. I had never strapped myself in because, if the boat ever overturned, I would go down with it, trapped in the seat. I would support myself with the pressure of the life jacket against the seat and the free foot on the footrest. In *Great Lakes* I was driving almost in a standing position, jumping up and down with the boat.

And I was missing not only the protective supporter but a motorcycle belt I always used and which had usually been put in the front seat before I entered the boat. I was taking a beating and wanted out. When the bridge came up, I went as fast as I could standing up and sat down only as we made the turn. But mostly the pain kept me standing and I have now the memory of Fallon counting, "One lap . . . two laps . . . three laps." The race was nine laps and by the sixth, I had no idea where I stood in the race. All I could feel were the pain and the desire to jump overboard.

But with only three laps to go, I decided to stick it out, going as fast as I could get the accelerator to move us. And then blessed relief. Fallon was shouting to slow down. We had finished the race and we had won. "The next boat is two and a half miles back," he told me.

I shut off the engine, looked down at myself, and noticed I was covered with blood. We went up to the starting barge for the trophy presentation and the picture-taking, and somebody covered me with a towel. The back seat of my pants was ripped apart and there was blood on my underwear. There for the presentation was Gar Wood, the man I had idolized as a boy, whose career I had decided to emulate when I was forty years old. Suddenly I wasn't hurting anymore.

Wood took a look at me and shook his head. "If you're the winner," he said, "I'd hate like hell to look at the losers."

I would meet my idol again the following spring under less than triumphal circumstances. I was more than ever convinced that I needed an Allison for *Tempo*, and over the course of that winter we had one installed in Freeport under the direction of Amp Worth, a top mechanic who used to work for Georgie Schrafft. If the boat performed the way I expected it would, I wanted to try to beat Wood's multiple-engine record of 124 mph. I already held the single-engine record of 101 mph.

Shortly before spring, I got a call from the Miami Chamber of Commerce. They heard I was after the world's record. How about attempting it in Florida? I had heard that Wood had set his record on Indian Creek in Miami Beach. I said I'd take a crack at it in the same waters during our Easter week vacation.

The chamber of commerce had done its work well. The papers were full of the assault Guy Lombardo was making on Gar Wood's record. Residents of the luxury homes on Indian Creek were playing hosts to guests who had risen at an ungodly hour to watch the attempt. The timer on my boat had been set for 7:00 A.M. on this Holy Thursday, and as I put the boat in the water on Seventy-fifth Street, one of the spectators wishing me luck was Tommy Dorsey. He had brought the entire band down and none of them had been to sleep after finishing a night's work in Miami.

The new *Tempo* with its Allison had still been untested, and, as with Al Fallon's *Miss Great Lakes*, I had never driven it. But I was cocky by now. If I could win a race in a boat that was totally unfamiliar, I felt confident I could push *Tempo* to the record.

I felt less confident when I took off and found that I could go only as far as a causeway bridge about two miles away. I also noticed there was a hospital on the other side of the creek and that made me feel a little better. Off I went and was at the bridge in a seeming instant before I had to turn back. The timers told me I had gotten up to 113 mph and I wondered how I could ever get more speed than that on such a short course.

After I eased back to the Seventy-fifth Street dock, I questioned the mechanics. How could I set a speed record on a course barely two miles long? One needed at least a four-mile run to try for a mile record. You needed at least three miles to get up to maximum speed and a mile to slow down before shutting off the engine. The mechanics shrugged. They were obviously telling me I had picked the wrong course to set a record. I believed them after two more attempts; the best I could do was 114.5.

I had upped my single-engine record considerably but was still short of the multiple-engine mark held by Gar Wood, who had a palatial home on Indian Creek and who had graciously provided facilities for reporters and photographers to watch the race and question me after it was over. I went over there, somewhat subdued, and Gar Wood looked at me quizzically.

"Whatever prompted you to try and set a record in this crick?" he wanted to know. I told him that to the best of my knowledge he had set the record on Indian Creek. He laughed. "You got it confused. I live on Indian Creek, but I never competed on it."

When I won the Gold Cup on my first attempt in 1946, I felt I was beginning a procession of victories that would last as long as I could race. But I would learn at considerable expense to my pocketbook and ego that boat racing is a speculative sport in which luck plays a major part. I would never win a Gold Cup again. The breaks of the game prevented it.

Although I won a number of races in 1949 and 1950, including the National Sweepstakes at Red Bank, I had come to the conclusion that *Tempo* had lost its racing trim after the Detroit accident. I did not compete in the Gold Cup those years, because I simply did not have the time to supervise the work needed to make *Tempo* a contender.

But in 1951, Danny Arena, with whom I had done battle in so many races, suggested that the Allison engine I had put into *Tempo* was too powerful for the twenty-four-foot boat. He volunteered to lengthen *Tempo* by six feet and I accepted the offer with gratitude. He completed the work in his shop in Detroit.

That was the kind of co-operation that made boat racing a joy. I had been helped by competitors before. Now I had a new boat that tested out beautifully and I was ready for the Gold Cup again. I was considered a favorite to win the 1951 race.

If I was the morning-line favorite, that pre-eminence didn't last long. Suddenly the cognoscenti began talking about a new boat from Seattle owned by Stan Sayres. The grapevine insisted that Sayres's boat had been tested out at 155 mph on Lake Washington and prerace tests in Detroit proved equally impressive.

The predictions about the race were accurate. By the third and final heat, only two boats remained: mine and Sayres's *Slo Mo*. The rest of the boats had broken down, victims of bad racing luck. We were to start the final heat at 5 P.M., and fifteen minutes before the race the committee was advising me I could win it by default. *Slo Mo* had broken an engine support and needed another half hour to repair it. I was being asked for permission to grant the delay. Otherwise the race was mine.

I never gave it a second thought. Of course, Sayres could have the time to fix his boat. I was not about to deny the excited spectators a chance to see what could be a classic race. It turned out to be a classic, but not because of the speed we were able to nurse out of our boats.

As I took off on a flying start, *Tempo* began acting like a car on an oil-slick pavement. The engine was racing, but the boat speed registered only 70 mph when it should have been at least 100 mph. Meanwhile *Slo Mo* was behaving erratically too. Sayres had to nurse his broken engine support. For the entire race, we kept our boats together and side by side at probably the lowest speed ever registered in the unlimited class. When it was over, the boat from Seattle had nosed out mine by a length.

And that would be the end of my Gold Cup racing. Seattle would be the home course for the next several years and I could never take time out from my summer work around New York to compete. Out of Seattle would come the champions of the fifties, helped by the fact that they could test their boats year round on Lake Washington. And from that city would come Bill Muncy, who would win more Gold Cups than any other driver. He would become the figure in speedboat racing that I had envisioned for myself.

I decided to take another crack at Gar Wood's record. By now the races I would enter, the records I would try to break had to coincide with the locations at which the band was playing. We were due to play the Cocoanut Grove, Los Angeles, in May; that wasn't too far from the Salton Sea, the huge lake in the California desert.

The last time I had tried for a record was on a Holy Thursday; this time I ventured a Friday, the thirteenth of May.

If that kind of date did not seem conducive to record-breaking, I had numerous friends in show business who were rooting hard for me. Frank Sinatra and Jimmy Van Heusen, the songwriter, flew overhead in a small plane that waved its wings in a good-luck gesture. Another single-wing plane from a nearby airfield floated down a tiny parachute that dangled a piece of wood at the end with the message: "Good Luck, Guy."

I had made all the necessary preparations this time. I knew my boat now, and I had more than enough water to push it to maximum speed. There was one slight hazard and that was that everything looked the same: the water, the land, the sand. To overcome that, we floated a sailboat in the lake as a marker.

But if I had learned anything about boat racing, it was that you had to have a target on land to ascertain your position on the course. I had surveyed the surroundings and picked out the V between two mountain peaks to set my sights on. But it didn't help. I got up to 119.7 mph, once again beating my single-engine record, but still leaving me 5 mph short of the multiple-engine mark.

In 1955 I would purchase still another *Tempo*, this one numbered VII, from a boatbuilder named Les Staudacher, who was becoming one of the most successful designers in the country. He had his business in an unlikely-sounding hamlet in northern Michigan, Kawkawlin. *Tempo VII* would win virtually every race it entered for the next two years—except the Gold Cup.

The one time my reputation as a boat driver coincided with the band business occurred in 1957 when the Royal Canadians were asked to play the annual boat show at Madison Square Garden. For me it was the best of two worlds. We would finish a set and I would wander around the exhibition floor looking at displays that ranged from race boats to yachts. The one I would come back to was an aluminum speedboat manufactured by Alcoa, and I soon became acquainted with the salesmen at the exhibit, who suggested that the company might be interested in having me drive a boat that could attempt a world's speed record.

I had tried that route, of course, and failed to achieve my objective of traveling faster on water than any other human had done before. And since my last attempt the record had soared dramatically. Donald Campbell, son of the celebrated Sir Malcolm Campbell, was now the world's record holder. He had recently driven a boat with a jet engine at the incredible speed of 248 mph. Young Campbell died later trying to stretch that record, but the risks involved in this business of getting more and more speed hardly crossed my mind.

I decided I would take another shot at it, if I could get an aluminum boat built with a jet engine. Alcoa was willing to furnish the aluminum. Les Staudacher was willing to design the boat and we would use a jet engine taken from a fighter plane that saw service in Korea.

The boat took almost a year to build. It looked somewhat like a pickle fork with tines on either side of the driver's seat. When the jet engine was completed and installed, Les took out a model of the boat to North American Aviation to have it tested in the company's wind tunnel. We were trying to learn how fast the boat could go before it would actually take off and fly. This kind of boat would be airborne perhaps 80 per cent of the time that it was in the water. But it had to have the proper aerodynamics to prevent it from acting like an airplane taking off at the end of a runway.

The tests showed that the boat was safe up to 460 mph before it would begin performing like a jet plane. But we never expected to go that fast. There were other dangers of mechanical failure at that speed. However, we felt confident it could go 300 mph, and after making some modifications suggested by the wind tunnel tests we decided on making a trial run in Pyramid Lake, Nevada.

I was playing in the nearby Lake Tahoe club owned by Bill Harrah, another speedboat enthusiast, and we had Les bring the boat out to test it at speeds up to 200 mph in Pyramid Lake. The lake was dead calm when he took off and I watched from an elevated bank with Lilliebell and Harrah. Les made two or three easy runs, getting up to 180 mph with no trouble, and all of us were pleased. I could hardly wait to get in the driver's seat myself. We were about to call it a day, when a photographer from *Popular Mechanics* magazine asked to take a photo of this wondrous aluminum boat in action. I went back to my hillside observation post and Les started up again. But by now Pyramid Lake was dead water no longer. A wind had blown up and there were ripples in the water. Where he could stop the boat in half a mile before, it would take him longer now.

He zoomed out, doing 200 mph easily, and from a distance he could see the photographer waving for him to get closer to shore. Les obliged. What he did not see was a small peninsula jutting out into the water.

By the time he spotted that tiny strip of land it was too late for him to stop. *Tempo Alcoa* hit the very tip of the peninsula, flew over it, and landed upside down on the other side. Lilliebell remembers that I screamed as I witnessed the boat somersaulting. I rushed down to the lake's edge, but I did not get there on my feet. Halfway down I stumbled and then I was tumbling down the hill, cracking into rocks and trees and landing finally in the water, bruised and bloody. Les Staudacher, meanwhile, was scrambling onto the dry land of the peninsula without a scratch. It was he who drove me back to a Reno hospital for patching up.

Les took the boat back with him to Kawkawlin and spent several months repairing it. The boat and the accident had received national press attention, and Alcoa would show it at the various boat shows around the country. By the following spring, we figured we were ready to try again, and this time we started testing in Saginaw Bay, near Staudacher's boatyard. But we could never be sure that we had repaired all damage. You just couldn't look inside the pickle-fork sponsons on either side of the boat.

I didn't want either Les or me to test the boat again with that amount of uncertainty over the state of its health. So we invested $2,500 in a remote control unit that North American Aviation built for us. The automatic pilot would start the boat, guide it, and steer it at the press of a button. When the logs were out of the bay that serves the lumber mills around it, Les took it out for a leisurely spin just to see how the boat would respond to the "slow" speed of 100 mph. He had no trouble.

Then we put the automatic pilot in and set the throttle at about half speed, which we guessed would be 150 mph. It worked and we pushed it to 200 mph. Finally we tried 250 mph, about three-quarter speed.

It went along beautifully and I couldn't wait to get into the driver's seat and skim along water at 300 mph. Suddenly a sponson came off, veering the boat to the right. And my dreams were going up in a huge splash of water; the two-ton engine was not turning with the boat. It had broken loose and continued up the bay for half a mile before it sank and disappeared.

What we feared had evidently happened. Being unable to look inside the sponson, we could not tell that the angles that held it together had been fractured to the point of breaking in the Pyramid Lake accident. When the boat reached 250 mph, it also reached the breaking point.

That was the end of *Tempo Alcoa*, which was hauled up from the bay a complete wreck. The Alcoa people were understanding; they were willing to start the project all over again. All of us knew that we could easily have reached 300 mph. But suddenly the entire business did not seem worth it anymore. A year had gone down the drain and so had considerable money. Lilliebell and my brothers were getting on my back: how could a man my age (I was over fifty by then) continue a hobby that could get him killed?

There were other considerations by now. The opportunity to race in the Gold Cup was no longer just a matter of taking a plane to Detroit and being back the same day. Seattle was now home for the big race. Commercialism was beginning to creep into the sport; more and more companies were sponsoring Gold Cup boats for the publicity value, and drivers were being paid to take dangerous risks to win the races. Where it had been purely an amateur sport before, it was becoming professional now, and I had to recognize the fact that my profession was leading a band.

I did not bow out of the sport altogether. I would fight for safety regulations and see many of my ideas put in. I would serve as judge and work on committees every time I could. Often I would resist going to races because the temptation to compete would almost change my mind.

Once I was sitting with Wilbur Shaw, the best-known auto-racing driver of his time, who had recently retired from the sport. We were at a dinner honoring Hall of Famers in all sports, and I asked him, "Do you ever get the urge to get back on the track, to show the younger drivers that you still can beat them?"

"All the time," he answered. "When I do, I just go up to my hotel room and take a nap for fifteen minutes. The feeling goes away."

And now I no longer had summers to spend free time in the racing business. In 1954, we began still a new career as producers of musical comedy extravaganzas in an outdoor stadium at Jones Beach. I began entering only races in the metropolitan area, in places such as New Jersey, that would enable me to get back to lead the orchestra for the production. I officially retired as race-boat owner and driver in the winter of 1963 after acting as an adviser on a segment of a television show named "Route 66." They filmed the racing-boat story in Tierra Verde, an island off St. Petersburg, Florida, where we had begun yet another career as part owners of a sumptuous motel.

And just not to forget about still one more sideline that was occupying my time during those years, the Lombardo brothers were operating a restaurant in Freeport. Even I had to admit there were no more minutes left in the day for Guy Lombardo to continue racing.

10. Off the Beaten Path

My brothers and I had to learn for ourselves a precept Papa must have overlooked. He had taught us to seek perfection, to be the best at anything we attempted. He had proved to me that "everything turns out for the best" after I dropped out of a short-lived banking career during my adolescence. That homily would carry me through future disappointments, frustrations, reverses.

What we had to learn on our own was that we could remain successful only by concentrating on what we knew. We would stub toes and come up limping when the band abandoned a formula that had brought us national attention; in Chicago a huge radio audience would dissipate during the brief period we discarded the identifiable sounds of Carm's sax and Lebe's trumpet in an effort to achieve a supposedly more sophisticated style.

Every mistake we made on and off the bandstand coincided with getting involved in projects that were foreign to us. Only one "turned out for the best" and paradoxically we might have been wiped out financially. We never made much money as producers of musical extravaganzas in the Jones Beach Marine Theater, but it remains the only Lombardo brothers venture, other than the band, that has lasted until today.

All those times we strayed off the beaten path may have been the result of our availability. Neither Carm, Lebe, nor I had ever developed a high degree of sales resistance, except in the band business. None of us were built to give a brush-off. There was always somebody in the crowded lobby of the Roosevelt Hotel to come up to us and address us by first name and we would always respond politely.

And then we didn't know how to walk away from the inevitable sales pitch. Everybody's mission in life seemed to be the enrichment of the three Lombardo partners. We would take to using the back entrance, but our well-wishers soon changed their lookout posts. Occasionally the ideas seemed to have merit.

In oil, we were told, lay the future of the country. That made sense, and we began investing with Depression money that was lying around dormant. We put up money for wells in Oklahoma, in Texas, and in Canada. Rarely did we hit a geyser of liquid gold. We were big in gold stocks, too, but never struck a mother lode.

Once it looked as if we had found a bonanza in an oil-well property in Alberta. World War II came along and drilling was discontinued; at the end of the war, we took our money out of the venture, which had expanded to oil-drilling operations on a nearby property. That well came in and everybody connected with it became millionaires.

Then there was the man who accosted me in the Roosevelt lobby and introduced himself as a Long Island neighbor. He had a solution for wealthy commuters fed up with the service on the Long Island Railroad and with crowded highway conditions. A drive by car from Montauk Point, at the eastern tip of the island, to New York took three hours. What he was proposing was an airplane shuttle service from Montauk to the Hudson River. The service would use seaplanes.

I knew Montauk Point from my cruises to the area on the yacht. I knew that the nearby communities of East Hampton and Southampton were populated with wealthy people who had homes in the area but rarely came out in the winter because of traveling time. It sounded like a good idea, and thus was founded the Long Island Airways at a considerable expense to the Lombardo brothers.

The airline struggled along for two years and we kept pumping money into it. I finally became disenchanted one day when I took a party of friends to Montauk for lunch. At about four o'clock we were ready for the forty-five-minute return trip when fog set in.

We finally rented a car, and I arrived after the band had started playing at the Roosevelt. That ended our career in the airline industry. I was never enamored of projects that disrupted the orderly operation of the band.

We even took a fling in the music publishing business. That one we figured we knew. Well, we might have known the mechanics of recording a song, the ingredients necessary to make it a hit. We knew music but we didn't know business.

We formed the Lombardo Music Company in the latter part of the thirties. We had an office in the Brill Building, and my sister Elaine ran it while we were on the road. We thought we could keep the entire profits of the Royal Canadians' records that were guaranteed big sellers. Why give a percentage to a publisher? Irving Berlin had gone from song-writing to music publishing; why couldn't we?

But we failed to strike oil. Our accountant decided after about two years that we ought to sell the company and take a tax write-off. A week after we sold it, one of the records we had produced suddenly took off. It was Ted Weems's version of "Heartaches." A disk jockey on a small station in North Carolina had been plugging it for weeks and by the time we had written off our company, the record was number-one in the nation. We had sold our company for $7,500 and "Heartaches" would be bringing in $7,500 a day for many months after that.

The idea for a new investment did not always originate with me. Sometimes it came from Carm and, occasionally, from Lebe. We invested equally and expected to take out equal profits. In almost every case, we lost most of the investment. But there were never recriminations or I-told-you-sos. We still believed that "everything turns out for the best."

Only in the entertainment business, which we knew something about, would the resistance to gimmicks stiffen. Even then there were times that I would finally bend to movie and television producers. They would convince me they knew better than I how to best present the Royal Canadians on the silver screen or the home tube. I would always regret bowing to the blandishments.

We made only two movies. The first was in 1934 on the occasion of our second engagement at the Ambassador's Cocoanut

Grove in Los Angeles. Paramount, which had been booking us into their theaters for stage presentations, talked us into making a film because we just happened to be the number-one band in the country and also happened to be handy for three months.

The opus was named *Many Happy Returns*, and if it was notable for anything it was the debut as a leading man by an English actor named Ray Milland. I never did know what the story was about, but the band got to play several numbers for Veloz and Yolanda, the dance team, and for George Burns and Gracie Allen, our favorite comedy team. The band would appear on the set every day, but we rarely had much to do. I used to spend most of my time on an adjoining lot where they were making a low-budget picture with a little girl as the central character.

That picture turned out to be one of the big money makers of the year. The little girl was Shirley Temple, making her debut in *Little Miss Marker*. *Many Happy Returns* surprisingly got fair reviews and grossed well. But my feeling about movie-making was that it did nothing for an established band. We had better things to do than provide accompaniment for singers and dancers.

We resisted making another one for more than ten years. Then we capitulated to pressure. Metro-Goldwyn-Mayer embarked on a campaign in 1943 to sign up every well-known big band it could get its hands on. Many of the Tin Pan Alley songwriters were out in Hollywood by now, and it seemed a profitable idea to build pictures around the orchestras who had become so well known on radio, on records, and on the stage. Xavier Cugat and Harry James were among the first to sign and become full-time Hollywood residents.

MGM executives came into the Roosevelt Grill almost nightly. They would sit with executives from the Music Corporation of America, which represented a number of stars appearing in pictures. The MCA boys would bring us over to meet the MGM boys, who would wonder why Guy Lombardo was resisting all offers to make his band even better known than it was. They talked fancy salary figures. Finally I signed a contract on the condition that we would make the picture only when we could clear our calendar to spend a month or so in Hollywood.

I procrastinated until the summer of 1945. I would tell them about this member of the band and that one being drafted into service. I didn't want to go out there without our vocalist, Kenny Gardner. Playing Washington one night, I received a wire from MGM saying that if we did not appear in Hollywood by August 7, 1945, they would consider it a breach of contract. We went out reluctantly by train and when we reached Albuquerque, New Mexico, we learned about the atom bomb dropping on Japan and ending the war. That made me feel better about doing something I really had no stomach for.

We were due on the MGM lot on a Monday morning at ten o'clock and didn't arrive at the Los Angeles station until three hours later. I called MGM to tell them we'd be there as soon as we checked into a hotel. Nobody knew what we were talking about.

Finally, I got hold of our MCA representative in L.A., explained our problem with a train that had been held up by the end of the war, and got a curious reaction. The agent told me not to worry, the picture wasn't scheduled for shooting for another three weeks. Relax and enjoy yourself, he said, you're getting $15,000 a week, starting now and for as long as it takes to finish the picture. I wished I were back in Freeport, enjoying my boat.

We had one of those charming cottages at the Beverly Hills Hotel, but I told Lilliebell I wouldn't know what to do with myself for three weeks of loafing. She suggested I walk down to the pool; she'd meet me shortly. That little walk would give me a lesson on Hollywood values. They did not coincide with my own.

I met, first, a violinist I had known in New York, a former member of the Columbia Broadcasting System's standby staff of musicians. He asked me what I was doing in Hollywood and I told him I was sitting around waiting to do a picture. He was enthusiastic about life on the Coast. "I'm making $30,000 a year, have a home in the valley, work only a couple of days a week. This is the life. You ought to move out."

I thanked him for the suggestion, moved on, and almost fell over a chaise longue occupied by a familiar face. Xavier Cugat, encased in sunglasses, was reading a movie script. He looked up, recognized me, and said, "Hey, Lombardo, what are you doing out here?"

I told him and he launched into a rhapsody that had a familiar ring. "Man, you got to move out here. I got myself a home in the valley, I make maybe $50,000 a year, I don't worry about paying musicians." And, continued the rising movie star, "You see how hard I'm working."

I told Cugie I liked it better in New York, and moved on to yet another reclining sun-worshiper on the other side of the pool. This happened to be a radio director I knew at CBS and he started spinning the same record for me. After I told him I was making a picture for Metro, he began enthusing, "You ought to stay here all the time. Me, I make $35,000 a year, I got a home in the valley and I spend more time at the pool than at the studio."

Lilliebell came into the pool area and we sat down under an umbrella. "I can't stick around here too long," I told her. "Or somebody is bound to sell us a house in the valley, wherever that is. Everybody is telling me how much money they make without working for it. This California is a lot of baloney, just like I thought."

We walked back to the cottage and Lilliebell said, "Well, your sister Rose Marie had more sense than you did. At least, she stuck to her guns."

My wife was referring to an incident that had occurred just before we left for Hollywood. Louis B. Mayer, the boss man at MGM, had come into the Roosevelt Grill to see the band that would be making a picture for his company. After the set, I visited with this man who was reputed to be the most powerful figure in the movie industry.

"Mr. Lombardo," he said, "I was enchanted by the girl vocalist with the band. She's beautiful. Who is she?"

I told him it was my sister Rose Marie, and he began enthusing. When she came to Hollywood with the band, he said, he was afraid she wouldn't be returning. "I will make her the biggest star in the business," he said.

I told Rose Marie and she wasn't one whit impressed. "I'm not going, Guy," she said. She had better things to do, like making a life with her new husband.

I agreed with Lilliebell and chafed during the three weeks before word finally came from the top. We were summoned to the office of Joe Pasternak, who would produce the picture. He was a very charming man; he asked how all my brothers were, neglecting to say hello to Carmen, who was with me. He told me how marvelous the picture was going to be; he had even imported a girl singer from England. Then, as an afterthought, he asked if I would mind adding three violins to my orchestra.

Now we hadn't had a violin in the band since I abandoned my own in Cleveland. I told him our listeners knew we weren't a string band. He turned on a little more charm. "Try it," he said. "How much can three violins hurt?" I looked at Carm and he shrugged. If Joe Pasternak wanted three violins we'd give him three violins. He had another inspiration. "And two cellos, let's have two cellos." We gave him two cellos.

We went to the studio the next day to work on an arrangement for one of our best-known numbers, "Humoresque." It really featured our twin pianos, but we made the arrangement to include the added instruments. Then we went into the recording studio to do the number that would appear in the picture. It looked like a convention of musicians. Besides our fifteen men were fifty others, the entire complement of the MGM Symphony Orchestra, one of the finest studio bands in the country. Joe Pasternak had had another inspiration.

They came equipped with harps, xylophones, a five-man percussion section, and every conceivable instrument. Our arrangement had included the addition of only the violins and cellos. I saw Pasternak and asked what they were doing there. He said smugly, "Wait till you hear."

The studio band also came equipped with a musical director, Geogie Stohl, whom I knew back in New York, and who had grown long hair since he came to Hollywood. He would lead his band and I would lead mine and we all played "Humoresque" together. Pasternak came up when we were finished, beaming, "What do you think?"

I answered grimly, "Joe, I have always liked the MGM Symphony, but why did you need our band? Who the hell is going to recognize us? Why did you bring us out here three thousand miles if all you wanted was one of our arrangements done by your band drowning out ours?" Don't worry, said this charming man, when it comes out in the picture, we would like it. I resigned myself to sweat out this torture, make the best of it, and hope we could soon go home.

It did give me the opportunity to compare our show business values with Hollywood's. The shooting started in a week and I watched developments. The imported English singer was a fresh-faced girl named Patricia Kirkwood, who had a beautiful musical-comedy voice. I watched as she torturously took lessons from Kay Thompson to become a kind of be-bop singer in the movie.

There was also this handsome young strawberry-blond actor, Van Johnson, the personification of a leading man. They made him a comedian in the picture and his career almost died before it started.

With Van Johnson mouthing the funny lines, what could the director do with another young actor who had been hired for the picture? That was Keenan Wynn, Ed's son, who had inherited his father's talent for comedy and had a face that demanded a charac-ter part. They made Keenan the leading man. I believe this brain-storm was hatched by Charlie Martin, a former radio director making his first movie.

So this comedy of errors had Van Johnson looking for laughs, Keenan Wynn handling the romance, Patricia Kirkwood trying to sound American and singing in a style she neither knew nor liked. It also had Guy Lombardo's band playing as backdrop for a studio band. The film, *No Leave, No Love*, was instantaneously forgetta-ble. To my knowledge it has never even appeared on a Late, Late, Late Show.

That should have taught me to follow my instincts and resist putting the Royal Canadians into a milieu that made no use of our talent. It did through the early years of television when they brought us dozens of ideas for presenting the Royal Canadians on the new medium. I resisted them all, signing finally for an NBC local show in New York in the fall of 1954. I had fought for a pro-gram that would simply present the Royal Canadians in a natural setting—playing at the Roosevelt Grill while people danced.

For two years, that show was rated number-one in the New York area. It became so successful that we taped it for syndication around the world. For the taped show, we used actors simulating the dancers in the Roosevelt, but other than that it was the kind of presentation that had made us successful. The show was seen by more people around the world than any other program on television.

And now the advertising agencies and broadcasting executives descended upon us again. We were the talk of the industry, even though we didn't even have a network show. The only trouble was that if you wanted to get on a network you had to have a gimmick. They were waving the red flag at a bull that had been burned before, but I succumbed to the picadors. We gave up the show from the Roosevelt and the taping for syndication around the world. Bigger things lay ahead.

The half hour they envisioned for us would have the Royal Canadians playing four or five numbers. The rest of the time was for our viewers. They were to write in letters about songs we played that reminded them of happy experiences. The best letter got a free trip to New York and a diamond ring. The program was sponsored by Geritol, and it was very popular with the old folks. It was a disaster. I spent more time reading letters and congratulating winners and presenting them with rings than I did leading the band. I had fallen for a gimmick and I would never sign for another TV show, except for guest appearances or our New Year's Eve broadcasts.

Nobody had to sell us on a project that took twenty years out of our lives and proved a costly mistake. We went into the restaurant business in 1949 almost as a lark. We had invested in enterprises we knew nothing about; at least we felt we had some knowledge about restaurants. We had certainly played in enough of them around the country, in clubs and hotel ballrooms. You might say we had been around kitchens for most of our lives. And suddenly we had the opportunity to become restaurateurs without coming up with a large outlay of cash.

At the end of South Grove Street on which I lived was an old seafood restaurant, Liota's East Point House, so named because it rested on a point of land jutting into the bay. All of us and our wives had eaten there, enjoying the wide porches set up as dining rooms with their view of the water and cruising boats. I had become acquainted with John Liota, the owner, who had been running the business for many years and was contemplating retirement.

"The town of Hempstead owns the land," he told me one night, "and I have seven more years to go on my lease. I'm looking for somebody to take it over till the lease runs out. All I'm asking is 7 per cent of the gross business which the new owner can consider as rent. However he wants to fix up the place is up to him. You know anybody?"

I talked it over with Lilliebell that night. How would she like a restaurant down the street that we would own, that we could invite friends and family for dinners and special occasions. She liked the idea, offered to decorate the place, suggested we could hire another member of the family to manage it. Bill Frey, husband of Lilliebell's sister, Viola, had managed restaurants around Cleveland most of his life.

Carm and Lebe were for it too. The three of us, like most show business people who eat on the road more than they do at home, all had favorite restaurants and ideas for incorporating the best points of the better ones. We took the Liota deal, figuring to do about $100,000 gross business. Freeport and Nassau County now had a new restaurant—Guy Lombardo's East Point House.

It took no great prescience to realize that we couldn't lend the Lombardo name to a broken-down, rather shabby building. We would have to do a certain amount of renovation. And in anticipation of doing a greater volume of business than John Liota, the tiny kitchen would obviously have to be enlarged. We called in brother Joe to give us the benefit of his architectural expertise.

The kitchen, Joe announced, was holding up the dining room, literally and structurally. We couldn't enlarge it unless we moved it, and if we did that the dining room would cave in. All that held up the kitchen was marshland, and the entire building might sink if we began moving rooms around. So Joe designed us a new restaurant.

It certainly was a beauty, shaped like a ship, with dining decks on three sides overlooking the water. The bar, warm and upholstered, was one of the largest in the county, and Lilliebell's decorating touches carried out the nautical theme. On a shelf in back of the bar reposed my speedboating cups and trophies, and a mural that covered an entire wall was a blown-up picture of *Tempo* VI winning the Gold Cup. We discarded all of Liota's furniture, replaced it with expensive new pieces, installed an all-stainless-steel kitchen, imported a chef and bar manager from New Orleans, and opened for business. Our lark had turned into a $300,000 investment.

The opening was attended with much fanfare. Our chef, Obie Smith, prepared a buffet that would have done credit to an ocean liner. I invited all the show business people I knew who were appearing in New York and the official families of the village of Freeport, the town of Hempstead and the county of Nassau. The town officials were particularly impressed. They now had a costly building on their land.

That first season the volume of business amazed everybody, especially my brothers and me. We had opened in the late spring, and by the end of the year some $800,000 had poured into the cash registers. John Liota had struck gold. Instead of the estimated $7,000 he expected in rent from his 7 per cent cut, he got $56,000. Our auditors told us at the end of the year that we had done fine. We had broken even.

The pattern was to remain that way for the next ten years or so. We never stinted on personnel; in fact we were one of the first restaurants in the county to sign up union waiters and bartenders. My instructions to Bill Frey, our manager, and Chef Smith were to buy only the finest provisions, the freshest fish and seafood. I had never been accused of cheating the public with our music and I wanted to maintain the same reputation in this new enterprise.

The customers would wait in line almost every summer night of the week. On weekends it was almost impossible to get into the place. No matter how busy, our captains would prepare dishes at tableside in chafing dishes, mix salads of an infinite variety of dressings and greens. And in the wintertime business would slack off drastically. Our costs would remain constant; I couldn't get myself to lay off a large number of help who weren't really needed in the slack season.

The investment kept growing. After a few years, we had to make alterations to accommodate the summer rush. We expanded an upstairs room into a catering hall, hoping we could book private parties in the winter. We put in a dance floor, and on occasion when we weren't working elsewhere we even booked the band into the room for special affairs.

We had almost half a million dollars in the East Point House when John Liota's lease ran out and we signed a new one for twenty years. The worst that could happen, my brothers and I figured, was that, if the financial strain of carrying the restaurant became too much, we could always sell and get most of our money back. Meanwhile, we loved the place, enjoyed coming to it, entertaining the people who were close to us. In 1954, when we began productions at Jones Beach, the East Point House would for many years be the setting for our opening night parties. And still later we would charter an old ferryboat and offer a package that included dinner at our restaurant, the boat ride to Jones Beach, and tickets to the show.

But the restaurant was beginning to take up time in an already crowded schedule. Bill Frey died, and I might be playing in Toledo and talking on the phone to Freeport with the chef, worrying about his problems and the others that always cropped up in restaurants.

We finally lightened the load, somewhat, by selling an interest in the restaurant to two young men whose family ran a successful night club in Brooklyn. They managed the place and lifted the day-to-day decision-making from my shoulders. But they faced the same problems we had. Business was good in the summer, bad in the winter, and there never seemed to be a profit at the end of the year.

They pulled out in the early sixties, and the Savarin Company leased the restaurant. That relieved us, finally, of management responsibility and gave us an annual rental that would take many years to make up our investment. A few years ago, Savarin gave up the ghost too, and presiding supervisor Ralph Caso, of the town of Hempstead, suggested that we become partners with Carl Hoppl, the county's largest restaurateur who had a chain of restaurants and concessions in county parks. I agreed and Hoppl was planning to rebuild the restaurant again, when one night the now-shuttered East Point House burned down.

Hoppl declared himself out of the deal, and I discovered to my dismay that Savarin had lapsed its insurance and that Hoppl had never taken out a policy on the property. I went to Ralph Caso, who had moved up to become Nassau County Executive, and he said there was nothing he could do. The deal he had made as Hempstead supervisor could not be honored now.

It was another lesson to be learned. You might convert a chicken coop into a castle, but if it was on leased land, you never owned it. So my brothers and I lost perhaps half a million dollars through ignorance. What may have hurt me even more was that all the mementos of my career as a racing driver went up in the fire, too. I was the principal mover in this disaster, but never once did Carm or Lebe express resentment. They remembered as I did the happy times we had in the place and we all preferred to forget the tragedy of it.

The East Point House would not be the first restaurant with which we were associated to suffer an unhappy demise. Along the way, while we were still involved with the East Point House, there came an offer for the Lombardos to associate themselves with a motel, dining room, and night club in Florida. No investment, just a chance to have permanent winter headquarters on an island with waterfront homes and a 50-per-cent interest in the profits from the motel's dining room and night club.

The offer came at a time when we were facing the unhappy prospect of giving up our base of operations in New York—the Roosevelt Hotel. By 1963 the era of the Big Bands was over and few hotels around the country still maintained name orchestras to attract the tourist trade.

New York was no longer the Fun City it used to be. People weren't going out as much at night. The night clubs were disappearing, the theater was suffering and the Times Square area had degenerated into an area for pickpockets, hustlers, and voyeurs frequenting the dirty-book stores and the new hard-core pornography being shown in the movie houses. Muggings were on the rise and many people simply feared to walk the midtown streets at night.

The atmosphere had affected a number of hotels that were beginning to suffer downtown blight and were losing customers to motels growing on the city's outskirts. Fewer tourists came to New

York anymore for a short stay—for instance, before taking off on transatlantic cruises. They went by planes now. The Royal Canadians were one of the last hotel bands remaining in New York, coming back to the Roosevelt every fall and winter. We always had four or five months in the big town and we had our homes on the island to come back to every night, and we were in the center of the entertainment business for our record and radio dates, for our new television career, for booking ourselves across the country when the Roosevelt season ended.

And now after thirty-three years, our New York base was threatened. The hotel was losing money, it was considering a change of management, we had heard they might no longer be able to afford us the next season. At that stage of our lives Arthur Etkus approached us with an alternative to spending our winters in New York.

He was a public relations counselor whom I had met a few months before. He had an idea for a new boat and asked me to come out to Cincinnati to see the prototype. I made the trip and told him the idea had no merit. Now he was working for the oil-rich Murchison brothers of Texas—Clint, Jr., and John—promoting a development they had been building for ten years and that now was in the process of completion. Etkus was grateful that I had made the trip to see the boat, and it had occurred to him that Guy Lombardo was ideally suited to help the Murchison brothers succeed in a business that had already cost them $20,000,000. In partnership with the father and son team who owned the Belanti Construction Company, the Murchisons had spent this fortune in building an island community in the Gulf of Mexico, at the foot of Tampa Bay off St. Petersburg. They had constructed the island by pulling together sixteen smaller ones, building miles of sea wall, dredging up millions of tons of sand from the bottom of the bay for fill.

Virtually completed, the island had been named Tierra Verde (Spanish for "green land") and awaited only residents to buy property and build houses and a community. A new highway connected it to the mainland and St. Petersburg, the retirement capital of the world. There were no unsightly telephone or electric light poles on Tierra Verde. All wires for TV, radio, or music connections had been buried underground. A golf course was planned. And building had started on a motel of fifty rooms with a small coffee shop for visitors who might want to spend a day or two deciding on Tierra Verde as a permanent retirement home.

Etkus described the planned community as the most modern and beautiful he had ever seen. Then he came to the point. He had just come from a conference with the Murchisons and Berlantis in which he had suggested that Guy Lombardo and the Royal Canadians be brought into the operation. A number of Canadian residents had already made inquiries about Tierra Verde as a place to retire. Who could pull them in better than the Canadian-born Lombardos?

What Etkus had in mind was to build a much larger motel than originally planned. It would serve as a resort complex for vacationers who would spread the word about the magnificence of Tierra Verde. It would include a dining room and a night club spacious enough for the Royal Canadians and name acts to appear nightly through the winter season.

All that would be done if the Lombardo organization agreed to come into the deal, which offered us a 50-per-cent cut of the food and liquor profits. The band would receive its regular fee.

What particularly attracted me about the offer was the timing. That late spring of 1963, with the prospect of no longer working at the Roosevelt Hotel for the winter, we would have to begin planning now to provide a substitute for that four-month period that had been locked into our schedule since 1929. Here was an offer that on the surface could erase the problem; if Tierra Verde was really the Shangri-La that Etkus was describing, we might even be on our way to that elusive fortune that had always escaped us. And with no investment.

Carm, Lebe, and I took an exploratory trip on a day off. We liked what we saw on Tierra Verde. The public relations man had not exaggerated. We met the Murchisons and the Berlantis and they showed us the new plans for an expanded motel that would cost $2,500,000. They said we could design the dining room-night club and would spare no expense to make it as fine a facility as could be found anywhere. They showed us the model homes already constructed and offered three of them to us to live in at no cost until we decided to build our own homes.

The island had unparalleled facilities for my speedboat hobby and Lebe's passion for fishing. Carm could swim and ride horseback on the beach. Our families could have winter vacations with us while we were working. The Murchison name inspired confidence; they were not known to embark on losing propositions. We agreed on the deal and promised to come back as often as possible to supervise the layout of the Port O' Call room, the showplace of Guy Lombardo's Port O' Call motel.

As we looked ahead, the sole remaining problem was the location of our telecast on New Year's Eve after we had terminated our association with the Roosevelt Hotel. That one was solved one summer weekend when Carm and Florence were entertaining Mrs. Winthrop (Bobo) Rockefeller as a houseguest in Woodmere.

She had been named chairman of a charity ball to benefit the Mental Health Association of New York. Just the other week, she told Carm, somebody had come up with a kooky idea that had elicited surprising support from the society ladies on the committee. The suggestion had been to run a New Year's Eve party in Grand Central Terminal. Where else could you book a party for several thousand people on New Year's Eve?

Furthermore, officials of the New York Central R.R. were not averse to the party. All they needed now, Bobo said, was a band like Guy Lombardo's.

Well, we just happened to have that night open for the first time since we had arrived in Cleveland. Carm got excited. The very idea of solving the logistics that would be involved appealed to him. He called me on the phone immediately. I agreed with him. I shared his zest and enthusiasm for trying something as new as it was exciting.

And so we booked Grand Central Terminal for $2,000 an hour and the railroad people figured out a way to reroute trains on the night that would usher in 1964. The only hurdle we had to overcome was that the giant station was not heated for scurrying commuters who breezed by in overcoats. We had to install heaters for the ladies who came in ball gowns.

That television show, broadcast by two hundred stations across the nation, may have surpassed all our other New Year's Eve programs in favorable mail. Viewers saw two thousand people dancing, sitting down at tables to box lunches of chicken, caviar, and champagne. "Auld Lang Syne" had suffered nothing by being taken out of a hotel and put into a railroad station. And Bobo Rockefeller would later report that the affair had raised $25,000 for the charity.

Our new winter home was formally opened the following week and business was brisk at the Port O' Call room. We put on names like Marlene Dietrich, Alan King, Dorothy Dandridge and played for several hundred people a night, most of them from nearby St. Petersburg and the West Coast towns as far away as Sarasota. The huge motel, however, was virtually empty. By next year when the golf course was built, we felt it would be doing capacity business. There were no profits from that first season, but the band worked those winter months and all the members in it enjoyed what amounted to a paid vacation on a paradisiacal island.

The next year the entire project collapsed. The Port O' Call room was still attracting people who lived in the area, but the rooms with beds remained mostly unoccupied. You couldn't always count on summer weather in the winters off St. Petersburg. The planned golf course was still on the drawing boards and that didn't help. A nine-hole Par 3 course was hardly a drawing card for golfers seeking a sun that did not always shine in December, January, and February.

Worst of all, the property and houses weren't selling. Perhaps the prices were too high in a market that had yet to contend with inflation. Waterfront plots were going for $13,500 and inland parcels were half that much. The Murchisons had two thousand acres to sell, but they had that $20,000,000 investment. If you paid that much for property, a proper house figured to cost from $40,000 to $70,000. People who wanted to retire could not justify that kind of expense in 1964 and 1965.

258 AULD ACQUAINTANCE

Later that season, a private plane piloted by the younger Berlanti and carrying his father crashed into the Everglades, killing both men. The Murchison brothers began looking around for a buyer to take the property off their hands. The Lombardo brothers, after two seasons of working in the sun, decided to accept a contract for December dates at the Waldorf Astoria. Henceforth that would be our home on New Year's Eve.

11. *The Jones Beach Extravaganzas*

I have to go back, now, to the story of our adventures at Jones Beach, which have continued through the present day. I became a producer in 1954, when we still had great hopes for the future of our restaurant in Freeport, when we had launched the highest-rated show on New York television and when the mere possibility of losing a little money was not a frightening prospect.

With all our other ventures we took on the added responsibility of putting on musical extravaganzas at the Jones Beach Marine Theater, an 8,200-seat stadium abutting a bay. We accepted the challenge primarily because it had been put to us by one of my heroes. Another reason may have to do with a common feeling among many star performers that their talent extended to the skills of an impresario. George M. Cohan was an early example. Later, fortunes would be made in television productions by such entertainers as Lucille Ball and Desi Arnaz, Bing Crosby, Danny Thomas, and Sheldon Leonard.

So it was flattering that a man like Robert Moses would come to us, asking to help him make a success out of a theater that had been built only two years before and had operated through two financially disastrous seasons. He was in effect telling us that he wanted our formula for reaching the top of the entertainment industry to work for his purpose of providing the public with spectacular shows at modest prices.

Moses was a hero figure of mine because of his penchant for

getting things done. Master planner and master builder, he had changed the face of New York City and New York State with his bridges, parkways, parks, and housing projects. Everything he did was accomplished with flair and imagination, and the Jones Beach State Park was just another example of his skill in converting a sand-dune wasteland into a public-recreation facility unequaled in the world.

His aversion to the cheap, the gaudy, the tawdry was in exact accord with my own ideas of entertainment for the public, and I had followed his career with interest and admiration. Apparently he had the same feeling for the Lombardos, and this was made clear when I received a phone call in Freeport one snowy afternoon.

The caller was Sid Shapiro, Moses' chief aide, chief engineer, and general manager of the Jones Beach State Park Commission. He said Mr. Moses had asked him to call us. He liked our style, our reputation for presenting good, clean entertainment. Could I come down to look at the Marine Theater? He'd meet me. I ventured out into a howling wind that blew snow flurries, and I remember thinking this was some day to look at an outdoor theater by the water.

What I saw upon meeting Shapiro was an open-air, concrete stadium with a sea of seats and, up front, a large number of boxes bordering on a lagoon that stretched for a hundred feet to a huge stage. In back of the stage was Zach's Bay. Shapiro gave me a brief history of the theater.

Moses had started building it in the thirties with the purpose of providing low-cost entertainment for boardwalk strollers and New Yorkers seeking a summer night's excursion. The building had been halted by World War II, and it had finally been completed in 1952 as a vehicle for water shows, patterned after Billy Rose's Aquacade in Flushing Meadows, a feature of the 1939 World's Fair.

It had been Moses' intention to retain Rose as producer of the water shows, Shapiro said. When Billy came out to inspect the theater, his immediate reaction was that the lagoon around which the theater was designed had to go. He called it a "dumb arrangement." He began planning his show off the top of his head,

Shapiro remembered, and on the assumption that the lagoon would be filled in and the stage moved closer to the audience.

He laid out a picture of a show that would feature a stage full of "long-legged beauties," and was rattling off a rapid-fire description of the pulling power of chorus girls, when Moses drew Shapiro aside and whispered, "Get rid of him."

For the next several months, Shapiro was told to forget about engineering. Robert Moses wanted him to find a producer. Instead of blueprints, he began reading *Variety* and other show business journals. He learned that the Shuberts were Broadway's top producers. So he tried to get them for Jones Beach and was turned down.

Then he read about peripatetic Mike Todd and the troubles he was having with bluenose groups seeking to close his "Peep Show" on Broadway. A day later Mike Todd, apparently convinced his show wasn't going anywhere, came out to see Shapiro. He promised that he would put on a clean show, and he advised Shapiro that he better hire him quickly because there remained only a few months to get a production ready for the Marine Theater's first summer season.

"That guy talked so fast and rattled off so many good stories, I decided with some trepidation to recommend him to Mr. Moses," Shapiro remembered. "And after all, we just didn't have anymore time to look around."

In the next two weeks, Shapiro was to get telegrams from Mike Todd abroad. One said he was bringing over the La Scala Opera Company from Italy, a cast of four hundred, on the S.S. *Rex.* All Shapiro had to do was get clearance for the artists from immigration authorities. That didn't work, and the next plan projected by Todd via transatlantic phone was a life of Verdi.

Finally with only a few weeks to go before the scheduled opening of the theater, Todd sent a two-page cablegram from Switzerland, outlining plot, songs, and scenes for *A Night in Venice*, a musical he predicted would provide a perfect vehicle for the lagoon to display colorful gondolas. He brought it in at the very last moment, without time for rehearsals, appeared on the stage to make announcements, and seemed to be having a ball. His constant companion was the beautiful young actress Elizabeth Taylor, whom he would later marry.

The opening of the show was attended by Billy Rose, who kept reminding Shapiro that the theater needed the lagoon "like a hole in the head." That was precisely the phrase Brooks Atkinson of the New York *Times* used in an unflattering review. Todd couldn't have cared less; he had picked himself up an angel, had a drawing account of $5,000 a week, a chauffeured limousine, and Liz Taylor at his side.

But A *Night in Venice* received no plaudits from the critics and not enough box-office money to break even on the production costs that first season. It was put on for another year and really incurred heavy financial losses. Robert Moses had had enough of Todd, and in the early months of 1954 he sent Sid Shapiro looking for me.

I had brought Lebert along with me and we listened to this tale of woe and to the icy wind howling over the stadium. I asked Shapiro, "You sure Mr. Moses wants me to do this?" Shapiro nodded, almost beseechingly; Lebe put his hands on his forehead almost in resignation. My brother knew I could not resist that kind of challenge, and I didn't.

I had no idea at the time of what kind of show we would put on. I thought about some kind of vaudeville show, maybe featuring acts that could work the lagoon—comic divers, water skiers, a boat regatta. I would hire scenic designers and a director and sit back and let them put on the show. But Robert Moses didn't want that kind of thing.

I called up a good friend of mine, Allan Zee, who produced the shows at New York's Capitol Theater. He'd produced other shows, could at least get us off the ground floor. He met us at the Roosevelt Grill, and we sat around after the band finished playing until about three o'clock in the morning, discussing possibilities. Finally he said he'd sleep on it, and I guess he never did get to shut his eyes. Four hours later he was on the phone. He had an idea about a modern Arabian Nights.

So with Carm accompanying us this time, we went out the next day for another freezing session at Jones Beach to plan how to put on the show and work out our band schedule. We were booked at the Roosevelt until March and had planned a tour that would bring us back in mid-May. That would give us six weeks to get the show together, a prospect that made Zee blanch. "Most big musical shows take at least a year to put together," he reminded us, also pointing out the poor quality of the production that Mike Todd had managed in a month.

We didn't have a year; we had six weeks. We had to cancel the tour we were planning after May and we had to renegotiate our TV schedules. We did have a big plus in that Carm offered to write the musical score with his partner, Johnny Loeb. We could get a professional to write the book and accompany us on the road to set the scenes for Carm's and Johnny's songs.

We figured it would cost about $150,000 to put on the show and that we could get investors to come up with most of it. We ended up with exactly $30,000 in outside capital, and by the time we were ready to go into production the costs had risen to $275,000, which the three Lombardo brothers had to put up.

That of course was exclusive of the ten weeks' salary we would have to pay a huge cast, including Lauritz Melchior, the operatic star, and dozens of technicians and stagehands. Our figuring had changed as we got into the planning of the show. We had never traveled second-class since our first vaudeville tour, thirty years ago, and we had to get the best players, the best scenic designers and scenery, costumes that wouldn't look like they were second-hand, and choreography to match Broadway's finest. We would have to take in $750,000 at the box-office to break even. And we had a ten-week season.

I had first met Lauritz Melchior in the VIP lounge at the Washington airport, where we were both returning home after performing at President Eisenhower's first Inaugural Ball. The dignity and humor of this giant of a man, the Met's reigning star, impressed me. We had to have a man of his stature and talent to star in the show, to play the Sultan.

Melchior turned us down cold. He had heard about the hastily prepared Todd productions; Jones Beach was too far from New York for him to travel every night; he wanted no part of it.

I sent Allan Zee, who would be in charge of production, and Johnny Loeb to see him in Los Angeles, where he was appearing.

Zee offered him $5,000 a week, a cottage on the beach, and a convertible to use all summer. Johnny Loeb played the score he had written with Carmen. The great Dane changed his mind and we had our star.

Our pit orchestra would be a combination of fine concert musicians plus the fifteen musicians in our band, including Carm, Lebe, and Victor. I would lead the opening National Anthem and overture and turn over the baton to our musical director. The pit band duties would pay my musicians as much as they would have earned on our summer tour, and it would keep the Lombardo sound in the production.

But I suppose the real star of the show was a whale that had been written into the story. The whale was a barge covered over with blue canvas and white polka dots and fashioned into the shape of the sea mammal. Christened "Polky" by Lilliebell, it came swimming into the lagoon carrying Sinbad and twenty-three sailors on its back. The shipwrecks thought the whale was an island and lustily sang the Lombardo-Loeb "A Whale of a Whale of a Story."

Polky furnished the sailors a bath every time he spouted and the audience a laugh every time he showed his bicuspids, one of which was a shiny gold tooth. They also appreciated Melchior's voice and the duet sung by the lovers from giant towers on opposite sides of the stage. We would always have to put on a feature to match Polky in succeeding shows.

We enjoyed good weather that first season with only a few rainouts, and when we totted up the receipts after Labor Day, we were more than happy to get our investment back. The show had made twenty-six dollars after all expenses. We paid the state thirteen dollars and my brothers and I split the rest.

We repeated the production the following year, happy that Bob Moses and Sid Shapiro were happy and that so many thousands of people had enjoyed it. The price range for tickets was from one dollar to four dollars and forty cents, we had put on the biggest musical in terms of cast and production ever seen, and we had met a challenge. With the cost of scenery and costumes no factor for a second production of *Arabian Nights*, we could even look forward to a big profit for our next season.

Even though we had paid back our investors in full for the first production, there were no takers for the 1955 show. We had to put up thirty-nine of our taped TV films as security for capital. The payroll was still constant and so were the operating costs. We got through July in fairly good shape, with attendance only slightly down from the previous year, and then we ran into August.

That was the month of the hurricanes. Never had so many of them come up from the Caribbean and the Florida coast as they did in those thirty days. There were at least five storms, closing up production for as long as four days each. I don't think we played more than ten days that August. My brothers and I lost more than $300,000, and we had to sell stocks and personal property to pay the creditors. I told Bob Moses we were through as producers. We had loved working with him and his staff, but we just couldn't afford to risk anymore money on the vagaries of weather in an open-air theater.

Well, Bob Moses had a reputation for moving mountains. He also should have been known as a Moses that couldn't be moved when he wanted to hold onto something. On parting, he said he'd never have another producer for his theater than Guy Lombardo and maybe after a few weeks I'd change my mind and come back again.

That's what it took, just a few weeks, and everywhere we played, we began getting phone calls from Sid Shapiro. "We can't break up the combination of Lombardo and Jones Beach," he'd shout into the phone. "Mr. Moses won't allow it. He says he's coming out to see you in Las Vegas when you play there, unless you change your mind by then."

Sid would do virtually all of the talking on those phone calls. I would interrupt only long enough to say, "No." Finally, to stop the everlasting calls, I sent Moses a wire. As firmly as I could put it, I advised him we would never return to produce shows at Jones Beach.

We began a month's engagement in Las Vegas, which was well on its way to becoming the nation's highest-paying town for entertainers, and we had hardly started playing our first set, when I noticed a familiar face from Jones Beach. It wasn't Bob Moses; it was Stan Polek, the head man for the night-by-night operation of the Marine Theater. I walked over to his table feeling that I owed him that courtesy, and I almost choked. He had a contract and a pen in his hand. I had to sign it, he said, or he'd never be able to go back and face Mr. Moses.

He kept following me around with that contract and pen for several days and I kept telling him to go back on the plane to New York. A gentle, nice, little man, Polek would look at me and say, "Guy, don't you know Mr. Moses doesn't know the meaning of the word 'no.'" I would tell him that I did and I meant it and he asked if he could meet me for lunch the next day. I regarded it as his last stand and, confident that there was no way he could sell me, I set a one-o'clock date.

After our show that night, I fell in with a bunch of entertainers from other hotels, and we traded show business lore almost until dawn. I got up at four o'clock the next afternoon with the feeling I had forgotten something. It came to me: the lunch date with Polek. I called him to apologize and told him to meet me at the swimming pool. He showed up, as usual carrying pen and contract.

That did it. Contrite about breaking an appointment, feeling sorry for this man who would have to go back and face the wrath of Moses, I capitulated once again. This time, I thought, I wouldn't blame my brothers if they called me an idiot or even if they refused to have a part in it. With Polek standing at the side of the pool and with me in the water, I signed the contract to produce the 1956 show.

Bob Moses had a pleasant surprise for us when we returned home. My brothers hadn't called me an idiot, although I'm sure they wanted to, and they hadn't pulled out of the Lombardo Jones Beach Production Company. Thus, they were as happy as I was to find that Moses had gone to Albany and found a way to protect us against losing as heavily as we had in 1955. From now on, New York State would advance $250,000 for our up-front production money.

We would have to pay it back if the show came up with a profit. But we actually were being insured against losses up to $250,000. Beyond that, we were responsible for further losses.

Feeling better about everything, we discussed with Moses ideas for our next production. He said he'd love to put on *Showboat*, but Oscar Hammerstein II, who had made a musical comedy out of Edna Ferber's book, had scoffed at the idea. He didn't believe it could be presented on other than a legitimate theater stage.

"Well, you're the man, Mr. Moses," I said, "who always says 'can't' doesn't belong in the dictionary. I think we can do it and better than it was done on the Broadway stage. After all they didn't have water for a showboat."

We proved it to Oscar Hammerstein. The first thing I did was shorten the lagoon and build a stage in front of the boxes. Now we would have two stages, the one in the back with scenery depicting our locale, and the one to give the audience a closer view of the action. They were now a hundred feet closer to the actors and singers and dancers, and we would use the back stage for spectacular effects and for scenes in which the entire cast might be singing.

And for *Showboat*, we presented even a third stage, right on the deck of the fabled *Blossom Queen*, the Mississippi River paddle-wheeler. For the first time in the twenty-nine-year history of the musical, *Showboat* would have a showboat. As usual no expense was spared. Designed by Albert Johnson, the boat was 140 feet long, 28 feet across, and 34 feet high. Along an 80-foot stretch on one side was a canvas drop that rolled up into a stage where most of the singing and dancing took place. When I saw it completed all I could think to say was:

"It's the biggest goddamned thing ever invented for a show."

We recruited Andy Devine, at the height of his popularity as a TV star, to play Cap'n Andy. I sat with Oscar Hammerstein and Edna Ferber, after directing the overture on opening night. Hammerstein kept shaking his head in wonderment, almost as if he had never seen his show before. Edna Ferber kept dabbing her eyes with a handkerchief.

We made what we considered a handsome profit that year, although it hardly matched what we had lost on *Arabian Nights*. The second year of *Showboat* we broke about even. We would find that second-year shows rarely matched the grosses of the preceding season, but it would take several years before we would finally decide on a policy of presenting a production for one summer only.

There developed, as one season rolled into another, what we would call our Jones Beach Navy, and in that respect my knowledge of boats came in handy. Every year we would try to outdo the one before in the type of craft we put in the water. For *Song of Norway*, which followed *Showboat*, we purchased the ship used in the Kirk Douglas film *The Vikings*. One night it sprang a leak to the lovely Edvard Grieg music, but a stagehand jumped into the water and stuffed his undershirt into the splitting seam. For *Hit the Deck* we came up with an actual speedboat race to provide an exciting finale written into a script that was never noted for its story line. And a battleship for sailors to tap dance on.

In 1961, two years after Hawaii achieved statehood, it struck Bob Moses that we ought to do a South Sea island book to honor the occasion. Carm and Johnny Loeb and I sat around our office in the amphitheater one night mulling ideas.

I had often wondered from whence came the inspiration for the story line that is fitted into a musical comedy. The only one I ever got came from a line in a song and out of that would evolve our 1961 production, *Paradise Island*.

Carm and Johnny had been busy talking about Hawaii and its people from what they had learned in the movies. For some reason a song kept running through my head, something about "bongo, bongo, bongo, I don't want to leave the Congo." I remembered vaguely that the premise of the song had to do with "rich men come for two-day vacation, I have vacation all my life."

I thought about it long enough to interrupt the song-writing team's quest for inspiration. "Look," I said, "we have these wonderful, happy people living on their island, fishing and swimming and dancing, doing what millionaires spend all their lives looking for, and we get this American tycoon discovering this Paradise Island when his yacht gets lost in a storm. Then he sees the possibility of making it a vacation retreat and he sells the king of the island on the idea that he will make him rich. And all of a sudden these people's lives change for the worse as civilization comes in."

The boys thought the story line was faintly reminiscent. But it was a takeoff point. Johnny Loeb's wife was interested in archaeology; she would do our research. And she came up with the tiniest island in the Hawaiian chain and its fables and folklore, including the intelligence that at one time a person who stumbled onto the island could never go back. And that there were Irish-type leprechauns on the island that came out at night and built fences.

So out of the research and with remnants remaining from my inspiration we fashioned a production, with Carm and Johnny writing a lovely score and with Billy Gaxton as the tycoon and Arthur Treacher as his perfect butler descending on the island. We imported dancers and a diver from Hawaii who jumped a hundred feet into the lagoon, carrying lighted torches. If anybody complained about the story, we didn't hear about it. The spectacle could not be matched.

The most spectacular of all productions was *Around the World in 80 Days*, originally produced by Mike Todd as a movie and the vehicle that had finally made him a fortune before his untimely death in the crash of his private plane. His son, Mike, Jr., owned the property and was happy to work on the show with us.

Imagine, if you will, a balloon and its gondola carrying actors, floating 150 feet into the air as part of a stage presentation. Or a railroad train being attacked by Indians, or a paddle-wheeler being taken apart timber by timber to provide enough fuel to get across the Atlantic. All of these things we could make believable with the unique character of our theater and with the ingenuity of our engineers.

If *Around the World* was the most spectacular, *Mardi Gras* was my favorite because it reunited me with Louis Armstrong. I paid my old friend $13,000 a week to appear with his quartet in a New Orleans story, with book and lyrics by Carm and Johnny. I never enjoyed anything more in my life than the "battle of the bands" we put on with my crew and his. Satchmo loved it so much he did the show a second year and this time we brought in an innovation. The Schaeffer beer people put in a giant tent into which people could come after the show for free dancing to both bands.

That policy remains today, with the Royal Canadians providing music for dancing for an hour. The tent is now also used when we've gotten through most of a show only to be interrupted by rain. We take the show inside and finish all the numbers that didn't get a chance to go on.

We would embark, finally, on a policy of reviving Broadway classics and shaping them with the spectacular effects our Jones Beach Navy could provide. Our eighty-foot barge could be made to look like anything from the baby whale in *Arabian Nights* to the alpine mansion in *Sound of Music*. For *Song of Norway* we would have a barge with its own ice-making machinery that played the part of a floating iceberg.

When we did *Fiddler on the Roof*, the barge carried a combination set: Tevye's house and barn rotating on a turntable to reveal the interior of a tavern. For *South Pacific* we had a genuine PT boat, and for *Carousel* we had an authentic merry-go-round built from scratch and costing about $10,000 to install on the stage. In all of these endeavors, the man most responsible for their success was Arnold Spector, who has been our managing director for many years now.

We have only had two or three years since the *Arabian Nights* fiasco when we lost money. Usually they were second-season jobs and ran up against foul weather. Now we limit productions to one year. Along about the first of August, we take a poll among dancers in the tent, asking what show they'd like to see next year. We had begun work on *Oklahoma* for 1975 when this book was being finished.

Since that policy started, we have always had a comforting advance sale of $200,000 or so before we even go into rehearsal, which is in early June. With it all, I would guess that the Lombardo Production Company has just about broken even for its twenty years in business. I'm delighted with that.

Of course, production costs have risen with the times and so have our admission prices, which now range from three dollars to six dollars. It now costs about $1,400,000 to produce one of our shows, and we still have to sweat out the weather. The first thing I do every morning of summer, these days, is turn on the radio for the weather forecast.

But I have found something in life out of putting on these shows. It certainly isn't money. There is the satisfaction of seeing all those nuts and bolts fitting into place to provide an audience an evening of entertainment I know they can't see anywhere else in the world.

There is the good feeling of mingling with some of the most talented performers in the world. We go after the best available if we think they fit a part. We wanted Yul Brynner for *The King and I*, but he was making a television series out of the show and it never proved a hit. So we starred a fine baritone named John Cullum, who proved such a hit we brought him back for *Carousel*.

The only time I ever had a problem casting one of the wonderful Oscar Hammerstein-Richard Rodgers musicals was when we put on *South Pacific*. Hammerstein had died and his son Bill had asked to direct the show after Rodgers had given us the rights to put it on. The man I immediately thought of for the lead was the brilliant Met baritone Jerome Hines.

We had set up an audition that Rodgers didn't attend, and young Bill was enthusiastic about our selection for the lead. Several weeks later we were at lunch at Dinty Moore's in New York. Carm and Bill and Arnold Spector were there, and all of a sudden young Bill asked me if I didn't think Jerome Hines had too much vibrato for the part. I didn't know what that meant. I had just heard him do *Aida* on the Bell Telephone hour and had never been so captivated. I told Bill that and it now developed that Dick Rodgers wanted Hines to audition for him personally.

We had already signed a contract for Hines at a salary of $2,500 a week, dirt-cheap for a performer who commanded $5,000 an appearance. Now how was I going to embarrass him by saying he had to audition again? Arnold Spector had the answer; he told Hines that Dick Rodgers had never heard him speak lines with actresses. Hines was very tall and Rodgers simply wanted to know if the height mattered.

Hines obliged, standing between two actresses, and Dick Rodgers watched, wondering what was going on. He had come to hear him sing. Then Spector called out to the baritone, who usually took an hour to warm up his voice before singing a note, "That was fine, Jerome," Arnold said. "Now would you do me a favor. Could you please sing a chorus of 'Some Enchanted Evening.' I want Mr. Rodgers to hear the best."

Jerome Hines didn't let us down. Maybe the flattery did it.

Richard Rodgers was much impressed and I was much relieved that my managing director's ingenuity had saved me embarrassment.

There are fine memories of all the wonderful performers who appeared with us through the years. I can never forget the courage of Elaine Malbin, who played the Indian princess in *Around the World*. She had to take Dramamine to keep her stomach under control every time she ascended the 150 feet into the balloon that was held up by a giant crane.

Several talented artists, who had been kicking around for years, were projected into stardom after appearing at Jones Beach. Joel Grey went from our *Mardi Gras* to leading roles on Broadway and finally to an Academy Award for his role in the film *Cabaret*. Robert Clary went from *Around the World* to a lucrative part in television's *Hogan's Heroes*.

There are whimsical memories to look back on, also. We had a veritable zoo for *Around the World*. Several elephants, camels, and horses. The pachyderms had the biggest problem, not so much because of their size, as for the fact they got seasick when we had to transport them to the back stage. They compensated for that by always trumpeting when Carm came down from our office to go home. Our cars were parked near the clearing we had set up for them. They knew Carm was the one who brought them apples every night.

For *Sound of Music* we had several sleek motorboats that would be used in an escape scene. The Trapp family was running from the Germans and the Nazi boat had a swastika flag on it. One day, I took it out for a ride in the bay, forgetting completely about that ugly emblem. Usually when I take a boat out on the bay, people recognize me and wave greetings. I didn't know why those greetings had turned to Bronx cheers until I docked the boat and noticed the flag.

But mostly I will remember the wonderful performers: Constance Towers, Kathy Nolan, Geraldine Brooks, Jules Munshin, Andy Devine, Billy Gaxton, Arthur Treacher, the marvelous Melchior, and Norman Atkins, the cantor in real life who played an island chief in *Paradise Island* and was on more familiar ground as Tevye in *Fiddler*.

We have been averaging about three hundred thousand customers a season, which rounds into an awesome figure of six million who have seen our shows since 1954. That's an awful lot of people to keep happy for twenty years. The happiest part of my role as an impresario is that they keep coming back, evidently pleased with low-cost, high-quality spectacles. That's what Bob Moses had in mind in the first place.

12. Retire? To What?

I will be seventy-three years old when this book reaches the market. The band and I travel for nine to ten months a year. The remaining time we are at Jones Beach in the summer, and, as noted, it is not entirely a vacation. If there were well-wishers in the lobby of the Roosevelt Hotel who used to greet me with sales pitches, now I am always running into concerned citizens anxious about my well-being. They want to know if I get enough rest. They ask when I am going to retire.

My good friend Jack Benny died recently. He had passed eighty and was still appearing on his "last-ever" television specials and on the circuit of show business dinners honoring performers. The younger comedians marveled that Benny always received the biggest ovation. They would ask him, probably in the age-old search of youth seeking to assume the old master's rung at the top: "When are you going to retire, Jack?"

He would give them that Benny stare, more recognizable and appreciated than the greatest of comedy lines. And he would say, "Retire? To what?"

He might have been speaking for Guy Lombardo. I have been blessed with good health. I have been further blessed with an occupation that enables me to make other people happy. Every night that I am out there doing what I know how to do, there is no need for a computer to tell me if I am succeeding. I can see it with my own eyes.

The couples dance by, older now than when the Royal Canadians first started. There are happy memories in their eyes. They are remembering love songs and sad songs and bouncy songs, and each one of them brings back the best times of their lives. They are having a party. And I, on the bandstand, am having a party every night I am working.

It certainly beats staying home wondering what television channel to turn to to kill one's time. How can one better enjoy himself than measuring the impact he is making in the always-crowded rooms we play—from one end of the country to the other and not neglecting the towns that lie between the two coasts of Canada.

I don't continue working because I have to. I don't need a monthly Social Security check and in that respect I am more fortunate than other senior citizens. I don't even feel like a senior citizen, and I am vain enough to be pleased that people tell me I don't look a day older than when they first caught my act thirty or even forty years ago. If they told me fifty or sixty years ago, I'd have to be suspicious.

Like the man-bites-dog story, there are certain other subjects guaranteed to get a play in your favorite newspaper. A person celebrating a hundredth birthday, for instance, is sure-fire copy. "To what do you attribute your longevity," the interviewer is bound to ask. The answers may be as diverse as one centenarian saying he never touched a drop and the other swearing that brandy keeps his heart pumping. If there is a recurring answer, it is that the birthday celebrant kept busy for as long as he or she could.

That, you may have gathered by now, has been my way of life throughout a career spanning sixty years. Even as a kid in London, when I wasn't practicing, I was rehearsing with Carm and Lebe and Enemy Kreitzer. We were all still in school, but time would have to be made to find bookings for our Lombardo concert company, to draft circulars and billboards, to write letters to dance halls and community gathering places within a fifty-mile radius of where we lived.

In Cleveland and Chicago there never seemed to be enough hours in the day. We started off playing for lunch and dinner and late-night dancing and still squeezed into our schedule room to

make records and appear on radio. We made a national reputation in New York, and all that meant was that we would have to
work even harder.

We never slowed down that way of life. In 1964, during the
New York World's Fair, we might have contented ourselves that
summer with our semivacation at Jones Beach, appearing only at
the Marine Theater between 8:30 and 12:30 nightly. During the
day we could have enjoyed our Long Island homes and hobbies.

But Robert Moses insisted that the Lombardos play at his fair.
And the General Cigar Company had built its Tiparillo Dance
Pavilion. They were the same people who had sponsored our first
Robert Burns show on radio. Almost over the phone we had committed ourselves to playing six nightly concerts. We would play
the overture at Jones Beach, I would hand over the baton to
Mitchell Ayres, our new conductor, and we would rush to our cars
for the twenty-five-mile drive to Flushing Meadows. Then we
would return to Jones Beach and play for dancing. That summer,
too, we had to concern ourselves with planning for our second
season at Tierra Verde in the winter.

I think that it was during that period that I found myself
almost too busy to notice the changes in our business. I knew that
most of the big bands were disappearing, but that seemed to make
no difference to the demands on us for more and more appearances. By now we had a commitment to appear in Las Vegas one
month a year, we were recording as frenetically as ever, and we
were booking additional tours.

The incursion of the rock-and-roll groups into our business had
already begun to make an impact before I realized it. Not that I
could have done anything to stop it. But I had begun to notice
that our records were not being played as frequently on the disk
jockey shows as they had in the past. Neither were the other
remaining name bands or the top vocalists like Sinatra, Como, or
Peggy Lee.

What you heard when you turned on the radio in your car was
electrically amplified noise. Out of the woodwork had come these
kids with electric guitars and new home-recording equipment and
made records in garages and basements and attics and the radio
stations couldn't wait to get their hands on them. The youth

market had always been the controlling factor in what was played on radio. It had been that way when we started and when the collegians began clamoring for our music.

And now, apparently, the young people were in rebellion against the older generation. They rebelled not only at the futility and horror of the war in Vietnam, but at all the values of their parents. Neat dress was to be ignored, hair was to be grown long, drugs would be tried, and this new sound called rock would become the national anthem of the young. Dancing, cheek to cheek and shoulder to shoulder, was for the old folks.

It could no longer be ignored as a simple fad that would pass away before the end of the decade. The Beatles—superb, imaginative musicians—had set a trend, and all over America parents were buying their teen-agers these electrically amplified guitars and young quartets were springing up to become idols for their peers and fodder for the promoters. The deejays wanted more and more records and the kids turned them out. Lacking the Beatles' talent, most would become stars for a week or two with a hit record and would fade into oblivion.

They almost canceled out the demand for music from the great songwriters of Tin Pan Alley, both in New York and Hollywood. Only a few new names in the industry would develop in the sixties, a Burt Bacharach, a Hal David, a Steve Sondheim. Songwriters didn't write for bands or vocalists anymore; the few hits they produced came from Hollywood theme songs or Broadway musical comedies. Good music virtually disappeared from the air because the radio industry was looking for rock. The long-haired kids in outlandish costumes were now the chief contributors to America's musical culture.

I am not ashamed to say that I neither understood nor appreciated the new cacophony they called music. I never heard a fine instrumentalist, a haunting melody, a lyric that made sense. I heard deafening noise and lyrics that were suggestive and worse. The verses were meant for those who understood the new drug-culture language and I didn't want to understand.

I have never resisted change in our industry, not through the beginning days when ragtime was replaced by jazz and the waltz replaced by the fox trot. We went through all those dance styles in the twenties, the Varsity Drag and Black Bottom and Charleston; in the thirties there would be the Big Apple and the Suzie, and the Lindy Hop; later, the Latin craze would descend on us with one variation after another. The best numbers of all of these we would add to our repertoire and put them alongside the beautiful waltz and fox-trot standards. And today we retain them all and there is no type of song that Americans have danced to in the last sixty years that we can't give our listeners.

That, of course, does not include hard rock numbers. In the first place, how do you dance to them? The kids do it by standing apart from each other and wriggling. No rhythm, no graceful steps in unison with one's partner. They wriggle. What bothers me the most is that a whole generation of young Americans have grown up without ever learning how to dance. I have seen young people in their late twenties and early thirties, on their own now and married, joining their parents perhaps for an anniversary at which we are playing.

They seem to be amazed that they are actually enjoying our music. They try to get up and dance as their parents are doing. And they don't know how. The rock beat they grew up with never taught them.

I am not enchanted, either, by what the rock revolution did to the American sense of style. I realize fashions change as they do in music, but I could never accept the standards of dress and appearance pioneered by the rock groups. The first requisite seemed to be an aversion to soap. Okay, the Beatles wore their hair long and that changed barbers to hair stylists. After fifteen years, I have learned to live with Prince Valiant hairdos, mustaches, beards, and sideburns. But nobody can ever sell me on an unwashed appearance.

For the Lombardos, neatness and grooming came with upbringing. Papa was in the business of designing the most fashionable clothes of the day. His sons and daughters would certainly be outfitted in the finest clothes available. Mama was everybody's old-fashioned mama who insisted on cleanliness. Her children never knew another way.

The stress on good grooming was a valuable asset in our career. We were always conscious of clothes and how they looked. No member of my band could appear in public with a spot on his jacket, a wrinkle in his pants, or shoes that didn't shine brightly. We looked good and the people liked it. So did the owners of the various clubs we played; they always wanted us back the next year, because as one of them said, "You guys add class to our place."

I had this fetish about designing smart new uniforms for every milestone appearance we made. For instance, when we made our plans to open the Cocoanut Grove in 1933, I took every member of the band to my favorite Broadway tailor, Mal Rutt. We worked out an outfit that would include white mess jackets, deep-maroon bow ties and cummerbunds, and black pants. In the height of the Depression those outfits went for $125 a man.

And to make sure the Hollywood celebrities got an unimpeded view of our style, we designed new music stands that were set low and invisible to the audience, so that our musicians would not be cut off below the shoulders. The only trouble was that in Los Angeles we couldn't find a maroon carnation for our buttonholes to match the tie and cummerbund.

We learned they were available in Denver; apparently they only grew in a colder climate. So we arranged for a daily shipment by airplane. That the Royal Canadians were so fastidious attracted the local reporters who had heard about the carnations flying over the Rockies every morning.

The resultant stories reached the eyes of a horticulture professor at UCLA. He wrote a letter to one of the papers saying that any kind of flower that could be raised in Denver could also be produced in Los Angeles. I understand he tried to grow them, but the maroon carnations were not in production by the time we left California.

I like to think that almost all the superstars of our business feel the same way about grooming. When Bing Crosby or Bob Hope or Frank Sinatra or Dean Martin comes into one's living room on television, they come dressed to the nines. They wear evening clothes as a mark of respect to the viewer. I probably am showing my age when I admit an intolerance toward a performer who might stand up and sing in a sweater and open-toed sandals.

I feel the same way about the lowering of standards in the material used by an increasing number of latter-day comics. I am not a prude. I enjoy a dirty joke as much as the next man. But I enjoy it in private and not in public. I don't believe blue material has any place on television or on any stage that attracts a mixed clientele, especially children. I know all about the new freedoms, the new sexual mores, women's lib, and the rest. I respect a person's feelings about these matters. But I am just not comfortable listening to a comedian spouting dirty lines. A woman in the audience might laugh at them. Another might be embarrassed and wish she hadn't come. I don't want to watch uncomfortable spectators when they came for entertainment.

I have used many comics in theater tours. The most memorable was the team of Burns and Allen. They never had to use a suggestive line to get a laugh.

I remember playing Broadway's Capitol Theater one week, and finding on our bill a rising young comic recommended to us by MCA. He played only one show. In that one he managed to cover every topic from intercourse to the habits of homosexuals. Apparently, the customers in a small Broadway supper club had loved the act. In the Capitol I saw parents walking out with their children.

I told him he would have to change his act for the next show. He refused. I reminded him that the people had come primarily to see Guy Lombardo and the Royal Canadians, but it made no impression. I called the manager and told him we wouldn't go on if this young man continued on the program. The comic got his walking papers. There might be room for that kind of act in a supper club or in a review; in those surroundings I would probably have enjoyed it too. But I would never allow blue material on a Guy Lombardo program.

But with all the changes in the business and with the new decade of the 1970's upon us, we had settled down to a regimen that still kept us as busy as ever. We still made records, although not in the volume of prerock-and-roll. The four months in the late fall and winter that had always been spent at the Roosevelt and for those two years in Tierra Verde were now taken up with a tour that would get us back to the Waldorf Astoria in December in time for the New Year's Eve telecasts.

The personnel of our band had undergone changes. Derf Hig-

man and George Gowans, and finally Enemy Kreitzer had retired
to their Long Island homes, and only Carm, Lebe, and I now
remained of that original crew that had migrated from London to
Cleveland. We would look assiduously for the best musicians in
the country to replace them, musicians who could and would
adapt to our style.

Even Las Vegas and Lake Tahoe, where we had worked at least
a month a year through the last fifteen, had abandoned the name
band shows and replaced them with the top vocalists and the top
comedians. We adapted. We booked more one-nighters and traveled more.

The schedule that has remained with us for the past five years
or so goes something like this:

Mid-June through Labor Day—Jones Beach Marine Theater;
six-day vacation and begin concert tour of Ontario, including London, through September; tour of Western Canada and states of
Washington, Oregon, and California, ending with concert at
Hollywood Palladium, October 19; fly back to New York for
week's vacation; start second concert tour in upstate New York,
continue through New England and East Coast to Florida; return
to New York for New Year's Eve; start tour of South through
month of January and end in Florida; play three-week engagement
at Galt Ocean Mile Hotel, Fort Lauderdale, for dining and dancing; tour rest of the country, Southwest and Midwest through
spring and start of summer season at Jones Beach.

In most of the towns we play concerts and in many, especially
in Florida, we play for dances at country clubs like LaGorce and
Indian Creek in Miami. We have been playing the same annual
dances for as long as thirty years. Larry Owen books the tour from
our New York office, and many times it is merely a repetition of
approximately the same dates as last year.

We travel in our own bus from one town to the other, a lux-
uriously fitted conveyance that could seat fifty, and is driven by
our long-time major-domo, Don Byrnes, who also sets up our
bandstands as soon as we arrive. If we begin a tour at some distance from New York, we fly to the first stop and Don will be
there waiting for us in the bus.

We follow a set routine. We arrive by bus for our new date,

usually in the early afternoon, check in at a motel, and Don drives us to the concert auditorium or dance engagement that usually lasts from about 9:00 P.M. to midnight. We get a full night's sleep and are off in the morning for the next city, usually a trip of about two hundred miles. All members of the band handle their own instruments and we never have a baggage problem.

Traveling across the country in short hops is infinitely more comfortable the way we do it now than it was the first thirty years. Our bus has reclining seats and enough of them so that if a band member's wife wants to come along there's always room. We hired Don in Toronto about fifteen years ago. He was driving a bus we had rented and Lebe, who had become our transportation expert, looked back from the seat he always occupies behind the driver. He whispered to me, "That's our man, Guy. You got to sign him up permanently. I'd feel confident if this guy was driving us to the moon."

Of course, this mode of traveling is expensive, too. We pay about twice as much per mile as if we rented buses from city to city. We stay only at first-class motels, having given up hotels to get away from downtown traffic and the blight that has afflicted so many big hostelries across the nation.

We may be the only surviving big name band that can travel across the country, night after night, because we can demand fees that are high enough to show a sizable profit over and above the enormous costs of the road. We have always paid our musicians the highest salaries in the business, and when you add on today's costs of transportation and lodgings, you are talking about a nut of about $10,000 a week. In the thirties you could get a first-class room for about four dollars a day. Today they cost twenty dollars.

My brothers never once complained about the additional traveling we were doing. They seemed to thrive on it. And then in the summer of 1970, I began to notice that something was bothering Carmen. He was getting irritable. He was acting the same way he did when I was spending so much time on my speedboats; I could only surmise that, like the last time, events were occurring to make him believe that something had come between us that we couldn't share.

We would come up to our office in the Marine Theater after a rehearsal and Carm would lie down on the couch, never speaking. I would begin a discussion about bugs in the show and what we had to do to remove them, and Carm would rarely answer. It began to worry me. I told Lilliebell and she told Florence, and between them they got Carm to visit Dr. Murray Israel, a local internist.

The doctor took X-rays and found a shadow in the stomach area. He recommended a specialist and I waited anxiously for Carm to come back and tell me the prognosis. Carm returned, still irascible, not spelling out what the specialist had told him. "He says something about I better cut down on smoking and highballs," he said. That's all I could get out of him.

The four of us, Lilliebell and I, Carm and Florence, took a short vacation to Aruba when the show closed. I really started worrying about my brother being sick when I noticed him in bathing trunks. No matter how much weight he had, Carm's face was always thin. Now it was thinner and I saw that his trunks were sagging. He had lost his behind and almost his entire stomach. I had noticed a similar change in Carm's song-writing partner, Johnny Loeb, who had died of cancer the year before.

I asked Carm how much he weighed and he said 145; he hadn't felt like eating much lately. His normal weight was 165. I started thinking about that shadow on the X-ray that he had dismissed so lightly. I told my brother that after the New Year's Eve show he was going down to see the renowned Dr. Michael DeBakey at the Houston Medical Center. This time Carm didn't argue or show exasperation.

It was DeBakey who had probably saved my life a few years before when he found an aneurism near my aorta and removed it. That was the only extended illness I ever had and now I was praying it would be the same for Carm. Now I realized why my brother had been so irritable in the summer. An illness was separating us, just like boat racing once had and that was how Carm reacted.

He went to Houston for a week of tests, and after they were over I got a call from DeBakey in Freeport. The doctor said he'd have to do a biopsy to learn if the growth in Carm's stomach was malignant. I guess he hadn't had time yet to tell Carm; my

brother called a few minutes later. "They can't find a thing wrong
with me in this hospital," he said. "I just called my travel agency
and had them book Florence and me for a cruise."

I flew down to Houston immediately; DeBakey had told me he
was planning to do the biopsy the next day. Florence and I sat in
a little waiting room, looking at each other, saying nothing. They
say when a person is at the point of drowning, his entire life
flashes before him. Well, in that operating room, they were determining Carm's future, and all I could see was this flashing picture
of what we had been to each other.

What I saw was a series of vignettes, and each one had two people in it, seemingly entwined like Siamese twins. Carm and I were
always together; in boyhood, practicing in Papa's shop, vying for
prizes; accepting with resignation the sissy outfits we wore for our
debut at a strawberry festival; trembling with anticipation of a
first ride in Papa's first car, which wouldn't start, and Papa in the
driver's seat and me trying to work the crank and Carm peering
under the car in back and finally the roar of the motor and the car
taking off in reverse, rolling over Carm; Carm picking himself up,
shaking himself off, saying, "Papa you were supposed to go forward, not backward."

The pictures moved ahead with the years, both of us forming
that kids' band and Carm going to Detroit to become a professional and returning to London to rub off what he had learned on
the rest of us; and always the traveling, sharing rooms, never more
than a few feet away from each other, or a few miles when we had
our own homes; Carm, who liked vacation traveling more than I
did, might be in Italy or the Orient, but there would never be a
day that he wasn't calling, wasn't keeping up to the minute on
what I had been doing.

There flashed by, even, a picture illustrating the last time I had
to be concerned about Carm's physical well-being. How long ago
was that? I remembered. It was twenty-five years ago and we were
the idols of Hollywood, playing the Cocoanut Grove and the Paramount Theater in Los Angeles and making a picture on the Paramount lot. And on his one day off a week, Carm had found a
beautiful retreat in the desert, a small community named Palm

Springs, ringed by mountains and containing two or three small motels.

He had always been a superb horseman, much more so than I, who preferred getting around with the aid of powerful engines. Carm had taken up the sport when Papa owned trotters and pacers, and it had been one of his means of maintaining physical fitness throughout his life. He was never sick; he was Carmen, the indestructible.

Lilliebell had joined him for riding most of the days he went off to Palm Springs; she was an excellent horseman, too. I had come along on one or two occasions, but my horse always led me back to the corral as they cantered ahead. We had met Sam Rosoff, the subway builder, during that stay in Hollywood. We had known him in New York and Carm had ridden with him in Central Park. Sam flew in a beautiful Arabian stallion just so Carm wouldn't have to depend on stable nags for riding the Palm Springs mountain trails.

On this Sunday, Carm had made the trip to Palm Springs alone. Lilliebell had been cautioning him against taking one rock-strewn trail that led up to a precipice. For Carm it was adventure. And that Sunday night, waiting for Carm to get back, my wife and I were listening to a Walter Winchell radio news broadcast. Winchell was back in New York, but his lead item was that Carmen Lombardo had been thrown from a horse and lay unconscious in a desert hospital.

The item was only partially factual. Carm had been thrown, his head had hit a rock, and he had been unconscious. But he regained consciousness, found his spirited stallion, and rode back to Palm Springs. And as Lilliebell and I frantically tried to find out where he was and to make arrangements to get there, Carm walked into our room with a bandage on his head.

The next night he was on the bandstand for our Robert Burns radio show and we were introducing our "hit of the week." We had planned the song a week in advance. As had happened so many times before, its title was of particular significance to Carm. The song was named "What Hit Me?" I don't remember if it ever became a best-seller; I do remember it broke up the audience, the band and my bandaged brother.

The past became the present when Dr. DeBakey came into the small room, still wearing his surgical gown. He looked at Florence and at me and found no way to soften the blow. "I hate to tell you this," he said, "but Carmen has cancer of the stomach and it may have already reached his liver."

I saw the blood drain out of Florence's face; she seemed to be aging before my eyes. I found enough voice to ask the doctor what could be done for my brother, how much chance he had.

DeBakey encouraged us. He said the hospital had the best cancer people in the world. Carm would get treatments. Perhaps cobalt would help. "It's just too bad," the doctor said, "that he waited so long."

Well, that was Carmen, too. He would share everything but his burdens. He just didn't know how to tell Florence or me, for fear of hurting us. Always the optimist, he was sure it would go away.

They brought him up in a couple of hours and he took Florence's hand. Then he asked me about a song we had been working on. Had we found the proper arrangement?

He spent the next month or so commuting between his treatments in Houston and the new home he had purchased for Florence in Miami. They had decided to sell the house in Woodmere, so that he could pass his last days in the sun.

Miraculously, it began to look like the treatments were working. He was gaining weight; by late spring he had rejoined the band and by summer he was in the middle of helping with the Jones Beach production. He was an entirely different Carmen than he had been the previous summer. His weight was up to 162 and he was bubbling with enthusiasm, immersing himself in his usual work load: producer, musical director of the band, songwriter. Every week he would go to a local doctor for an injection prescribed by DeBakey and every three weeks he would go back to Houston for tests. The last time, he went back as we were wrapping up the Jones Beach season. DeBakey told him he could make the Canadian tour in September. All he would have to do was go to a doctor every week with the prescription for his injection.

I felt like a man who had been given a reprieve from the electric chair. I was never so happy in my life. Carm sent a large check to the Houston Medical Center as a donation for giving him back his life and we proceeded to Canada, together again.

Into the latter stages of the Canadian concert tour, we had landed at the Vancouver airport in British Columbia and I headed for our hotel while Carm proceeded to the address of a doctor who would give him his shot.

Later when I walked into his room, Carm was lying on the bed, shaking like a leaf. He was having his first bad reaction since he had begun the treatments and I called the doctor, who told me to go to a drugstore for a prescription. By the time I got back again, Carm was calmer, optimistic as ever. "The doctor must have given me the wrong injection," he said.

A few days later we were in San Francisco and Carm looked up the doctor who had been recommended for him in that city. He came back and I noticed that his eyes were yellow; the doctor had told him to go back to Houston for an examination. I knew it was the beginning of the end. Carm stayed in Houston for a time, commuting again between the hospital and his home in Miami. He insisted, however, on coming up to New York to play for New Year's Eve.

All of us had to look away when Carm walked onto the bandstand for rehearsals, carrying his instruments, hardly weighing more than a hundred pounds. But at the rehearsal and at the performance at the Waldorf, only his physical appearance would cause a stranger to suspect he was sick. He played that flute and that sax; he stood up with the trio and sang "Seems like Old Times," he barked orders, he kept telling the new men in the band not to forget to smile.

The New Year's Eve that ushered in 1971 would be Carm's last appearance with the band. For me, it would never seem like old times again, but we pushed on from city to city. In Las Vegas, he came out to see us and sat in a chair, crying as we made a recording of the last song he ever wrote: "Look What We've Done to Our World."

He had written it while he was dying in Miami, but it was not a dying man's song. It was a song by a man who concerned himself with the problems of the day. In 1970 the problem that had begun to dawn on thinking people was ecology, and Carm was writing a theme that was contemporary, as he always had done before. The verse goes:

"God gave us the lakes and the rivers/ And then colored them to match the sky/ He filled them with birds and with fishes/ It was their home to live and to die/ On the land he created the forests/ The wildlife to run and to play/ Then along came Man never knowing/ He would end all this freedom some day/ The beautiful skies lost their color/ The rivers and lakes became grey/ He abused the land and the forests/ Never knowing there would come a day/When air would become polluted/ The rivers and lakes would decay/ I know that Man didn't mean it/ He thought Nature would wash it away/ And look what we've done to our world."

We had first heard the song in Savannah, Georgia, where we were playing in a ballroom. Carm had struggled into a plane for his first trip since coming back to Miami. He had set himself a deadline to finish the song and hear it played just once by the band.

We had copies of the music and the verse for Kenny Gardner to sing. We were in the middle of a set when Carm came in and he handed Kenny copies to pass around to the musicians. "I want to see how it plays," Carm said.

We played it and Kenny sang the beautiful verse and the dancers stopped dancing to listen. They cheered for ten minutes. Kenny, a cheerful sort who rarely shows emotion, broke down. I had to turn away from the applause. The only member of the Royal Canadians who wasn't crying was Carm. He just sat there, taking it all in, as if he was ready now for whatever lay ahead.

At the funeral that April in Freeport, Florence appeared thankful, too. "The songs, Guy," she told me. "They kept him from thinking about the pain those last few months of his life. He wrote six of them besides the ecology thing. He would be lying in bed with a piece of fur under him to make it more comfortable and then he would get up and start pacing around, the old Carm thinking about nothing but his music. The songs kept him alive an extra four months, I think."

Although we recorded the ecology song before Carm died, I never had it published. That period just holds too many painful memories for me and one of them is that Victor quit the band shortly after the recording session in Las Vegas.

Vic had replaced Carm as our first sax and we had had an argument at the recording session. Shortly after, on the bus taking us to a date in Wisconsin, he announced he was leaving the band. He and I began scuffling and Lebe stepped in to separate us, and Don stopped the bus. The peacemaker was the only one injured. He hit the metal railing of the seat and fell, groaning in pain. They taped him up in a hospital for three cracked ribs and I insisted Lebe return to New York till he got better.

Vic and his wife, Ginny, left on the same plane the next morning. I was stuck in the middle of Wisconsin without a first sax or first trumpet to play that night's engagement. Larry Owen shipped out two replacements from New York who arrived just in time for the date.

I love my brother Victor but I have never asked him to return to the band. I suffered with him when Ginny died recently, and I am happy that he now has his own crew and a regular job at the Drake Hotel in Chicago. Meanwhile I could never get myself to publish Carm's last song. The memories were too painful.

Two people have given me the will to go on as long as I can. That I did not seriously consider retirement after Carm died is due to my brother Lebe and my wife Lilliebell. They set examples of courage and determination that I had to follow.

If Carm was almost a twin brother with whom I was constantly battling and making up, it was Lebe who cemented our solidarity. He often shamed both of us by the way he bounced back after personal tragedies that might have embittered a saint. He never permitted the pain to alter the sunniest disposition I have ever encountered. To this day, I have yet to hear Lebe bad-mouth another person.

Lebe has been married three times and raised two families. When he married Carol Williams in Cleveland, he completed the conversion of the three Lombardo brothers from bachelors to husbands in the space of a year. Carol died before their seventh anniversary and Lebe tried to hide his sorrow from us. He never wanted to be an object of pity.

In the mid-thirties, he married a Bradford, Pennsylvania, oil

heiress, Helen Healy, who gave him four children. They lived in a
fine house on the North Shore of Long Island and seemed to be
sharing an idyllic existence. One night, playing the Roosevelt, a
process server walked up to the bandstand and handed Lebe a
summons.

"They're divorce papers," he told him. "Don't go home tonight."

I don't know how Lebe got through that set. He was shaking,
wondering what had gone wrong, steeling himself to finish the
night until he could go home and find out what had happened.
He never did find out, except that Helen said she wanted a
divorce and that he couldn't enter the house.

His wife moved the children to San Francisco, and Lebe was in
agony that he could only see his three sons and daughter on occasional holidays and on weekends when we were playing the
Coast. Carm and I both knew what he was suffering, but he
would never let it show on the outside. He would come back from
the visits, describing how the children were growing, showing their
pictures.

After Helen married a publisher, Lebe made another trip to see
the kids, and this time he was genuinely happy when he returned.
He had been afraid they would forget their father now that their
mother had a new husband.

"They all love me, Guy," he said. "They weren't giving me a
story. You can tell about these things. They want to see me more
often."

His pride and his love for those children kept him going. Only
once did I have to fear that my brother would crack under the
strain of tragedy. That was when we were playing Las Vegas in
the sixties. The hotel's public address system called for Lebe to
pick up a telegram at the desk. It notified him that his daughter,
Susan Ann, a beautiful young woman now, had died in a flu epi-
demic that was ravaging San Francisco.

I doubt if even Lebe could have withstood that new shock had
he not now been married again and building another family of
two girls and a boy. I had introduced him in 1953 to an attractive
young model from Texas, a girl named Peggy Landers. They fell
in love and were married. Later Lebe bought a big old house on

an Amityville, Long Island, canal and spent his summer days fishing with Peggy and the children, Lizanne, Gina, and Carmen. Often his sons from San Francisco would come for vacations. They were the twenty happiest years of his life. Once he admitted to me, "I never thought I could make it, Guy, but everything seems to have a way, like Papa used to say, of turning out for the best."

Lebe will have to believe that even more than I do. Peggy died in 1973 of cancer. She was in her forties. We buried her in a December ice storm on Long Island and left immediately to play another date. That's the way Lebert wanted it. On the trip south, I tried to bring up the subject of retirement. He wouldn't discuss it. The band is his life as it is mine. Lizanne and Gina are teen-agers, and young Carm at twelve is beginning to show all the drive and talent of the uncle for whom he was named. My brother Lebe keeps playing his beautiful trumpet and worrying about the band. You would never know to look at him that he is anything but the happiest of men.

Lilliebell and I were never blessed with children. Both of us wanted a family and we began to wonder when we arrived in New York why she had never become pregnant. We went to doctors, took tests, were told nothing was wrong with either one of us, and to be patient. When we went to Hollywood in 1933, the movie people insisted we see a renowned doctor who had had success with actresses resigned to childlessness. More tests and one night the doctor came to the Cocoanut Grove and told me not to worry, we'd have children. He was giving Lilliebell treatments. They didn't help either.

Lilliebell has enough love in her to accommodate more than the family we could never have. She spread it around everything she touched. She was another daughter to my mother and father, and a sister to all my brothers and sisters. A lifelong empathy for pets often filled our house to the dimensions of a menagerie.

She would sit in our back yard and a stray dog or cat would run by. If it came back, Lilliebell would call the local animal shelter. If the shelter couldn't accommodate another stray to give out for adoption, Lilliebell would take it in. She always had her own pedigreed dogs and cats, never less than six or seven. The strays would get equal treatment. Sometimes there would be fourteen or fifteen of them in residence at the same time, not to mention birds and a pet monkey.

Lilliebell's favorite dog during the forties was a beautiful Doberman pinscher pup my father had given her. He obeyed every command, was as docile as a poodle. He used to kiss her good night. And one night, he accidentally bit her cheek. The vets ordered the dog destroyed and Lilliebell was inconsolable.

One night I came home and she was on the long-distance phone to California. She had read about a police chief in a small town who had ordered a dog destroyed, a move that had split the townspeople into two factions and generated much publicity. I didn't know whom she was talking to, but I knew I wouldn't want to be on the other end of the phone. She was certainly chewing out somebody. When she hung up, she said, "That guy will think twice about killing a little dog that never harmed anybody." The next week she showed me an Associated Press story saying that the chief had changed his mind.

Another time she asked me to mail a letter. I noticed it was addressed to Doris Day, whom I knew as a band singer but hadn't met since she had become a movie star. I asked Lilliebell since when she had started communicating with her. "Oh, for a long time," she said. "Doris is doing a wonderful job for homeless animals. I send her checks."

Lilliebell had learned to cook shortly after we were married, and perhaps our happiest memories were of the early days in Chicago when all the members of the band lived in one apartment building on the South Side and when we would come home after the Granada closed to find a spread she had prepared. Almost every night was a party we could look forward to after a day's work.

When we took over George Gershwin's penthouse suite on Riverside Drive, it was Lilliebell who earned a reputation as one of New York's best party givers. Every Sunday night was open house at the Lombardos' and it was at these gatherings that I would meet and cement lifelong friendships among the show business community.

Later in Freeport, the parties would move to our home by the water, and when the guest list got too big we'd simply head over to our restaurant down the street. It was Lilliebell who insisted that our chef prepare such dishes as lobster Lombardo ("the sweetest lobsters this side of heaven") and Royal Canadian seafood platter.

She is a woman of great resolution and strong will. Her values have always been the same as mine, and if I ever bent them a little I would have to answer to Lilliebell. I considered her the best judge of what was good for the Royal Canadians and what was not. If she was not along with us on a trip, I would call every night. She would give her reaction on the radio show we might have just finished. If she didn't like a certain song or its presentation, she'd tell me. She was invariably right.

And throughout the large Lombardo family, it was to Lilliebell that every one of us would go with a problem. My brothers and sisters and their wives and husbands respected her judgment, her advice and, above all, that great big heart. I cannot conceive of another woman so perfectly suited to help carry the Lombardos through everything we achieved and everything we suffered.

Lilliebell doesn't travel with us much anymore. She has had a painful back condition for the last few years. It has impaired her mobility and she is more comfortable at home. I worry about her and I miss not having her near me as I used to when we had many more lengthy engagements in places like California, Nevada, and Florida.

But, like Lebe, Lilliebell doesn't want to discuss retirement. She knows me well enough to imagine what inactivity would do to me. She is content to stay in Freeport with her friends, human and otherwise, and to remain the judge of what is good for her husband and his band. She gives me the will to go on.

Lately I have been noticing a small movement back to the music that has filled my life. I think the young people are beginning to discover the beauty of a melody, drowned out these last fifteen years by the barbaric noises of their rock idiom. When the Beatles put out a haunting tune named "Yesterday," a few years back, the kids grabbed onto it, possibly because it had been produced by a group they idolized. They may not have realized that the song was in the same genre that yesterday's Tin Pan Alley writers were continually producing.

And in the last year or two, the youngsters discovered ragtime. One of 1974's biggest hits was the theme of the movie *The Sting*. It had been adapted from a Scott Joplin ragtime song written before World War I. Suddenly, the youth market was on a Scott Joplin revival kick. They were clamoring for the kind of tunes my London Concert Company was playing before the Jazz Age came in.

I was riding in a car with a friend and his teen-age son, recently, and the radio was playing Jerome Kern's "Smoke Gets in Your Eyes" and Cole Porter's "I've Got You Under My Skin." Both songs had been made into records by a rock group. Now they were being played in the Big Band style of the forties.

The boy turned to his father and me triumphantly. "See that," he said, "they're playing those songs for the older people. They've taken our songs and slowed them down."

Of course he wouldn't know that those beautiful classics had been written more than forty years ago and that he had never been exposed to them through all the junk rock the kids were fed. The point is that some of the junk is now being replaced by the standards I knew, even if I shudder at the tempo and lack of musicality. More and more I have been seeing young people in their twenties, accompanying their parents to one of our dances or concerts. They seem amazed that they enjoy the music we play.

I am also encouraged by the reappearance of bands that play under the names of their former leaders, like the departed Tommy Dorsey and Glenn Miller. It makes me happy to see Duke Ellington's name kept alive by his son, Mercer, who is now playing more engagements than Duke could in his later years. I have the feeling that young people as they grow into adults will begin to look for music again, and the bandleaders if they keep coming back will provide it for them.

Meanwhile it seems to be my lot in life to keep the torch alive. The Royal Canadians remain the only name orchestra to bring dance music nightly to the millions of people who grew up on it, who hardly ever hear it anymore until we hit their town.

I could never dream that big when I was growing up in London, wondering whether I wanted to be a champion bike rider or a prize fighter or a banker. Even when we had set our sights on making something of our orchestra, how could I dream that someday I would be in places to meet Presidents and two sets of Great Britain's royal families and the bandleaders I worshiped as a boy and the songwriters whose music we tried to play and the most glamorous names in Hollywood and in industry.

How could I dream that my orchestra would lead me to these places and also give me the opportunity to embark on a speed-boating career which would make my name almost as well known for winning races and breaking records than as a bandleader.

And how could I, who gave up high school to become a bandleader, ever aspire to an honorary doctorate in music? That occurred several years ago and may have been the most rewarding moment of my life. It happened in my home town of London, at the University of Western Ontario, where my father once outfitted medical students with white jackets. I wish he could have been alive to see it, the boy from Lipari who came to Canada so the sons he would have could learn music.

But always in the end, the great places, names, and honors would mean not nearly as much as the millions of faces looking up at me happily and dancing to our music. And out there in homes around the country, there would remain many of the 300,000,000 Guy Lombardo records to ensure that the music of the Royal Canadians would never die.

And each succeeding New Year's Eve broadcast is heard by more people than ever. The one ringing out 1974 reached 55 million people and as usual the ratings left no room for argument. We were Number One.

I answer well-wishers a little bit differently than Jack Benny. I say to them:

"Why should I retire when every night I meet another Auld Acquaintance. And when every night is New Year's Eve."